DAILY LIFE OF

NATIVE AMERICANS IN THE TWENTIETH CENTURY

DONALD FIXICO

The Greenwood Press "Daily Life Through History" Series

GREENWOOD PRESS
Westport, Connecticut • London
Library of Congress Cataloging-in-Publication Data

Fixico, Donald Lee, 1951–
    Daily life of Native Americans in the twentieth-century / by Donald Fixico.
        p.   cm.—(The Greenwood Press "Daily life through history" series)
    Includes bibliographical references and index.
    ISBN 0–313–33357–2
    1. Indians of North America—Social life and customs—20th century.   2. Indians
of North America—Rites and ceremonies.   3. Indians of North America—Politics
and government.   I. Title.   II. Series.
    E98.S7F59   2006
    305.897′0730904—dc22   2006001178

British Library Cataloguing in Publication Data is available.

Library of Congress Catalog Card Number: 2006001178
ISBN: 0–313–33357–2
ISSN: 1080–4749

First published in 2006

Greenwood Press, 88 Post Road West, Westport, CT 06881
An imprint of Greenwood Publishing Group, Inc.
www.greenwood.com

Printed in the United States of America

The paper used in this book complies with the
Permanent Paper Standard issued by the National
Information Standards Organization (Z39.48–1984).

10 9 8 7 6 5 4 3 2 1

To RD Beloved brother

CONTENTS

PREFACE

This book is designed to provide an introduction to the big picture of real Indian life in the twentieth century. At the same time, the purpose is to provide the historical context for the primary issues and problems confronting modern Native peoples. This effort involves covering the complexity of native life from over 200 reservations and leading to urbanization in every major city in the West while presenting the new adjustments of more than 500 Indian tribal groups' whose people endured assimilation and assault of various federal Indian policies.

This complexity made it a challenge to pull together an understandable presentation to anyone curious about American Indians after the so-called Indian wars were over in the late nineteenth century. I hope that the following pages share insights into the Indian experience and what it was like to be Indian over the course of the last 100 hundred years.

Chapter 1, on family and women's roles, addresses the essential social and cultural unit of American Indians while emphasizing how native people have changed traditions in adapting to a mainstream environment. Economics and urbanization are the focus of chapter 2, which stresses that it is these two influences more than anything else that have brought great change to American Indians. Chapter 3 discusses language, oral tradition, and education. It is through education that American Indians have been changed by outsiders such as instructors and officials at boarding schools. However, American Indians have also used education as a tool since the 1960s to bring about change for the better in their lives. Chapter 4, on material life, discusses the physical changes in Indian people's lives and how this has been exhibited through the twentieth century. Chapter 5 covers the political dimension in the lives of American Indians, noting the inside of tribal governments and communities, national Indian organizations, and the service of native peoples in the military.

The next collection of chapters address how native peoples have been influenced by the outside mainstream and how they adjusted to welcoming new things, ideas, and inspiration from other people. Chapter 6 is about the recreational part of native lives and the enjoyment of sports. Notable individuals have played in professional sports and competed in the Olympics since 1908. Chapter 7 introduces the strength of native communities in their beliefs culturally with Christian influences and maintaining an indigenous ethos of looking at the world and universe. Culture expressed through art, artifacts, music, and entertainment is covered in Chapter 8. Indian cultural expressions are intermixed with mainstream influences, yet much of this is a new kind of traditionalism of native and modern collaboration. Literature and the media are the subjects of Chapter 9 and how American Indians have been presented in these two forums of the American mainstream. This includes the outside world of European and Japanese interests in American Indians.

The remaining five chapters are reminders of the internal strength of Indian communal life. Chapter 10 is about the natural environment, resources, and how native peoples have maintained homes and made new ones by sustaining their identities. Chapter 11 takes us further into Indian life and describes humor from an their perspective. Chapter 12 is about the growing Indian gaming industry, how it started, and its impact on Indian country. Native medicine is a pillar of the internal strength of Indian people and chapter 13 discusses this including how external diseases have made Native American health vulnerable. Finally, chapter 14 is about "being" Indian and what it feels like to be Indian during the modernization of the twentieth century.

The following pages are an extraordinary story of internal life of a minority group living in indigenous land of its own while working, living, and playing in a mainstream world much of the time and sustaining native communities most of the time.

I want to express appreciation to various individuals whose works I revisited to read and to think about during the process of compiling, shaping, and writing and revising the following chapters. Many of these scholars are also good friends, such as Charlotte Heth, Donald Parman, Francis Paul Prucha, Tom Hagan, Brian Hosmer, Colleen O'Neil, Philip Deloria, Margaret Connell Szasz, Peter Iverson, Tom Holm, Terry Straus, Vine Deloria Jr., Laurence Hauptman, Blue Clark, James LeGrand, Brenda Child, Tsianina Lomawaima, David Wilkins, Fred Hoxie, Alison Bernstein, Kenneth Philip, Wayne Stein, Elizabeth Cook-Lynn, Jay Miller, Collin Calloway, and many others who have written about modern American Indians. I also want to thank Sarah Colwell and Bridget Austiguy-Preschel at Greenwood Press for supporting my manuscript and Apex Publishing for helping to turn it into a book.

Closer to home, I would like to express appreciation to President Michael Crow of Arizona State University, Provost Milton Glick, Dean David Young, Divisional Dean Debra Losse, and Noel Stowe, the chairperson of the history department at Arizona State University. I am grateful to the ASU Foundation for providing my distinguished professorship. I am also grateful for the conversations about Indian issues with my colleagues in American Indian studies, notably Eddie Brown, James Riding In, Carol Lujan, Myla Vicente Carpio, and Susan Miller. Across ASU, I appreciate the conversations and discussions with David Beaulieu in the school of education and Kevin Gover in the law school. I want to thank my research assistant, Kristin Youngbull, who has helped to track down a lot of information for me as well as make continual runs to the Hayden Library on campus. In addition to Kristin, I want to acknowledge the mutual support of my current doctoral students, Azusa Ono and Tamrala Swafford. I am especially grateful to my wife, professor April Summitt, whose words of support and concern encouraged me throughout the entire project. I am also grateful to my son, Keytha Fixico, who has patiently waited to go for ice cream or play golf with me while I completed tasks for this book. Also, I am grateful for the support from my parents, John and Virginia Fixico, and for the knowledgeable insight they were able to provide concerning community activities among Indians in Oklahoma.

Donald Fixico
Arizona State University

INTRODUCTION

This book is about American Indian lifeways and how Indian values have changed from traditional ones to new ones that have enabled them to live in the twentieth century. It is also about how the federal government has impacted Indians' lives through policies and programs designed to improve livelihood. The federal government's influence has frequently been negative, and native peoples have learned to endure federal paternalism while maintaining tribal ways. Simultaneously, they have amended many of the old ways while embracing new technologies of the twentieth century.

Why has the federal government been such a big part of American Indian lives? An acute decline in economic prosperity among Indians during the nineteenth century led, in the late 1800s, to a desire on the part of government officials to help Indian communities. The continuous aim of federal assistance to Indians has been to change the latter—to transmute native peoples into white Americans. In the view of white Americans, the Indian was either a noble savage or primitive savage, but was in either case viewed as uncivilized, as defined by prevailing standards in U.S. society. Little effort was made to understanding the lifeways of tribes from any region of the country. Popular thought among bureaucrats promoted the idea that the Indian "savages" could be civilized through education, farming, and Christianity. The predominant Euro-American culture, including its political and religious beliefs, was fundamentally different from native Indian communal life.

The history of Indian wars is well known in general and the United States signed many treaties with Indian tribes. From the late 1700s to 1890, Indian nations fought over 1,500 wars, battles, and skirmishes to defend their lives and homelands. Starting in 1778, Indian nations continued to make treaties until 1870. After that, Indian tribes made agreements with the United States with the last one being with the Mountain Ute Indians in l917. In all, 389 treaties, ratified by Congress, were made between the tribes and the United States. The treaties legally obligated the United States to fulfill its promises. Education, annuities, and the cession of Indian lands were the most common treaty provisions. This was a sovereign-to-sovereign relationship, according to law, comparable to treaties between foreign nations; and this relationship is the basis of Indian rights today. In the end, Indian communities had survived the catastrophes of removal to the West and war.

The Indians' new homelands in the west were soon threatened by the advent of the transcontinental railroad, initially created by the meeting of the Central Pacific Railroad originating from Sacramento and the Union Pacific Railroad coming from Omaha. They were joined at Promontory Point near Ogden, Utah, in l869. Within the following years, four more transcontinental railroads connected the West with the East. Watching from a safe distance, the Indians observed the whites' activities: settlers clearing land for homesteads, miners erecting camps, and towns springing up, all brought about by the railroads. In the path of the white man's progress, the buffalo and other wildlife quickly began disappearing, as settlers built homesteads, ranchers herded cattle, and miners claimed certain areas of Colorado, Arizona, Nevada, and California. The west was rapidly changing. The railroad industry helped at least 12 territories to become states between l867 and l912.

During the 1800s, peyotism surged among Indians in the Southwest and its practice spread throughout the plains and eastward among the Oklahoma tribes. Based on a ceremonial ingesting of a hallucinogenic plant, members of some tribes combined this with Christianity to form a new religion. In the early 1900s, the peyotists fought for legal recognition to establish the Native American Church (NAC). With the aid of ethnologist James Mooney and the decision supporting peyotism reached in *Woody v. United States* (1964), the Native American Church had a thriving membership of well over 250,000 by the mid-1990s. The deep spirituality of Indians was retained amidst the multitude of white man's religions.

A major piece of legislation in 1887 again caused major changes in Indian lives—the General Allotment Act, or Dawes Act. On the reservation of Sisseton and Wahpeton Sioux in Minnesota, 2,000 Indians were the first to be assigned individual land allotments in 1887, leaving 660,000 acres in surplus. The act stated that the U.S. president could allot reservation lands to Indians, without their consent, and that those Indians who follow the provisions of the act would be granted U.S. citizenship citizens (excluding the Five Civilized Tribes—Cherokee, Chickasaw, Choctaw, Creek, and Seminole) and a few other tribal groups until amendments were passed). Normally, the head of a family received 160 acres, persons over the age of 18 received 80, and the children received 40 acres apiece.

Commissions were in charge of distributing the lands after survey crews had dissected the reservations. Federal officials kept tribal rolls to record who received allotments. Amendments followed the Dawes Act to allot lands to tribes excluded from the 1887 act. In 1906 the Burke Act amended the Dawes Act to grant U.S. citizenship at the end of the trust period rather than at the beginning. Tribal lands were held in trust with the U.S. government because they were defined by treaties. This gave the U.S. government the responsibility to protect all Indian lands held in trust. Furthermore, Indians did not have full ownership over their allotted lands. Full U.S. citizenship granted them complete ownership of their allotment unless a court appointed a guardian to them. Unfortunately the majority of allottees could not read and write English, much less have business knowledge necessary to develop their properties. By delaying citizenship, allottees were under the protection of the United States, but for many the Burke Act came too late when shrewd opportunists manipulated them out of their lands. Amidst the graft and corruption, Indians kept their sense of belonging to community, the essence of their identity.

From 1887 to 1934 Indian land as a whole diminished from 139 million acres to 48 million acres. Of the 91 million acres lost, two-thirds disappeared during the first 10 years of the allotment program, even though only 5 million acres were actually allotted in this period. Tribes such as the Five Civilized Tribes experienced debauchery and fraud, a tragic situation described by Angie Debo in her book, *And Still the Waters Run: The Betrayal of the Five Civilized Tribes.* Finally, the Meriam Report of 1928 surveyed the poor living conditions on the Indian allotments and remaining reservations and recommended the allotment program be stopped. In 1926 the Northern Cheyenne Allotment Act distributed lands to the Northern Cheyenne, the last tribe to be allotted land during 1930–31.

The early decades of the twentieth century were clouded with negative repercussions of the allotment program. While the majority of the population stayed entrenched on their allotments and on tribal reservations, a small steady stream of Indians moved away due to World War I. An estimated 10,000 Indians fought in World War I, and they experienced living in the American mainstream as servicemen. With the granting of U.S. citizenship to the remaining Indian population, Native Americans faced the worse of the Great Depression with the rest of the country. America did not come out of the Depression until the outbreak of World War II. Approximately 25,000 Indian men served in World War II. Another 40,000 to 50,000 worked in the war industries. This large outpouring of Native Americans from Indian country to join the war effort produced the first "urban Indian" generation. A change in federal Indian policy resulted, and the government's relocation program started officially in l952. This new program contributed to a dramatic urban shift in the American Indian population of approximately 1.5 million people. The U.S. government wanted to improve the lives of Indians by arranging jobs and housing in cities to escape poverty on the reservations. At present, more than two-thirds of the population resides in cities like greater Los Angeles, which has an estimated 50,000 Indians, the largest urban Indian population. Other metropolitan areas with Indians include Chicago, 13,000; Oklahoma City, 15,000; Denver, 15,000; and the San Francisco Bay Area with 18,000. Additional large urban Indian populations reside in Minneapolis, Seattle, Albuquerque, and Phoenix. But instead of the population becoming assimilated into the urban mainstream, an Indianness of community identity has survived through the concentrated settlement of Indians in enclaves more commonly know as ghettoes.

Undereducation, inadequate qualifications for well-paying jobs, poor housing, inconsistent employment, and alcoholism remain consistent problems for urban Indians. Federal assistance came as early as 1956, when the Indian Vocational Training Act authorized three kinds of programs to train Indians in job skills. But, for the most part, urban Indians themselves and concerned individuals have initiated alcoholism treatment programs and Indian neighborhood centers such as St. Augustine's Indian Center in Chicago that offer temporary shelter, meals, and counseling. Indian centers also exist in Kansas City, Seattle, Dallas, Los Angeles, Oklahoma City, and other cities. Efforts have been made to help the elder Indians to live in the cities as well. Still, too often, American Indian populations in the cities reside in urban ghettoes, but this is changing as the people become more educated and qualify for professions.

Government legislation and other actions have sought in some cases to offer Indians financial reparations. With the introduction of the Indian Claims Commission Act in 1946, the federal government was called upon to settle numerous disputed Indian land claims. For instance, until its discontinuance in 1978, the Indian Claims Commission reviewed 125 claims and awarded $669 million to tribal groups for past injustices and broken promises. Another federal bureaucracy, the Bureau of Land Management, created five major dams on the Upper Missouri River that compensated Sioux families who had to move. The bottom line called for dollars and Indian removal to produce hydroelectricity and water reservoirs. A similar case was the Kinzua Dam project, completed in 1966 on Seneca lands, which were flooded in the name of progress. Several court cases came to the legal forefront in the 1970s, chief among them the Maine case involving the Penobscot and Passmaquodies, who wanted a return of land instead of being compensated in dollars.

The Indian–land relationship is of a depth that bureaucrats seem to have taken lightly. In the view of traditional Indians, maintaining this relationship is essential to life on this planet, or else the consequences will be grave. For instance, kinship is bonded between the land and communities through generations. This fundamental structure is disturbed when the federal government intervenes to decide an issue such as the ongoing Navajo-Hopi Joint Use Area in northeast Arizona. In 1996, the government engineered a settlement agreement between the Navajo and Hopi tribes resulting in a shared common land area that both tribes claimed was theirs originally.

American Indian groups hold specific philosophical and spiritual views of the land and environment in which they live. Such views guided the people's lives in conjunction with the environment as they believed they were guardians of the land. Throughout the first many decades of the twentieth century, only a few non-Indian individuals, such as Ernest Thompson Seton, naturalist George Bird Grinnell, and sociologist John Collier, understood the deep Indian attachment to the environment.

In the first part of the century, Indian water rights were tested in *Winters v. United States* (1908), in which the Gros Ventre and Assiniboine Indians on the Fort Belknap Reservation in Montana argued their rights to the Milk River flowing adjacent to their land and the Supreme Court ruled, in essence, that Indians are entitled to the use of water needed to support the viability of reservation land. In its affirmation of the Indian view that reservation land and water are one and the same, *Winters* proved to be the most important legal case in Indian water rights thus far. Other cases in which the Indian–environment relationship with regard to water have been legally disputed include Pyramid Lake in Nevada destroying the fishing subsistence of the Paiutes, the return of the Taos Blue Lake to the Taos Indians in 1971, and the famous "Boldt Decision" (1974, *U.S. v. Washington)* that granted several tribes in Washington State the right to use traditional net fishing on local rivers.

Since the 1970s the most serious Indian environmental concerns have involved energy companies mining coal and uranium and drilling for oil and gas on Indian reservations. In fact, the Four Corners area, where the boundaries of New Mexico, Arizona, Utah, and Colorado meet, has become the world's largest strip-mining operation and currently no less than 25 energy companies seek to mine coal in the sacred Black Hills of the Sioux in South Dakota. With approximately one-third of the coal in the West on reservations lands, it is no wonder that the Council of Energy Resource Tribes (CERT) was formed in 1975 to protect the interests of its 25 original members.

Learning to live with the environment, rather than choosing to alter it, has remained a fundamental characteristic in the Indian–environment relationship. In spite of the many negative events affecting Indian–white relations, Indian people have kept their native identity as they stood at a threshold of major irreversible changes in the late twentieth century. The projection for the twenty-first century is that they will remain basically

Indian people because of the legacy of community and the guiding influences that perpetuate native community existence. The Indian identity
has, it should be noted, changed, but it remains basically "Indian." The
evolving of this identity through community is the saga of the survival of
Indian people as told in the following chapters. They are about the daily
lives of American Indians and how the federal government and other
external influences have brought considerable change to their communities on reservations and in urban areas.

CHRONOLOGY

1887   The General Allotment Act is passed. Also known as the Dawes Act, this act divided Native American reservation land into individual allotments, with allotted land to be held in trust by the government for 25 years. After land was allotted to the Native Americans on a reservation, the surplus land would be bought by the government and then sold.

1903   In *Lone Wolf v. Hitchcock*, the Supreme Court rules in favor of Hitchcock. This ruling gives Congress the major authority in determining Native American affairs as well as the ability to abolish or change treaties.

1901–03 Amendments to Dawes Act affecting Choctaws, Chickasaws, Cherokees, Creeks, and Seminoles in Indian Territory.

1906   Burke Act provides for the Secretary of Interior to grant "competent" Indians with land allotments fee-simple title to their lands to sell or lease.

1907   Oklahoma is formed out of what was known as the Indian Territory.

1908   The Supreme Court rules in *Winters v. United States* that Native Americans living on reservations have the right to water for agricultural needs. This ruling created what is known as the Winters Doctrine and allows Native Americans to appropriate as much water as needed for both agricultural and economic needs.

1912   Jim Thorpe, Sac and Fox, and Potawatomi, wins two gold medals for the pentathlon and decathlon at the Olympic Games in Sweden.

1919   American Indian Citizenship Act of 1919 grants U.S. citizenship to honorably discharged American Indians in World War I.

1921   The Snyder Act obligates the Interior Department to provide social, health, and educational services to Native Americans.

1924   All Native Americans are given U.S. citizenship under the Indian Citizenship Act.

1928   Lewis Meriam and his committee publish "The Problem of Indian Administration." In it they report on the alarming death rates, inadequate education, and horrible living conditions among American Indians. The Meriam Report advises Congress to allocate money to counteract these problems and to reform the Office of Indian Affairs.

1934   Indian Reorganization Act (Wheeler-Howard bill) enables Native American tribal governments to create their own constitutions, membership, and laws and encourages tribal leaders to form business corporations.
        Johnson-O'Malley Act authorizes the federal government to provide health, education, and social welfare services to Native Americans through state and territorial contracts.

1935   Will Rogers, Cherokee humorist and rodeo star, dies in plane crash with aviator Wiley Post.

1936   Oklahoma Indian Welfare Act provides Indian reorganization provisions to Oklahoma tribes.
        Alaska Reorganization Act provides Indian reorganization provisions to Alaska Native communities.

1941–45 An estimated 25,000 Indian men and several hundred women served in the U.S. armed forces in World War II.

1944   Tribal leaders meet in Denver, Colorado, and create the National Congress of American Indians.

1946   Congress creates the Indian Claims Commission to hear and address final tribal land claims against the United States.

1946–49 The Bureau of Indian Affairs (BIA) is reorganized into 12 area offices amid the 90 reservation offices, including the original

Washington office. Much of the authority of the commissioner of Indian affairs is transferred to the 12 area offices.

1947   The Hoover Commission is formed. This commission suggests that Native Americans be assimilated as soon as possible. The commission thinks that the federal government should stop funding Native American programs once trust status of their land ends and families begin to relocate off the reservation.

1952   Relocation Program is provided to all American Indians in rural and reservation areas to escape poverty for jobs and temporary assigned housing in cities.

1953   House Concurrent Resolution 108 passes in Congress to end the unique government-to-government trust relationship that existed between Native American governments and the federal government. The federal government terminated the legal status of Native Americans as tribes.

Public Law 280 allows five states (Alaska added as sixth state) to have criminal and civil jurisdiction on reservations within their boundaries.

1954–62   During this so-called termination era, Congress endeavors to end federal responsibility for Native Americans as stated in treaties and to end health programs and sovereignty.

1956   Indian Vocational Act to train native peoples for jobs.

1961   Individuals representing 90 tribes meet at the Chicago Indian Conference and makes out an agenda that focuses on achieving improvement in academic opportunity for their children, job training, reservation housing, medical services, economy, and employment rate.

National Indian Youth Council forms in Gallup, New Mexico, and questions the attempts of former advocate groups and their ways of dealing with Native American problems.

1962   The federal government forces New Mexico to allow its Native American populations to vote in elections, both state and local.

Institute of American Indian and Alaska Native Art established in Santa Fe, New Mexico.

1964   Tribal governments receive funds directly from the Office of Economic Opportunity (OEC) to help reduce poverty among Native Americans. Community Action Programs become the main source for funds and the principal organization used for controlling these funds. Such allocation of funds directly to the tribal governments becomes the main example that the self-determination policies try to follow.

1963   The terminated Menominee tribe of Wisconsin is restored to
            federal recognition by the leadership of Ada Deer, a tribal
            member with the support group DRUMS. Later, Deer became
            the first Native woman appointed as Assistant Secretary of the
            Department of the Interior over Indian affairs.

1964–74   Beginning in the mid-1960s, new state laws and court rulings
            begin to restrict Native Americans in Washington from using
            traps and certain types of nets. Washington Indians start to
            assert treaty rights dating back to the 1850s. This fishing rights
            dispute is sent to higher courts and ruled on in 1974 in *U.S. v.
            Washington*. Called the Boldt Decision, it confirms Indian treaty
            rights and declares that American Indians in Washington have
            the rights to at least half the fish in many of the state's rivers.

1965   The executive director from the American Indian National
            Congress and tribal representatives affirm their opposition in
            front of a U.S. Senate subcommittee against the Colville tribe
            termination during the termination era.
                LaDonna   Harris   organizes   Oklahomans   for   Indian
            Opportunity

1966   February: Nisqually tribe members are arrested, along with other
            "fish-in" protesters, for illegal net fishing at Green River and
            Columbia River in Washington. The Nisqually contend that they
            have the right to fish this way according to their 1856 treaty.
                April: Robert LaFollette Bennett is appointed as the BIA com-
            missioner and becomes the second Indian person to ever hold
            that position.
                September: The Navaho establish the Rough Rock
            Demonstration School by contracting with the BIA. This is the
            first school, in modern times, to be completely controlled by a
            tribe.
                October: The members of the Alaska Federation of Natives
            meet in Anchorage to discuss plans for conserving their land.
            Their main issue at hand is how to stop state land claims until the
            controversy of what "aboriginal title," which is given to those
            Alaskan Natives who did not sign treaties with the federal
            government, means.

1967   January: In order to improve educational services to Native
            American students, the BIA creates the National Indian
            Education Advisory Committee.
                February: The senate in Iowa revokes a law that prevented
            the sale of alcohol to Native Americans.
                March: A bill is passed to allow the Indian Claims Commission
            to function until 1972.

June: The U.S. Claims Court upholds a previous decision made by the Indian Claims Commission that stated that the Seminole of Florida, according to an 1823 treaty, have claims to 32 million acres.

August: Eight Sioux tribes get $12.2 million in compensation from the Indian Claims Commission for lands totaling 29 million acres taken from them by deceitful treaties in the nineteenth century.

1968   March: In his speech to Congress, President Lyndon Johnson gives his "Forgotten American" speech concerning Native Americans.

March: President Johnson creates the National Council on Indian Opportunity, which is responsible for improving Native American livelihood.

April: The American Indian Civil Rights Act gives Native Americans living on reservations under tribal governments many of the same civil rights that all persons under state and federal governments have according to the U.S. Constitution. It also abolishes Public Law 280 and requires updated versions of *Indian Affairs: Laws and Treaties*, by Charles Kappler, and *Handbook of Federal Indian Law*, by Felix Cohen, to be published by the Secretary of the Interior.

May: President Johnson signs a bill honoring the centennial of the peace treaty between the federal government and the Navajo.

May: In *Puyallup Tribe v. Department of Game*, the Supreme Court rules that the state of Washington can ban net fishing by Native Americans in the name of conservation.

July: Dennis Banks, George Mitchell, and Clyde Bellcourt found the American Indian Movement (AIM) in Minneapolis, Minnesota, to improve social services for urban Indians and stop police from harassing Native Americans.

October: A $5 million settlement, for the illegal taking of nine million acres of land by the federal government in 1874, is awarded to the Yavapai tribe of Arizona.

San Francisco State University begins its American Indian Studies program.

1969   N. Scott Momaday wins Pulitzer Prize for Literature for *House Made of Dawn*.

March: President Richard Nixon signs the Office of Minority Business Enterprise into existence. Its goal is to make sure that minority-owned businesses receive a share government contracts and purchases. The act also calls upon the government to aid tribes in developing their reservation economies.

March: The trial of seven Mohawk protesters begins. These individuals were demonstrating against the Canadian custom duties on Mohawk goods. They stated that the Jay Treaty of 1794 allows border tribes to freely pass the borders and exempts them from paying import and export taxes on their goods.

May: The Indian Claims Commission awards the Klamath tribe of Oregon $4.1 million dollars because of bad surveys that were conducted on their reservation by the government in 1871 and 1888.

August: Louis R. Bruce, A Mohawk-Oglala Sioux and one of the establishers of the National Congress of American Indians, is appointed as commissioner of Indian affairs by President Richard Nixon.

University of Minnesota, University of California–Berkeley, and Trent University in Canada begin American Indian Studies programs.

1970   Native American Rights Fund officially opens in Denver, Colorado.

LaDonna Harris founds Americans for Indian Opportunity.

1971   Alaska Native Claims Settlement Act gives Alaska Natives 44 million acres and $962 million dollars for relinquishment of the remainder of their claims in Alaska.

1972   AIM leaders Dennis Banks, Russell Means, and others lead several hundred Indians and supporters on the Trail of Broken Treaties march to Washington, D.C., and takeover of the BIA building.

American Indian Higher Education Consortium organization of tribally controlled colleges.

D'Arcy McNickle Center for the History of the American Indian opens at the Newberry Library in Chicago as a prominent research center.

1973   Takeover of Wounded Knee, South Dakota. AIM members confront FBI, military, and government officials.

1975   American Indian Self-Determination and Education Act establishes prevailing Federal-Indian policy of Indian self-determination for tribes to develop governments independent of the U.S. government.

Council of Energy Resources Tribes (CERT) founded in Denver, Colorado of 25 member tribes to protect their natural resources against mining companies.

1977   American Indian Science and Engineering Society founded in Boulder, Colorado.

1978   American Indian Religious Freedom Act protects Indian religious rights and sacred sites.

American Indian Child Welfare Act ensures that adopted Indian youth are raised in their tribal cultures.

Oliphant v. Suquamish Indian Tribe rules in Washington state that tribes cannot prosecute non-Indians committing crimes on tribal lands.

Santa Clara v. Martinez favors the Santa Clara Pueblo in New Mexico to make its own laws without federal intervention.

1979   Establishment of Federal Acknowledgement Branch, which regulates and processes federal negotiations with new tribes.

Seminole Tribe in Florida starts first Indian bingo operation, leading to big bingo and gaming operations for 189 tribes by 2000.

1982   *Merrion v. Jicarilla Apache* case involving taxation of non-Indians on their reservation.

1988   Passage of the Indian Gaming Regulatory Act regulates the Indian gaming industry through the National Gaming Commission.

1987   *California v. Cabazon Band of Mission Indians* in southern California rules that the Cabazon tribe can legally operate card playing games.

1990   Native American Grave Protection and Repatriation Act (NAGPRA) protects and respects Indian burial sites and starts repatriation movements to return artifacts and burial remains to native groups.

1992   Mashantucket Pequot open Foxwoods Indian Resort and Casino in Connecticut;

Public Law 102–573 amends Indian Health Care Improvement Act to increase health services to Indians including urban Indians to the highest level; Ben Nighthorse Campbell, a northern Cheyenne, elected to the U.S. Senate, representing Colorado.

1998   Organization of the NAMMY (Native American Music) Awards.

2002   Sand Creek site returned to Cheyenne and Arapaho tribes.

2004   Grand opening of the Smithsonian's National Museum of the American Indian in Washington, D.C.

1

FAMILY, WOMEN'S ROLES, AND SEXUALITY

THE FAMILY UNIT

The universal social unit among American Indians has always been the family. Among native people, relationships are very important and the idea of togetherness extends to their view of the natural world. The socio-cultural entity of family is the most important element for sustaining life. Indian people see themselves in terms of relationships within a greater whole called the community or tribe. This social context of family is the integral unit of togetherness and it is much like any family unit among all ethnic groups, yet it is different according to the cultural meaning of each tribe. Understanding relationships remains germane to a healthy native extended family. One's place in the extended family is still defined by kin-ship relationships among all involved.

More precisely, the Indian family is an extended family, especially during the first two-thirds of the twentieth century. Unlike the family unit in the American mainstream, the extended family has been a continual norm among almost all Indian groups. Native Americans will recall their younger lives when a grandparent, uncle, or aunt lived with them. No one, especially the elderly, should be left to care for themselves alone. These special relatives were a part of the family and played important roles that contributed to the stability of the entire family.

The Lakota use a term, *tiyosapaye*, that refers to their extended family based on the concept "all my relations." The concept of *tiyosapaye* connects families with their relatives to bond them together as a support unit.

In the *tiyosapaye,* an individual member is understood to have a political and social obligation to help immediate family members and relatives and in return identity is rendered to all of those who belong to this socio-kinship unit of the Lakota extended family.

It is important to be "connected" to community, for this links one to the present, the past, and the future. Connectedness is a part of the Indian way of life. The worst that could happen to a native person is to become disconnected from one's family and community. It is membership in these kinship groups that renders identity to each person, providing a sense of place, role, and responsibility. Therefore, belonging and kinship are pertinent to the Indian way of life.

Achomawi mother and child. Courtesy of Library of Congress.

Hunting and farming was much easier when practiced by several extended families, or even the community. Working as a group and for the best interests of the group was the philosophy of Indian tribes. This key idea has sustained this way of life for centuries. Friends were outside the kinship group, but they were important members of the community. An internal dependence on relatives and friends developed. Relationships became stronger.

Individuality was less stressed as a value until the federal government's actions resulted in an upheaval of traditional lifeways with the passage of the General Allotment Act (or Dawes Act) in 1887 that called for allotting tribal lands to individual tribal members. The allotment system disrupted the traditional family unit by geographically separating its members. The government expected allottees to work on their own lands. Indian people had always hunted, farmed, worked and went to war in groups. The strength and efficiency of more than one person logically dictated a philosophy that one person could not survive as well as many people could. Prosperity occurred with group cooperation. Thus, cooperation and working together remained as a central cultural norm to the Indian way of doing things. Native people recognized that maintaining relationships was imperative for the sustained togetherness as it had always been in the past.

Pueblo Indian children. Courtesy of Library of Congress.

Group orientation helped to define identity and role for each person. This gave overall purpose to life. Beyond extended families, each person belonged to a clan or society making Indian life systematic and complex. Belonging to a community, clan/society, and extended family provided security and safety for everyone—child, teenager, adult, and elder.

Relatives   Cousins and close relatives are a part of the immediate orbit of extended families. It is a part of the norm to have relatives constantly around. In fact, growing up with cousins living nearby is a part of Indian life. In this way, it seems that everyone is related to each other. This also means that everyone knows each other and who their people are. And, belonging is pertinent to Indian people. Belonging to a community means security and protection. A person is never alone in such an existence.

Blood relations insured membership in the extended family even at the risk of disagreeing personalities. Blood relations were the strongest kind of relationships, whereas symbolic relationships were reinforced by the usage of kinship terms. Calling people "cousin," "aunt," "uncle," "grandmother," and "grandfather" helped to integrate and sustain non-blood-related relationships within the communal scheme of life.

Clans and Societies   Outside of the extended family, a network of kinship contained other extended families. Clans or societies represented the next sociocultural unit. Clans were animal and sometimes plant or certain named groups, such as paint or hair, where a person inherited membership through the father or mother. In communities, societies were age-groups or associations based on certain deeds performed by individuals. These groups and extended families made up communities that are also called bands, towns, or tribes. The majority of American Indian tribes consist of several communities or more. There may be several—20 or more—clans or societies in tribes. Members of clans studied their clan totems to learn their strengths and practice them, for example, the way a wolf hunted. Societies provided comradeship and built trust among members of similar talents.

Most eastern woodland Indian groups and Pueblo groups of the southwest have clans that are named after animals and plants. Western groups like the Plains Indians possess societies such as the age-group societies of the Lakota, military societies among the Cheyenne, and medicine societies among many Plains people. The Cheyenne have dog soldiers, who are devoted warriors of high rank, to protect the tribe. They are well known for their warriorship. Other societies of the Cheyenne are Fox, Elk, Shield, Dog, and Bow-string.[1]

Originally, the elders of the Muscogee Creeks in Oklahoma say there were 12 clans of animals and plants in the Muscogee worldview. More clans developed to accommodate the expanding Creek universe as the people learned more about flora and fauna. At one time in the Southeast, the Muscogee had as many as 22 to 24 clans before their removal to west of the Mississippi River. Bear, deer, tiger, snake, and wind are some of the clans.

In the Great Lakes region, the Ojibwa or Chippewa have a sophisticated clan system. Their clans represent an important social order with five major phratries (division of related clans). The phratries consist of Awause (fish), Businause (Crane), Ahahwauk (Loon), Noka (Bear), and Monsone (Marten). The Chippewa have as many as 23 clans, including the catfish, merman, sturgeon, pike, whitefish, sucker, crane, eagle, loon, goose, cormorant, bear, marten, wolf, lynx, moose, rattlesnake, beaver, gull hawk, and reindeer. One of the nearby tribes, the Potawatomi, has a similar maze of phratries and clans. Their six phratries consist of water, bird, buffalo, wolf, bear, and man. At one time, the Potawatomi had as many as 23 clans, including the buffalo, grizzly bear, moose, otter, muskrat, marten, red carp, black carp, golden carp, and thunder.

In Michigan, the Ottawa had clan-type subgroups. These subgroups contained the Kiskakon (bear), Sinago (black squirrel), Sable (sand), and Nassauakueton (fork), which also made up the four communities of the Ottawa or Odawa. Furthermore, the four communities or villages acted as one in a most effective alliance.

Clans united native peoples with the natural universe as it seemed all of life and the known existence was contained in such a totality. Indian people study animals and plants for their patterns of growth and cycles of migration and life. In the same light, human beings are in the Natural Order, bonding humankind with the rest of the world in a Natural Democracy.

While blood kinship was stressed, symbolic kinship substituted when necessary. Symbolic cousins are also a **Non-Blood** part of Indian life. While kinship relations are important **Relationships** for solidifying relationships in indigenous society, obtaining allies is important for survival and to maintain harmony with nearby communities. Friends not related by blood are called cousins as a means of giving depth to relationships and making them a part of the community. symbolism is an integral part of Indian life as well as ceremony. Ceremonies are held to acknowledge symbolic relations and recognize the significance of relationships. Positive relationships are what held extended Indian families and their communities together.

The integration or adoption of other people was very important to sustaining the population of a tribe or com- **Adoption of** munity and for other reasons. In the case of the Comanche **Outsiders** during the early 1800s, as much as 40 percent of their bands' populations came from captives taken in raids. Adoption in this situation was for sustaining the necessary population of the various bands of the Comanche to continue their raiding economy during the late 1700s and early 1800s. Casualties suffered while raiding other tribal communities, Mexican settlements, and Texan homesteads threatened the numbers of the Comanche bands. For these raiders, a constant flux of new people coming into the bands was a way of life. Cheyenne, Kiowa, and Apache were also raiding tribes of the Plains where the region proved difficult to live off of so that taking from other peoples meant that the strong survived. Scarce natural sources of food forced plains tribes to take from others.

Ceremonies marked the adopting of captives or unrelated persons into an Indian family. As a part of the adoption procedure among the Sac and Fox of Oklahoma, clothes and necessary items like hunting equipment for boys and young men and cooking utensils or sewing items for girls and young women were given to the newcomers. In most cases, adopted newcomers replaced someone who had died in a family. The newly adopted person was welcomed and given a name as a part of the procedure for becoming a part of the family. The Sac and Fox are not alone in this ceremonial adoption process; other woodlands tribes, such as the Shawnee, had a similar procedure. The Sac and Fox continue the practice of adoption to the present. The loss of a family member is the primary reason for a ceremonial adoption, although it is not legal according to U.S. law.

Alliances   In the negotiations for alliances, kinship terms like *brother* are used to form brotherhood relations with other Indian groups. A historic example of this kinship terminology is the "Three Fires" of the Great Lakes in Michigan where the Oldest Brother is the Ojibwa, the Middle Brother is the Ottawa, and the Youngest Brother is the Potawatomi, meaning that all three brothers came from the same fire. Throughout the history of American Indian, the usage of *brother, father,* and *children* are found in tribal relations and relations involving tribes with the United States.

The history of the American Indian is one of many alliances of long duration as well as temporary ones. Known alliances were among the League of the Iroquois, Muscogee Creek Confederacy, Cheyenne bands, Comanche bands, Sauk and Fox, Cheyenne and Arapaho, and many others.

Grandmother and Grandfather   The grandmother is the matriarch of a family or more than one family. With many years of experience and collected wisdom, such a woman is admired and respected. To be called "grandmother" is an earned position based on respect from younger women and relatives. The native woman elder commands respect in the matrilineal type Indian communities, although she may also be heavily criticized for her personality and actions. Like anyone else, grandmothers have personalities and other people may not always agree with them. Grandmothers with strong views are especially susceptible to criticism. Matrilineal communities empower grandmothers especially by passing cultural and political inheritances through the mother's side of the family.

Traditionally, the grandmother has a collective wisdom of political and medicinal experiences that help to protect her relatives. As head of the extended family and related families by blood, the grandmother wields a great amount of influence and political power.

In addition to her status of respect, the grandmother drew upon her wisdom to take care of the sick and suffering members in the extended family. She had many years of experience with cures and means for improving the health of those who fell to illness. Her collective knowledge of herbs, plants, and the earth in general enables her to be a provider of good health and to maintain well-being in the extended family. Naturally, grown daughters defer to their mother's role due to the grandmother's experience and wisdom. In time, their turns come when they will be grandmothers to their grandchildren and perhaps even take on an extra role as the grandmother to other children.

The grandfather has played a different role in comparison with the significant role of the grandmother. In patrilineal societies (ones where all inheritances are passed down on the father's side of the family), the grandfather plays an integral role in the community. He is revered for his wisdom and longtime experience, and his advice is respected. Often in the absence of a father killed in war or an accident, the grandfather played the father role to guide the lives of children. The grandfather was a tribal elder and like the grandmother, he possessed much wisdom and life experience to help his family and community.

The domesticity of Indian life focused on traditional ways of native culture. This effort became increasingly challenged as Indian families learned to adjust to new lives on an estimated 291 reservations and over 300 including state Indian reservations by the end of the twentieth century.

Life for native people called for achieving balance to avoid chaos and confusion. The young are guided by the elders, whose responsibility is to maintain peace and order.

The Family in the Early- to Mid-Twentieth Century

Traditionally, elders advised, taught, and encouraged the correct ways of doing things in hunting, war, and in life in general. After 1900, the elders continued to advise youth in both the old ways and new ways of living in the American mainstream. In many ways, the roles of the grandmother, grandfather, and elders in general have become more demanding because these older individuals have less experience with the mainstream culture after World War II and the urbanization of the 1950s and 1960s. Yet, it was not too long ago that grandmothers and grandfathers were dealing with the federal government interventions concerning boarding schools and tribal land allotments.

The Dawes Act of 1887 has had a tremendous negative impact on the well-being of Indian people. Although not all tribes were affected, the majority of the Indian population underwent allotment via this act or amendments to it or by way of similar act, such as the 1899 Nelson Act that allotted the White Earth Chippewa Reservation in Minnesota. Land allotment called for change in culture, philosophy, and ethos, and it changed Indian families from living communally to living individually. Furthermore, it led to displacing Indian people from the earth as they knew it.

Naturally the environment remained an integral part of Indian life as the twentieth century began to unfold. Many native people recall the woods, meadows, and grassy areas that they played in and how they grew up entertaining themselves when they were not with grownups. They had few toys and most of them were handmade, whittled figurines or hand-sewn dolls. Little boys played with bows and arrows and Indian children played outside most of the time. Nature was their playground. Growing up on the Great Plains or the Great Lakes, in the Southwest, Pacific Northwest, California, or the Eastern woodlands, had a permanent influence on Indian youth and their families.

Cultural values remained more traditional as the American Indian population entered the twentieth century. This would change with increasing contact with the outside world. Community as the most important social unit remained the same until after World War II. The service of Indian men entering military service and native women going to work in the war industries represented a pivotal point for tremendous change as American Indians kept less and less to themselves. Economic needs made working in the mainstream almost a necessity, thereby causing change to the sociocultural infrastructure of native communities.

A family gathering place was essential to the rhythm of daily life. This was the front porch during the warm months of late spring, summer and early fall. For the rest of the year the kitchen table or the living room near a fireplace or woodstove was the gathering place for the family to talk and share stories about relatives, friends, and the past.

The oral tradition continued to be a mainstay of the Indian family. Practiced in the form of storytelling, the oral tradition has captured modern American Indian history with a revival of stories being told. As a cultural norm, stories were the fabric of native social life until the introduction of television into Indian homes beginning in the early 1960s.

The Modern Indian Family   To understand the modern life of Native Americans it is necessary to understand how the Indian family itself has changed. The nuclear family—meaning parents and children—became the normal Indian family unit as a result of Indians becoming a part of the American mainstream. But "normal" is not the reality for many Native Americans, especially in the last quarter of the twentieth century. With the constant problem of alcoholism and the increase of drug usage in Indian communities, many native families are maintained by a single parent. In a similar fashion, Indian society mirrors the mainstream with divorce becoming more of a common occurrence.

Having insight into why the Indian family changed is also important to understanding Indian people. First of all, Indians are used to change and they have been adapting to new conditions as new situations mandated changes. Although traditionalism is strong, they have worked out ingenious methods of combining tradition and new ways. They have adopted technology, many have converted to Christianity, and most have become mainstream educated. While undergoing the transformation into a new social unit, namely the American nuclear family, the Indian family has retained its integral self based on quasi-traditional values.

Family values began to change in the twentieth century with each new Indian generation of youth. World War II had the most significant impact on altering these values. In addition, the adoption of various forms of technology has transformed the traditional family into a modern one.

The breakup of the Indian extended family unit occurred with increasing contact with the American mainstream. Alcoholism and drug addiction in the last part of the century were main contributors to the decline of the extended family. This unfortunate pattern has become an infrastructural norm where the customary father role is missing. The incidence of Fetal Alcohol Syndrome (FAS) has increased among Indians, especially on reservations. This condition became a rising problem, especially after World War II, as alcoholism increased among native people on reservations. World War II changed people's lives as reservations lacked adequate jobs and Indians were undereducated and lacked job skills. Indians felt frustrated on reservations and in cities. FAS has become generational as FAS children grow up to have children of their own.

Adaptability has been a necessary skill among American Indians for their survival and prosperity. In fact, this cultural borrowing has been a way of life among Indian groups in that they acquire new ways and material items that will make life easier. By borrowing technology and ways of doing things from the mainstream on their own, native peoples have decided to adopt to modernity.

Cultural materialism had a significant impact on American Indians with increased contact with the mainstream. By adopting cultural items from the American mainstream, Native Americans began to change their own lives. For example, Indian people began dressing increasingly like white men and women.

Technology has been an important factor causing this change in the Indian family. Like the white American family, modern innovations like the automobile, electricity, and modern gadgetry to make life more comfortable has affected Indian life. Similar to the glass beads introduced during the fur trade era between Indians and whites, other non-Indian items like the sewing machine used to create patchwork designs on Seminole clothing in Florida and the automobile adopted by most modern

Indians have radically altered the both lifestyle of native peoples and the material culture they in turn produce.

The reservation Indian family has remained as the mainstay of the traditional ways of culture. The continual practice of certain rituals and ceremonies has perpetuated age-old values and ideas about life. Such values and ideas have shaped thought according to each native community within a particular region of the country. Traditional by nature, the Indian family on reservations or in historic home areas is less prone to influences for change from the outside.

On the other hand, the urban Indian family has been the most susceptible to change from old tribal ways to new ones in the attempt to thrive in metropolitan areas. In fact, most of Indian families have changed considerably, as roughly two-thirds of the total Indian population lives in urban areas. Former values on reservations and in rural areas did not always make sense in towns and cities. Traditional ceremonies could not be conveniently held in cities. Sweat baths and visiting sacred sites could also not be done. Hence, new cultural norms began to replace old tribal ways of life.

WOMEN'S ROLES

The role of the American Indian woman has changed considerably during the twentieth century. As a result, the matriarchal system began to dissolve. This change is the result of continual contact with the mainstream. At the other end of modernity stands the traditional Indian woman.

The traditional Indian woman was an iconic strength of American Indian people. She remains in this special status although much has changed during the last part of the twentieth century and in the early years of this century. Through her, culture is perpetuated, although it is changed by the surrounding influences from outside of the native community.

The working Indian woman began to become more visible following World War II. Many native women had worked in the war industries and this gave them important exposure to the American mainstream and the confidence to work outside of their homes. Unfortunately most Indian women worked at low-level labor jobs. They continued to work in jobs requiring little education or skill.

The new Indian woman represents something of the past and the present needs of Indian families. She has two full-time jobs: her paid employment, and taking care of her children and husband. Working in mainstream occupations requires her to communicate assertively in the course of teaching, solving problems, giving presentations, and sharing her expertise. She is bicultural in knowing the ways of her people and those of the mainstream business world. She has a high school education and most likely some college or even a college degree. By the 1990s, a noticeable number of Indian women held final graduate degrees and law degrees, and a small number were physicians.

The works of Native women writers, in addition to providing a valuable female perspective on native life, offer a treasure of knowledge about native life in general. The earliest Indian women authors include Humishuma (1888–1936), Ella Deloria (1888–1971), Pauline Johnson (1861–1913), and Sarah Callahan (1868–1894). Humishuma, who was also known as Chrystal Quintasket, wrote because she wanted to preserve knowledge of the Okanogan. She published a novel, *Co-go-wea, the Half-Blood* (1927), which brought her national attention. Ella Deloria was a research assistant to anthropologists, leading to her own scholarly work on linguistics and the folklore of the Dakota Sioux. Pauline Johnson, a Mohawk actress born in Canada, wrote books of poetry for Canadian readers. Sarah Callahan, a Muscogee Creek, wrote *Wynema: A Child of the Forest* (1891), perhaps the first novel by an American Indian woman.[2]

This early generation of native women writers paved the way for modern writers of poems and novels. Prominent contemporary authors include Paula Gunn Allen, Diane Burns, Gladys Cardiff, Nora Dauenhauer,

Hopi Indian women grinding grain. Courtesy of Library of Congress.

Charlotte de Clue, Louise Erdrich, Rayna Green, Joy Harjo, Linda Hogan, Wendy Rose, Carol Lee Sanchez, Mary Tall Mountain, Judith Mountain Leaf Volborth, Annette Areketa West, Roberta Hill Whiteman, and Shirley Hill Witt.[3] These native writers continue the tradition of using story to tell about tribal ways and human experiences that they grew up with.

SEXUALITY

Sexuality among American Indians has changed in major ways during the twentieth century. Once a forbidden subject, constant exposure to the mainstream has made sexuality a more open topic of discussion. Television commercials, magazines, and movies have persuaded native peoples to see themselves in a mainstream manner. Fewer and fewer cultural ways involving sexuality have been maintained as more young Native Americans see themselves as a part of the mainstream or somewhere in between tribal and White ways.

Berdache is a Lakota term for a man who is actually a woman. He leads a life that is not of the cultural norms for men. His roles and responsibilities in the community are those of a woman and he has a place in society. The Lakota observe that such a person exists and is different, and that this difference may lend special power to the berdache.

Traditionally, Indian tribes recognized homosexuality and it had a place in society. The tribal view was that everyone had a role in the community, including those outside of the norm. Special attention was given to people who were different for there had to be some purpose for their differences, such as their gift of prophecy, healing powers, or other special talents.

Mixed Marriages Keeping the blood pure, with the goal of preserving tribal identity, was supported by arranged marriages within tribes until about the 1940s and 1950s, after which government-sponsored Indian boarding schools and native service in World War II began to soften tribal differences and more Indian mixed marriages became more common.

Marriage between members of different tribes has been a normal occurrence over the years, but this change accelerated in the twentieth century with the introduction of the Indian boarding school, which was attended by students from several tribes. It is quite common for Indian husbands and wives to have met their significant others while going to boarding schools at Haskell Indian School in Kansas, Sherman Institute in California, Chilocco Indian School in Oklahoma, and various other places. Many boarding school couples even continue to live in the area of the schools, making their homes there and raising families. For example, many students from southern and central plains tribes like Cheyenne, Kiowa, Comanche, and Apache have attended Haskell at Lawrence, Kansas and decided to live there after getting their education. In such cases, native young men and women uniting in mixed tribal marriage raised families while promoting an *Indianness,* a generic Indian identity. In turn, this rising new Indian identity contributed to the decline of tribalism in Indian Country. Naturally, the decline of full-bloods of one tribe has declined with the increase of mixed tribal marriages.

As a result, the makeup of the Indian population has changed with many more mixed-bloods (Indian and non-Indian as well as among different tribes) than full-bloods. In between, are full-bloods of more than one tribe. Tribal members marrying other tribes have been a steady pattern since the nineteenth century and before. This is not a new phenomenon for the twentieth century, but it became more evident as a cultural pattern as more Indian people met other Indians from other tribes. Naturally, native peoples married other tribal people in the same region, but as World War I and World War II dispersed Native Americans throughout the country, the experience provided opportunities to meet Indians from other tribes for the first time in their lives.

The increase of tribal colleges has also changed the demographics of the Indian college student. As a result, at least half or more of today's American Indians in colleges and universities are women. This is also apparent at the graduate level as more native women began seeking advanced degrees during the last two decades of the twentieth century. This trend has continued in the first decade of the twenty-first century as more and more of the same Indian women have found themselves becoming single parents raising children.

While the federal government's attempt to force most Indian tribes to send their youth to boarding schools beginning in the 1940s was met with limited success, by the end of the 1960s, the Indian people themselves began to believe that possessing an education was the key to a better life. Native people in most tribes began to believe this, making this change a general Indian value rather than a tribal one.

The postwar era in the second half of the twentieth century has marked a modern American Indian history in which Indian people have initiated much change. For example, the explosion of tribal colleges in the 1960s and 1970s was a part of the urbanization of American Indians. Starting in 1952 as a federal program introduced to all Indians, "relocation" brought about the largest demographic shift in modern Native American history. Perhaps as many as 100,000 participated in relocating to urban areas. This incredible geographic transformation enabled Indians to meet other Indians from different tribes. Cross tribalization occurred, causing a pan-Indian effect thereby substituting the mainstream presumption of a generic Indian identity. Naturally, intermarrying within a tribe decreased and mixed-tribal marriages became a common occurrence as the urban Indian population soared to surpass the number of native peoples living on reservations. In addition to this aspect of cross-tribal marriages, many Indians began to marry partners from other racial basis.

CONCLUSION

The American Indian family changed considerably during the last half of the twentieth century. Indians were becoming like non-Indians as the two separate cultures began to remain in contact on a daily basis. Due to external influences from the larger mainstream such as materialism, stereotypes, and daily jobs in the business world, Indian families were forced to adapt to a new socioeconomic environment. Soon, they accepted these new ways as necessary for prospering and not just surviving in the twentieth century. Such changes altered the nature of the American Indian family as it began to mirror the mainstream family. Basically, available technology and continual exposure to the non-Indian world has had a permanent influence on native families.

NOTES

1. E. Adamson Hoebel, *The Cheyennes: Indians of the Great Plains* (New York: Holt, Rinehart and Winston, 1960), 33.

2. Rayna Green, ed., *That's What She Said: Contemporary Poetry and Fiction by Native American Women* (Bloomington: Indiana University Press, 1984), 3.

3. Ibid., v–xi.

2

ECONOMICS, RURAL, URBAN, TAXATION, TRADE, AND TRANSPORTATION

The continuous contact of American Indians with mainstream society caused the greatest change of values among Native Americans during the twentieth century. Simply, the willingness of American Indians, their families, and communities to adopt mainstream values has enormously affected Indian economics. Perhaps an important question to ask is how and why Indians wanted to change? Why did they leave reservations to live in cities? It would be wise to discuss possible answers for rural and reservation life in Indian Country compared with urban Indian life in the cities, which did not begin noticeably until after World War II.

On the eve of the twentieth century, in Chicago on April 10, 1899, Governor Theodore Roosevelt of New York gave a speech entitled "In Praise of the Strenuous Life." A persistent Roosevelt said,

I wish to preach not the doctrine of ignoble ease but the doctrine of the strenuous life; the life of toil and effort; of labor and strife; to preach that highest form of success which comes not to the man who desires mere easy peace but to the man who does not shrink from danger, from hardship, or from bitter toil, and who out of these wins the splendid ultimate triumph. . . . As it is with the individual so it is with the nation.[1]

Several years earlier, Roosevelt assessed the situation facing many Indian people, saying that the federal government had done much to help them. Now, "we must turn them loose, hardening our hearts to the fact that many will sink, exactly as many will swim."[2] The brutal honesty of Roosevelt's words described Indians to be on their own in learning the ways of the white man, but also losing their old ones along the way. Such a transformation was not easy and came with unpredictable hardship.

American Indians are traditionally a communal people whose identity and way of life depended largely upon group emphasis. This concept detours from the American mainstream's focus on individuality. President Theodore Roosevelt characterized this lifestyle as "rugged individualism." Indian people quickly learned about the "rugged" part as their reservations began to be surveyed into parcels called allotments of 160 acres with 60 acres on the average to be assigned respectively to individual Indian men and women.

Federal–Indian relations in the late nineteenth century involved the General Allotment Act of 1887, or Dawes Act. This legislation had the greatest impact on the economies of all tribes. In essence, tribal lands became vulnerable to white opportunists. The majority of Indians continued to live according to tribal ways while they also realized that jobs nearby would help feed their families. In 1900 an estimated 60 percent of Indian males aged ten years old or older were categorized by the U.S. Census Bureau as being "gainfully employed." For the next 15 years, this percentage increased only 5 percent.[3]

American Indians of the West whose previous lives were mobile and dependent upon horseback found farming and raising stock to be incongruent with their lifestyles and fundamental cultures. Under the land allotment program, agriculture consisted of livestock grazing, dry land farming, and irrigation of crops. Unfamiliar with farming techniques and susceptible to opportunists native peoples were left with the poorer grade of land to farm. In regard to potentially productive Indian land, non-Indians leased 60 percent of the irrigated lands and 76 percent of dry farm land.

On May 21, 1908, the U.S. Senate amended the Dawes Act by removing restrictions from allotted lands belonging to members of the Five Civilized Tribes of Oklahoma: Cherokee, Chickasaw, Choctaw, Creek, and Seminole. Among the five tribes, some allottees had coal and oil under their lands, leading to significant royalties being paid to them. For the 1898–1899 fiscal year, the federal government collected $110,145.25 in royalties for the Five Civilized Tribes. In 1903–1904, royalties soared to $277,811.60 and then decreased to $273,196.82 in 1907–1908. Natural gas became a part of the old industry during these years. By 1907 as many as 4,366 oil and gas leases had been signed, covering 363,000 acres belonging to the five tribes.

Becoming wealthy overnight, the oil-rich Indians bought anything that they wished. Often, they gave cars, horses, and clothes away that they grew weary of. The ease of their accumulation of material goods confused their cultural values with traditional ones. For perspective, not all members of the five tribes had oil under their allotted lands. Less than one-fourth of the members of the five tribes actually benefited from oil. It would normally be thought that they were fortunate, but the majority of

Indian reservation at Tejon Ranch in California, 1900. Courtesy of Library of Congress.

the oil-rich Indians became victims of opportunists. Most oil-rich Indians could not read or write English for having never gone to school.

A Muscogee Creek woman named Wosey John Deer had oil on her land. In the custody of a guardian, W. J. Cole of Sapulpa, Oklahoma, she invested in high-bred cattle and had other livestock. Wosey could not read or write English and fell vulnerable to Cole's influence. She could afford anything so on one occasion Wosey had one of her prized $500 bulls butchered for a barbeque. Her wealth brought misfortune as opportunists harassed her for money. Friends once found her beaten up. In the end, Cole convinced Wosey to divorce her husband, Albert Deer, to make it easier to manipulate her.

Another Muscogee Creek, Willie Berryhill, left an estate of more than $40,000 when he died. This was an enormous sum during the 1920s. Surrounding people fought over his estate, some claiming that he owed them and others that he had promised them money. On a whim, another wealthy Creek Indian purchased a wooden horse to put in his yard and later acquired two record players to play just two records. Whims and desires produced irrational actions. Royalty money had brought convenience, comfort, and grief.

Man plowing his land on Sacaton Indian Reservation. Courtesy of Library of Congress.

Oil also had a major impact on the Blackfeet Reservation in Montana. In 1910 the Blackfeet Reservation had been allotted to tribal members, and oil divided the tribe over whether or not to drill wells and how to distribute the income. A mixed-blood group of Indian and non-Indian wanted oil production and a primarily full-blood community opposed it to protect the tribe. In 1914 about 1,189 full-bloods lived on the reservation with 1,452 mixed-bloods. During the early 1930s, oilmen drilled wildcat wells on the eastern boundary. Original projections declared that the Blackfeet would receive a rich steady increase of per capita payments from the tribal oil royalty. This did not happen. The payment for 1955 totaled nearly $2.5 million, which amounted to $225 per tribal member. An additional $75 was paid to each member, but the Blackfeet never experienced oil windfalls like the Creek and Osage Indians of Oklahoma.

In the Southwest, Navajo women developed fine weaving skills into small profits to supplement family incomes based on herding sheep. In the late-nineteenth through mid-twentieth centuries, an estimated 100,000 Navajo women wove one million textiles. This enormous effort included saddle blankets and rugs. In 1890 white traders shipped textiles worth about $24,000. Forty years later at the beginning of the Great Depression, this amount grew to about $1 million. During these years, a weaver earned about $200 per year.

In Indian Country during the first two decades of the century, the haves and have-nots existed. Most of the latter consisted of full-bloods as money and properties changed hands and more mixed-bloods became experienced at handling their own business affairs. The federal government directed its court system to deem Indians without English skills to be "incompetent," thereby a court assigned a guardian to legally protect the assigned Indian person from opportunists. This incompetent/competent system lasted until regional agencies took over the affairs of individual Indians in the 1930s, although most native people handled their own affairs after World War II.

BEGINNINGS OF URBAN LIFE

Economic conditions on reservations have changed considerably throughout the last 100 years. With each new generation of young Indians, more left reservations and traditional homelands to find jobs, usually in towns and larger urban areas. This demographic movement began in the early years of the Great Depression after the horrific stock market crash on Black Tuesday in October 29, 1929.

When John Collier was appointed in 1932 as the new commissioner of Indian affairs for the FDR administration , a new era of Indian history began. As a means to bring relief from the Depression, President Franklin Roosevelt started the Civilian Conservation Corps (CCC) in 1934. As a part of the CCC, an Indian Division began that assigned jobs to Native Americans in 17 states. The CCC-ID encouraged Indian men to leave their homes to work, creating a stream of off-reservation employment. Indian workers helped to build public buildings, bridges, highways, and other common projects on their reservations and for the rest of the country.

The federal government's efforts toward economic relief for the country were interrupted by the outbreak of World War II. The attack **Effects of World War II** on Pearl Harbor by the Japanese forced the U.S. into the war, and 25,000 American Indian men and 700 women served in the armed forces. They became soldiers, marines, and seamen, while an estimated 40,000 Indian women and elderly men worked in the war industries as a part of the effort to save the country. Indian women and men who were not eligible for the draft made soldiers' uniforms, jeeps, tanks, and guns, and they worked in related areas for the railroad and local communities. With what few funds they had available, they bought war bonds when the government launched a national campaign to persuade the public to buy bonds to support the war effort. Ira Hayes, a Pima Indian from Arizona, was a part of the tour of men who raised the American flag on Mount Suribachi following the bloody fight against the Japanese at Iwo Jima in the Pacific, where more

Apache Indian laborers. Courtesy of Library of Congress.

than 6,000 Americans died. American Indians were now a part of the mainstream workforce as a result of World War II and the way back to traditionalism was farther away and not reachable for many.

In 1950 the typical Indian family living on the Yankton Reservation in South Dakota earned $730 annually. Annual income was less than $1,000 for other reservations, such as the Crow Creek Reservation, where one-third of the Lakota families earned less than $500. Gradually, income on reservations increased as unemployment dropped to 57 percent in 1969. Reservations economies could not keep up with the growth of the rest of the country as high unemployment remained constant in Indian Country.

Urban economic life proved to be considerably different from rural reservation life. Indians were in contact with whites and the rest of the mainstream on a daily basis and adopting new values. The federal relocation program started in 1952 brought American Indians to cities in large quotas throughout the 1950s, 1960s, and early 1970s. Initially started as an experimental program to bring relief to Arizona and New Mexico from the blizzard of 1947–48, the federal government moved Navajos (Diné) to Salt Lake City, Denver, and Los Angeles in 1951. The following year, the government extended the relocation program to all of the Indian population, finding them jobs and temporary housing in urban areas. Soon, the Indian relocatees found themselves being given a ticket to take a bus or drive their car to Chicago, Denver, Los Angeles, Seattle, Minneapolis, San Francisco, and other major metropolitan areas, mainly in the West. In the 1960s, members of different tribes found new homes primarily in their regional city.

A fascinating example of Indians in the urban workforce is that of the Mohawk Indians, who **The Mohawk Ironworkers** found a daring line of work in high steel. They traveled to major cities to help build tall buildings as other Indians relocated to urban areas during the 1950s and 1960s. In fact, since the 1890s, Mohawks working in high steel began moving to Syracuse, Rochester, and New York City for employment. Their introduction as ironworkers began much earlier, in 1886 on the St. Lawrence River between the United States and Canada.

Mohawk ironworkers consisted of a band from the Caughnawaga Reserve, located on the south shore of the St. Lawrence River. Long ago they had become Christians and became known as the praying Mohawks and have since moved to other cities—Brooklyn, Buffalo, and Detroit. Their dangerous occupational history began in the spring of 1886 when the Dominion Bridge Company built a railroad bridge across the St. Lawrence River for the Canadian Pacific Railroad just below their village. The Dominion Bridge Company, the largest iron and steel construction company in Canada at the time, hired the Mohawks as laborers to unload materials. Eventually the Mohawks began to come onto the bridge being constructed to deliver materials to the workers. They proved to be agile walking on the beams of the bridge and over 70 continued to work for the company.

On August 29, 1907, during the construction of the Quebec Bridge, which crosses the St. Lawrence nine miles above Quebec City, a span of the bridge collapsed and 96 ironworkers fell 350 feet to their deaths into the river. Of the dead, 35 Caughnawaga Mohawks were counted in the worst bridge construction tragedy in modern history.

The horrific accident did not stop the Mohawks. By the mid-1920s, three or four of the Mohawks' crews worked on building Rockefeller Center in New York City. More crews arrived as the Mohawk ironworkers worked for big steel companies like Bethlehem and American Bridge. Other companies like Lehigh Structural Steel and Harris Structural Steel hired Mohawks when they saw how the other companies benefited from the skills of the Mohawks. Their numbers increased as did their reputations while working on other high steel projects like the RCA building, the Cities Service Building, and the Empire State Building. Their ongoing success in the industry found them working on the Daily News Building, the Chanin Building, the Bank of the Manhattan Company Building, the City Bank Farmers Trust Building, and the George Washington Bridge. Mohawk ironworkers also helped to construct the Bayonne Bridge, the Passaic River Bridge, the Triborough Bridge, the

Henry Hudson Bridge, the Little Hell Gate Bridge, the Bronx-Whitestone Bridge, the Marine Parkway Bridge, the Pulaski Skyway, the West Side Highway, the Waldorf-Astoria, London Terrace, and Knickerbocker Village.[4] They have also worked on the CN Tower in Toronto, George Washington Bridge and the World Trade Center in New York, and the Golden Gate Bridge in San Francisco. The Mohawks developed a reputation in an occupation that few other groups dared to follow. Heavy steel work in the air attracted other Iroquois Indians—the Onondaga, Seneca, and Tuscarora, who also became skywalkers.[5] This Mohawk tradition continues today.

URBAN LIFE

During the course of the federal relocation program, from 1952 to 1972, more than 100,000 Indians moved to cities. The first two generations of relocatees unfortunately lacked the education, skills, and experience needed to secure employment. Although they lagged behind other Americans working in cities, urban Indians earned 20 percent more income on an annual average than those on reservations. However, in comparison with the average white American family and other minorities, the American Indian earned a lower salary. In the early 1960s, the Indian family earned $1,500 per year compared to the mainstream family income at $5,000. The federal government sought to do something about this.

One year after the end of World War II, the Bureau of Indian Affairs (BIA) introduced vocational education to Navajo and Hopi students at Sherman Institute in California. The new five-year program provided special education, job training, and off-reservation job placement. The program called for relocating the Indian young people to Phoenix, Denver, and Los Angeles and expanded to include Minneapolis, Milwaukee, Chicago, Dallas, Oakland, and San Jose. On January 16, 1952, Secretary of Interior Oscar L. Chapman and Secretary of Labor Maurice J. Tobin announced the government's approval of the first American Indian apprenticeship program in history. This was a ten-year program to help the Navajo and Hopi peoples by providing them with 28 skilled trades, including machinist, automobile mechanic, bricklayer, tile setter, and stone and block mason. Other trades included carpenter and cabinet maker. Plasterer, cement mason, electrician, and electric motor and transformer rewinder were other trades. Yet more trades were power lineman, telephone lineman, telephone cable splicer, P.B.X. installer and repairman, telephone repairman, four types of operating engineer, lather, painter, resilient floor covering and carpet layer, plumber, pipe fitter, roofer, and sheet metal worker. The government extended this opportunity to all Indian men and a total of 442 Native Americans were provided direct employment services.

The recovery of America from the demands of war production provided jobs in urban areas such as Chicago for large companies including Caterpillar Corporation, General Motors, Inland Steel, St. Joseph's Hospital, and the Wells Manufacturing Company. In Chicago employed Indians could expect to earn $1.41 an hour (nearly $3,000 per year) on the average in 1955 and over $2.00 per hour (or more than $4,000 per year) in 1960 compared to the average income on a reservation at $1,500 annually.[6] The 1960 Census recorded an estimated 600,000 Indians with an estimated one-third living in urban areas, with Los Angeles home to the highest number of urban Indians. In another effort, the government offered the Adult Vocational Training Program, which provided over 50 different courses of study in vocational and technical schools for 4 to 24 months after a medical examination was passed. In 1963 the program encompassed three general types: direct placement in jobs without vocational training (1,678 persons); on-the-job training (545 persons); and vocational training prior to employment (2,885 persons).[7]

The government decided that Indians needed jobs. In a memorandum from 1964, Secretary of Interior Stewart L. Udall called for a ten-year plan "to raise the standard of living on Indian reservations above the poverty line." The idea was that while urban Indians would be taken care of under the relocation program, reservations needed to be brought into the industrial economy. On December 3, 1964, Secretary Udall announced a plan of $500,000 for a plastics molding plant at Durant, Oklahoma, to provide jobs for 100 Indian men and women. Plans included 40 other such plants that had been established with federal assistance, providing employment to 1,500 Native Americans on or near reservation communities.[8]

As a new beginning, the Interior Department announced on August 16, 1965, that the BIA would renew contracts totaling more than $150,000 with six manufacturers to provide on-the-job training for 236 Indians. The government sought to prime the economic pump. As a part of the BIA's emphasis on jobs for Indians and preparation for urbanization, the new commissioner of Indian affairs, Robert L. Bennett, an Oneida from Wisconsin, announced that two new employment assistance centers were scheduled to open in Oklahoma City and Tulsa.[9] Almost two years later, the BIA announced a renewal of a number of contracts for job training for Indians that totaled nearly $3 million. The largest contract renewal named Philco-Ford Corporation's Education and Technical Services Division for their factory in Madera, California, involving $1,728,600.[10]

The BIA's effort was a part of President Lyndon Johnson's War on Poverty program. Mounting anti–Vietnam War and civil rights protests demanded the president's attention. One full-blood from the Minnesota urged the president, "please do not forget the American Indian people in the urban areas of our nation." He applauded Johnson's request to Congress to provide $516 million to alleviate suffering among Indian people via federal programs.[11] In 1967 an estimated 90 percent of Indian housing, mainly on reservations, was substandard and unemployment among Native Americans averaged 46 percent. The average income for an Indian family stood at $30 a week, in comparison to $130 a week for the average non-Indian family.[12]

In California during the late 1960s, urban Indian income varied across the country. An employed Indian in Los Angeles/Long Beach earned $5,922 per year and $6,503 in San Francisco/Oakland. In San Diego, urban Indian men earned $4,143 annually; in Phoenix, $3,786; and in Tucson, Arizona, $2,731. The following list illustrates urban Indian incomes for various cities.

City	Income 1960	Income 1970
San Francisco	$3,349	$6,175
Chicago	3,473	5,896
Los Angeles	3,423	5,690
Seattle	2,321	5,439
Minneapolis	1,978	5,366
Oklahoma City	2,658	5,087
Albuquerque	2,392	4,322
Buffalo	3,712	3,996
New York	3,660	2,854
San Diego	2,070	2,854

Unemployment has constantly plagued both urban and rural Indians when compared with other groups. For example, in comparison with whites and African Americans during 1940 to 1970, the Indian unemployment rate rose 16 percent. In search of jobs, a large migration of Indians from rural areas accounts for most of this statistic. In their searching, Indians found themselves working at unskilled jobs, often in seasonal work and prey to high rates of layoffs. Nonetheless, in comparison with African Americans, Indians in cities had a 10 to 15 percent higher unemployment rate.[13]

Urban Indians in Oklahoma, Texas, New Mexico, and Arizona had the lowest rates of unemployment. Specifically, the unemployment rate was 3.8 percent in Dallas. High rates existed in Minnesota, Washington, and Oregon. For California, with the largest Indian population during these years, the unemployment rate was at the middle of the scale.[14] At this time, with Indian workers dispersed all throughout cities at their jobs, no one could really measure the success of Indian employment in urban areas. A federal task force called for the assessment of employment rate and investigation into the cause of unemployment.

In 1976 the Task Force Eight of the American Indian Policy Review Commission concluded that "Indian people in substantial numbers came to urban areas because of a lack of employment in addition to other social and economic problems existing on the reservation, but have failed to make a desirable transition because of a lack of necessary and sufficient, continued support from the Federal Government, coupled with the indifference and misunderstandings, by and large, existing in the communities in which they have chosen to live."[15] The misunderstanding of Indians stems from a lack of information about them and their various cultures, which remain so far removed from mainstream values. As a result, a welfare status emerged for many urban Indians, which has been accompanied by public criticism of native people. In trying to do well in urban adjustment, Native Americans have been recipients of social services, especially after the 1960s. In another light, an estimated 15 percent of all urban Indian families received welfare assistance that averaged $1,471. With each decade, Indian family incomes increased. For the rural areas and reservations, the average income rose from $3,509 to $6,600, which was an increase of 90 percent.

The poor adjustment of many Indians to urban living compelled American Indian businessmen to petition the federal government for control of the relocation program. Although this attempt failed, the Urban Indian Development Association, an Indian group, submitted a plan to the commissioner of Indian affairs whereby the BIA would turn over to the association the Employment Assistance (Relocation) Program. After two preliminary meetings with positive tones, nothing happened, in spite of the general effort of the Johnson's War on Poverty program.[16]

Many Indians in cities had traded reservation poverty for urban poverty. Poverty became a part of their new urban culture. For 1970, the census reported that 15 percent of all urban Indian families received public welfare, approximately three times the rate for the rest of the entire urban population. Furthermore, the economic status of all Indians continued to be well below the total national population. In regard to urban Indian families, one-sixth earned an income under $3,000, while on the reservation one-third of the Indian families earned an income under $3,000.[17]

Being Indian in the 1970s meant being poor in general. Frank Love, the Executive Director of the American Indian Center, believed that "Indianness" meant being poor. Unfortunately he also thought that potential employers made the same assumption when hiring, causing Indians to have a psychological disadvantage. Native Americans had the lowest-paying jobs, forcing them to live in substandard housing. As Indian families sought each other out, Indian ghettoes began to develop. Certain neighborhoods became known as Indian areas; Franklin Avenue in the Twin Cities was called the "Reservation," and the Mission area in San Francisco became known as the "Little Reservation." Urban Indian communities began to increase but reamain poor.

Impoverished urban Indian areas were naturally associated with welfare assistance. But urban Indians did not always qualify for such assistance. Federal welfare regulations required complete information and various facts for receiving Aid to Families with Dependent Children (AFDC) and assistance from other programs. Native people learning about city life found it necessary to keep records about their employment, medical records, family history, and financial information, a practice previously unfamiliar to them.

A part of the welfare system required working with social workers. Native peoples have always relied upon each other and now they were forced to trust strangers in order to obtain social services. This did not always work very well until trust began to develop between the Indian family and social worker. Often a barrier of communication initially occurred due to language and cultural differences. One alternative was for Indian social workers to help native families, but the number of these individuals was too small during the 1960s and 1970s to serve all native families in need.

Limited education added to the difficulties of American Indians. In the 1960s, an estimated 55 to 60 percent of reservation students completed high school. This meant that almost one-half of the students dropped out of school. By 1970, urban Indians 25 years and older had an average of 11.2 years of education. The average was even lower on reservations, at 8.7 years. To make matters worse, one in eight rural Indians had no schooling at all, compared to one in forty Indians living in cities.

An estimated 1,500 Indians had entered the federal Vocational Training program by mid 1959; the program enabled almost one-half of urban Indian workers in the 1970s to become craftsmen, foremen, or operators. Obtaining vocational training did not solve employment problems for many Indians. Some vocational training schools hired untrained instructors, including Indians themselves. Some schools lacked proper state accreditation. Another problem arose when the schools had insufficient funding sources to help their Indian students. One young native woman wanted to enroll in college and the vocational training school put her husband in sheet-metal training classes. After six months, he was told there was not enough money to finish his training. The school got him a menial job paying $1.50 per hour. The couple did not have enough money to send the wife to school so the husband quit his job and found a higher paying one. He enrolled in another vocational course to complete his training.[18]

Although many urban Indians enrolled in job training programs in the 1970s, not many completed the training, or were placed in jobs as a result of the training. Two-thirds failed to complete job training, another 7 percent had been trained as beauticians, 18 percent as clerical workers, and 8 percent as medical assistants. An estimated two-thirds of Indians women were housewives, or unemployed, while 9 percent were in trade school or other educational programs. Furthermore, Indian women in cities began moving into the labor force at the same rate as the women of the general population.

In 1970 urban Indian unemployment was more than twice the total national average. On the average, Indian men of 16 years and older had a 11.6 percent unemployment rate—higher than the rate for the rest of the nation's male population, which stood at 9.4 percent. In comparison, the Indian male situation was worse. Native men had the lowest rate of male participation in the workforce for any group in the nation. For Indian women, the unemployment rate was 10.2 percent, twice as high as for all women. In addition, from 1960 to 1970 the urban Indian population increased from 30 to 45 percent as more Indians left the reservations and rural areas to find jobs in cities. People between the ages of 18 to 40 years accounted for the exodus from reservations Towns close to reservations could not meet the employment demand as more young Indians moved to cities. Too often, the initial jobs did not last. One urban Indian complained, "You get placed on the job, and your first job don't work out, where are you? Several thousand miles from your home and broke."[19] Most urban Indians found jobs in cities not so far from their reservations. This decision allowed them to spend less money to go back to their homes on the reservations. This made cites like Duluth, Minnesota, preferred over Minneapolis; Rapid City over larger areas in South or North Dakota. Living near one's reservation permitted temporary escape from the pressures of urban living. One could return to the reservation for financial help and to maintain friendships, thus creating a migratory pattern for a balance between life on and off the reservation.

The majority of urban Indians in the 1970s and 1980s were blue collar workers. New stereotypes developed about American Indians, convincing company management and supervisors to believe that Indians lack creativity and ambition because they are not as talkative and outwardly competitive as their mainstream coworkers. Traditionally Indian people are mostly introverted, preferring to be with other Indian people. To Indians it is important to work together as a group and maintain positive relationships within their communities. Indians have been restricted to blue collar jobs because of the old myth that Indians work best with their hands. While it is true that they have always been clever and talented in producing arts and crafts, the mainstream has failed to recognize the abilities of American Indians for their abilities in leadership and administration.

FEDERAL SELF-DETERMINATION

In 1975 the federal government announced a new Indian policy called American Indian Self-Determination that was supported by federal government in that year. Tribes were given more support as termination was denounced as the previous policy in favor of American Indians and their tribal governments having more control over their lives. From 1953 to 1971 the federal government implemented an

Indian policy called termination that involved withdrawal of federal trust repositories to tribes as promised in treaties.

Tribes became more enterprising as their governments entered the bingo era of the late 1970s, which turned into casino businesses in the 1980s. Reservations began to close the gap between income comparisons with urban Indians. Still, an estimated 32 percent of Indian men and 37 percent of Indian women who lived on or near a reservation were employed by federal and local governments, compared with 16 percent of men and 17 percent of women residing in urban areas.

In 1979 a white household earned 37 percent more money than an American Indian household, creating a $9,829 difference. By 1980 the gap between whites and Indian families increased to $14,102 or a difference of about 54 percent. Low Indian incomes created Indian ghettoes in cities. For example, on Chicago's north side, a concentration of Indian live in a dilapidated eight-square-mile area called Uptown. Although Indians were dispersed throughout the city, during the 1970s about 55.5 percent of the original urban Indian population lived in the Uptown district. Uptown is an area 11 blocks wide and 19 blocks long. The census for 1970 reported approximately 4,000 Indians lived here although the population was closer to 12,000 to 16,000.[20] Due to moving from one place to another, the Chicago Indian community averaged 0.45 moves per year or one move every 2.2 years.[21] Chicago has been a main target city for Indian relocation since the early 1950s. The Indian community's various social activities such as dances, softball, canoeing, bowling, and cultural activities attracted many native people to live there.

In Los Angeles, the Indian districts included Bell, Bell Gardens, and Huntington Park. Bell Gardens was the heaviest populated Indian neighborhood in Southern California, located several miles southeast of downtown Los Angeles. Initially, refugees from the Dust Bowl days, consisting of mainly poor whites from Oklahoma, Arkansas, and Texas arrived in the area, but more Indians moved in after World War II. The influx of Indians led to the creation of a couple of Indian churches with the Indian Revival Center (Assembly of God) being the largest and most active Indian congregation in Los Angeles during the late 1970s.

Another area of urban Indians lived in a low-rent district approximately four miles west of central Los Angeles. Bordered by Western Avenue, Beverly Boulevard, Figueroa Street, and Pico Boulevard, this was the original location for relocated Indian families coming mostly from eastern Oklahoma and the Southwest. Small wooden houses and rundown apartments made up the neighborhood, along with several Indian churches and a number of Indian bars.

In the Bay Area of Northern California, the Mission District was known as the Indian neighborhood. Also known as the "Little Reservation," the area earned a reputation for its activism during the late 1960s and 1970s.

Towards the end of the twentieth century, the district began to lose its Indiana presence with other ethnic groups moving into the area.

Six blocks around Baltimore Street in Baltimore, Maryland, is the home of the urban Lumbees and other Indians. In what is known as East Baltimore, the urban Indian districts consists of East Baltimore Street as the east and west line with Broadway on the west side, Patterson Park Avenue on the east, Fayette Street on the north, and Pratt Street on the south. This is an old housing district with many large homes divided into apartment units. The 1960 census disclosed that 40 percent of the houses were declining or dilapidated with most of them in need of painting, plastering, and repair to kitchen and bathroom fixtures.

In Minnesota, the area along Franklin Avenue in Minneapolis was known as the "Reservation." During years of relocation in the 1960s, the neighborhood consisted of rundown apartments. The American Indian Movement (AIM) originated in this area in an effort to improve relations with the police and better the livelihood of the Indian community.

In spite of the Civil Rights Act of 1964 and the Fair Housing Act of 1968, which stated it is against the law "to discriminate against any person in terms, conditions, or privileges of sale or rental of dwelling, or in the provision of services or facilities in connection therewith, because of race, color, religion, or national origin," prejudiced landlords continued to discriminate against Indians and other minorities.[22] Many landlords discriminated against Indians who had children, and the requirements of credit checks, security deposits, and advanced rent made housing beyond the reach of some Indians.[23] Even when Indians could afford the rent, living conditions in apartments were not good. Cities had housing codes, but officials could not be everywhere to enforce them, thereby allowing landlords to neglect maintenance. Such neglect included mice, cockroaches, poor insulation, broken windows, outdated plumbing, heating insufficiency, substandard electrical wiring, and other problems. Most Indians did not complain for fear of being evicted from their apartments. In the late 1960s, one St. Paul agency responsible for housing codes in the city speculated that Indians failed to apply for services because they were (1) unaware of them, (2) afraid to complain, and (3) accepted that they were expected to live in rundown conditions.[24]

In response to poor housing conditions, a group of Indians in Minneapolis completed their own study on their housing situation. Out of a survey of 345 households, they reported that 48 percent of the housing units were overcrowded and 12 percent were extremely crowded. Rent for housing consumed 34 percent of their total income. A 50 percent annual turnover rate showed a high rate of moving. Hot water was lacking in 1.4 percent of the housing, there was no water at all in .2 percent, and residents in 10 percent of the 345 households shared a toilet with other families.[25] In 1973 in Minnesota, the Housing and Redeveloping Authority estimated that of 87 family units in apartment projects on the near north side in

Minneapolis, 9 percent of the dwellers were Indian and about 13 percent of the residents were Indians (38 families) in scattered housing units throughout the city.[26]

In 1970 the federal government estimated over 750,000 American Indians represented the total native population and that over 38 percent on reservations and in urban areas lived below the poverty level. Conditions had not improved since the 1960s. On reservations the situation was worst, with over 54 percent of the Indians below the poverty level.[27] Because the conditions were worse on reservations, the federal government turned its attention away from urban Indians. In 1976 the BIA started a Home Improvement Program with a budget of $11 million.[28] The program intended to help reservation Indians while neglecting the urban Indian population with no clear explanation. The government seemed convinced that better and more jobs would solve the Indian problem in cities and on reservations.

In 1974 the Department of Labor implemented the Indian Manpower Programs under the Comprehensive Employment and Training Act (CETA) of 1973.[29] This opportunity for job training was intended to increase Indian employment to help families and improve housing conditions. As progress seemed to be made with more Indians at work, another problem arose. The Indian rate of birth was much higher than the average for the total U.S. population. An estimated 5.2 Indian children were born in rural homes compared to 3.4 to 3.6 for all women in rural areas. The birth rate among urban Indian women was 3.8. In 1970 birth rates for three major urban Indian centers were Los Angeles/Long Beach 3.4; Oklahoma City, 3.4 and Chicago, 3.0.[30]

In another comparison during the mid-1970s, on the Navajo Reservation the median age of residents on or near the reservation was 19.6 years. In comparison, the median age figure for the entire United States was 28 years.[31] The Indian population was young and it was growing.

Ironically, 75 years earlier it was thought that the Indian population would vanish by the end of the nineteenth century. In the 1970s, a large growing Indian population on the reservations and in cities was evident. More jobs were needed. In Chicago about 70 percent of the Indians were of the working class.[32] Following old tradition, Indians enjoyed working with other Indians as an Indian working class began to emerge. Many native people found jobs through friends as urban Indian communities began to grow as well.

In the early 1970s, one of the unanticipated employers was the federal government itself. During these years, 14,714 native people worked for the BIA in regional offices throughout the country. Another 1,942 worked for the bureau on a temporary basis. At the BIA in Washington, thirteen Indians, one Alaska Native, and four non-Indians held the top management positions in the central office.

For fiscal year 1971, the BIA funded 204 industrial and commercial enterprises located on or near Indian reservation in 23 states including

Alaska. The government employed 13,494 people, of whom 6,443, or about 48 percent, were Indian. In this effort, native people owned or operated an estimated 17 enterprises.

As of 1975, American Indians had the lowest individual income of any group in the country, with 55 percent of all native households earning less than $4,000 per year. Forty-six percent of urban Indian men earned annual incomes below $4,000. One in six urban Indian families earned an income below $3,000, although one in three rural Indian families had an income under $3,000. In another light, 26 percent, or 80,000 urban Indians, lived in poverty. Of these people, 6,300 were 65 years old and over; 29,000 were children under 18; and 6,500 were female heads of households.

An urban Indian culture of living below mainstream standards for most native people began to develop since the beginning of the relocation program. As a result, the public began to associate urban Indians with poverty, creating an image of poor Indians living in cities. The reasons for this impoverished image can be explained by the enormous cultural adjustment to a new lifestyle in the city that Indians were required to make . While retaining many of the tribal ways and values, urban natives now lived in a mainstream value system that was different. The loss of contact with natural home spaces of nature and the earth disconnected urban Indians from their previous identities. Like anyone, Indian people needed to be with other Indians. Like the Irish immigrants who gathered in cities such as Boston on a daily basis and the Chinese in San Francisco, Indians met on street corners and in bars to talk, forming new friendships and reaffirming old ones. Unfortunately, public opinion formed a stereotype of the drunken Indian in the city.

Unfamiliar conditions trapped native peoples in the cities. Unaccustomed to the ways things worked in the urban mainstream, Indians became disenchanted with their housing and jobs. Meanwhile, family and friends kept their spirits up enough to endure each day until things got better. In an interesting way, the Indian ghettoes became home spaces like those left on the reservation and in rural areas. Home spaces were Indian-only and were places where Indians felt comfortable among each other. They were reservations of space in cities. Much like their communities back home, urban home spaces were the same except that the urban Indian neighborhoods became intertribal. Often certain tribes were evident in a neighborhood, but it also had members from other tribes.

Two interesting examples involve urban Indians and another minority group. In the 1970s, the Mission District in San Francisco consisted of urban Indians from various parts of Indian Country. Samoan population moved into the area, which was located in a poor section of the city. The situation resulted in a turf war between the two sides, as both claimed the area. Bars in particular became the battleground as both groups asserted their identities through threats and violence. In Seattle the Indian Center was located on the east side of the city north of the city center. In addition, the Seattle Indian Health Board was a part of the Indian district. Close by, a Chinese community began expanding in the late 1980s, creeping closer to the Indian neighborhood.

AN URBAN INDIAN MIDDLE CLASS

The last two decades of the twentieth century witnessed increased adjustment to city life by American Indians. More native peoples attended college and worked at high-paying jobs. Since then, and perhaps as early as the 1970s, a class difference developed among urban Indians. College-educated Indians have become professional people working as lawyers, teachers, and the like. The results have been the emergence of an Indian middle class in the cities.

Moving to the city represented an enormous decision on the part of many Indian people who held inspired hope for a better life. Leaving relatives and friends behind, a new generation of urban Indians wanted something better. They were not the same as other Indians who volunteered for relocation and accepted whatever job and housing was provided to them by the relocation workers. The mainstream society had influenced these enterprising individuals, who also wanted something better for their children. They wanted a formal education to qualify them and their children for well-paying jobs. They saw education as the key to their success. In the process they borrowed many values from the urban mainstream culture.

As the urban Indian middle class emerged, some individuals became members of the mainstream middle class and disregarded tribal ways. One might say that they became absorbed and assimilated into the cultural mainstream and were Indians only by race. Others of this status choose to retain their Indian identity and moved back and forth between Indian activities and mainstream life. Hence, it is not always easy to pinpoint who actually belongs to the urban Indian middle class.

Information for the 1970s disclosed that Indian professionals, nationwide, consisted of 2 podiatrists, 3 veterinarians, 6 dentists, 30 pharmacists, 115 physicians, and about 191 people of Indian descent who held a Ph.D.[33] There were likely more Indian professionals than exhibited by these numbers, but the 1970s was also a time when native people, especially mixed-bloods, preferred not to be Indian, due to the militant actions of AIM. This sector of Indian people had graduated from high school and college. They entered the professional workforce alongside other Americans as an increasing number of minorities began to complete college and seek well-paying jobs. The emergence of an Indian middle class began to close the monetary gap between Indians and whites.

In the last quarter of the twentieth century, Indian people began to make choices of their own about whether to live as a member of a tribe, as Indian, or simply to disappear into the mainstream. Indian self-determination in the 1970s also included self-identification with most Indian people preferring partial assimilation into mainstream America. Of their own choosing, they adopted cultural items and values of modern life while retaining some native values and cultural ways.

Long ago, trade relations were important to Indian groups as new cultural items, especially technology, were exchanged among tribes. This form of cultural borrowing has consistently been a native way as people controlled the change in culture that was introduced to them. Naturally they traded for certain goods that they preferred and believed would improve their life.

The impact of Indian gaming has been substantial on Indian economics and will be covered in more depth in a later chapter, but it deserves mention here. Per capita payments from gaming profits have enabled native peoples to visit friends and relatives on an as-needed basis. This opportunity supported the image of American Indians as a mobile people who have never been permanently attached to one place.

American Indians are great travelers and their need to visit relatives who moved from homelands changed the cultural norm of being confined to living on reservations. American Indians have never been stationary people to the extent of always living an entire lifetime in one house. Even the Eastern woodlands people who have townlike communities used to have summer sites where they traveled to hunt and live to allow the main community site to replenish its store of wild game.

The proverbial "Indian car" has been a modern characteristic of American Indians throughout the last 100 years. It has symbolized the poor conditions of Indian people. On reservations, the Indian car has become an icon representing both poverty and ingenuity. The battered but still running vehicle proclaims the resourcefulness of American Indians to keep their worn out cars going with the least amount of money as they have very little to spend on maintenance.

In 1979 the average yearly income for American Indian families was $13,724, compared to $19,917 for all U.S. families. About 23.7 percent of Indian families lived below the poverty line, compared to 9.6 percent for all families in the U.S. In 1980, the unemployment rate for native people 16 years old and above was 13.2 percent, compared to 6.5 percent for the entire American population. Overall, only 55.5 percent of Native Americans who were 25 years or older were high school graduates compared to 66.5 percent of all Americans.[34] In the last decade of the century, more Indians were at work. In 1990 the percentage of American Indian at jobs increased to 69 percent.[35]

At the end of the twentieth century, some Indian people did very well, some had moderately well paying jobs, and most did not do so well. In 1989 one-third of American Indians lived in poverty, compared to 30 percent of African Americans and 10 percent of whites. The 1990s revealed little improvement.

FEDERAL ASSISTANCE FOR TRIBES

During the 1990s, American Indians experienced a lot of support from the federal government. The federal government attempted to help both specific tribes and Indians in general. On October 23, 1992, Congress passed the Indian Employment, Training and Related Services Demonstration Act, P.L. 102-477. This was an "act to demonstrate how Indian tribal governments can integrate the employment, training and related services they provide in order to improve the effectiveness of those services, reduce joblessness in Indian communities and serve tribally-determined goals consistent with the policy of self-determination."[36] On the same day, Congress enacted the Jicarilla Apache Tribe Water Rights Settlement Act, P.L. 102-441. This law was an act "for the settlement of the water rights claims of the Jicarilla Apache Tribe against the State of New Mexico, the United States and other parties."[37]

In another case to help specific tribes, Congress passed the Three Affiliated Tribes and Standing Rock Sioux Tribe Equitable Compensation Act, P.L. 102-575, on October 23, 1992. This effort was an "act regarding that Congress declares that the Three Affiliated Tribes are entitled to additional financial compensation for the taking of one hundred and fifty-six thousand acres of their reservation lands, as the site of the Oahe Dam and Reservoir, and that such amounts should be deposited in the Standing Rock Sioux Tribe Economic Recovery Fund."[38] On the same day, Congress helped another tribe with passage of the San Carlos Apache Tribe Water Rights Settlement Act, P.L. 102-575. This measure was an "act regarding that Congress declares that the Secretary of the Interior will authorize the actions and appropriations necessary for the United States to fulfill its legal and trust obligations to the Tribe as provided in the Agreement's provisions of this law."[39]

As a means to help tribes in farming, Congress passed the American Indian Agricultural Resource Management Act, P.L. 103-177, on December 3, 1993. This effort was an act "to improve the management, productivity, and use of Indian agricultural lands and resources."[40]

On October 25, 1994, Congress enacted the Indian Self-Determination Contract Reform Act, P.L. 103-413, as one of the most comprehensive modern laws to assist tribes in helping their people. This act was "to amend the Indian Self-Determination Act to specify the terms of contracts entered into by the United States and Indian tribal organizations under the Indian Self-Determination and Education Assistance act and to provide for tribal Self-Governance."[41] Another major legislative measure was passed by Congress on March 14, 2000, the Indian Tribal Economic Development and Contract Encouragement Act, P.L. 106-179. This important law tried "to encourage Indian economic development, to provide for the disclosure of Indian tribal sovereignty immunity in contracts involving Indian tribes, and for other purposes."[42]

TAXATION IN INDIAN COUNTRY

Non-taxation on reservations existed in that they had a legal relationship only with the federal government. State governments had no legal treaties with Indian tribes, thus exempting tribes, not Indian individuals, from taxation. This legal exemption changed during the last 25 years of more of the twentieth century as states increased their legal relationship with Indian tribes.

Tribal taxes were imposed on non-Indians on reservations in the early 1980s. Congress passed the Indian Mineral Development Act and the Indian Tribal Government Tax Status Act in 1982. In 1982, the Jicarilla Apache drilled oil and gas wells using tribal funds. The Fort Peck Reservation tribes formed a joint venture with U.S. Energy. In 1985 the U.S. Supreme Court ruled that the Navajo tribe had the right to impose taxes without the Secretary of the Interior—a victory for sovereignty and other tribes.

As the growing Cherokee tribe of about 102,000 sought to establish its governmental authority, it found conflict with the state government of Oklahoma. In February 1990, the Cherokees proposed a compact with Oklahoma whereby "the state might benefit from taxes collected by the Cherokee Nation on businesses owned by the tribe or its members." Although representatives from the governor's office met with tribal officials, no one from the Oklahoma Tax Commission attended the meeting. Wilma Mankiller, principal chief of the Cherokee Nation at the time, noted that other tribes had negotiated compacts with their home states since tribal health clinics and similar tribal facilities were licensed by state governments. In addition, non-Indian merchants had complained that they lost business to Indian smoke shops which did not pay any taxes. As a response, the Cherokee Tribe created their own tax commission to oversee the taxation of smoke shops and bingo halls on Cherokee land.[43]

On an individual basis, American Indians pay taxes like everyone else who works in the mainstream. Naturally, this obligation to the federal government includes income taxes to the federal and state governments by law. As individuals living in the mainstream, American Indians pay property taxes and other taxes as deemed by law.

CONCLUSION

The economics of American Indians have changed considerably during the twentieth century. Indians became a part of the workforce, but usually in labor-type positions that were often seasonal. Naturally this has meant that American Indians are the first to be laid off, along with other minorities who usually lack sufficient education, job skills, and work experience. In spite of these continual drawbacks, each generation bettered itself with more education and job training. Finally, an Indian middle class began to emerge following World War II. Following the 1960s and 1970s, the number of Indians in professional positions increased, but these numbers are not great in comparison to other people of color in the U.S. It is interesting that native people have two choices as they become college educated and obtain well-paying jobs. Professional Indian people can likely find jobs working for their tribes or they can find positions in the capitalistic system of the American mainstream. While some people might call this assimilation, in that native professionals appear to live like white Americans, the truth is that most of these successful individuals live a lifestyle that combines tribal ways with those of the mainstream culture.

NOTES

1. Quoted in Diane Ravitch, ed., *The American Reader: Words That Moved a Nation* (New York: HarperCollins, 1990), 191.

2. Quoted in William T. Hagan, *Theodore Roosevelt and Six Friends of the Indian* (Norman: University of Oklahoma Press, 1997), 23.

3. C. Matthew Snip, "Economic Conditions," In *Native America in the Twentieth Century: An Encyclopedia,* edited by Mary B. Davis (New York: Garland, 1994), 176.

4. Edmund Wilson, *Apologies to the Iroquois.* With a study of "The Mohawks in High Steel" by Joseph Mitchell (New York: Farrar, Straus and Cudahy, 1960), 23.

5. Mary B. Davis, ed., *Native America in the Twentieth Century* (New York: Garland, 1994), 278.

6. "Model Urban Indian Center Program," Urban Indians, Box 114, Folder Urban Indians 3 of 4, White House Central File, Leonard Garment Papers, Richard Nixon Materials Project, National Archives.

7. Lawrence Clinton, Bruce A Chadwick, and Howard M. Bahr, "Urban Relocation Reconsidered: Antecedents of Employment among Indian Males," *Rural Sociology* 40, no. 2 (Summer 1975): 118–19.

8. "Another Industry Established to Increase Indian Employment," news release from Department of Interior, December 3, 1964, Box 47, Folder 57, Carl Albert Papers, Departmental Series, Carl Albert Center, University of Oklahoma, Norman.

9. "Two Indian Employment Aid Centers to Open in Oklahoma," news release by Department of Interior, January 12, 1967, Box 116, Folder 17a, Page E, Belcher Papers, Carl Albert Center.

10. "Multi-Million-Dollar Indian Training Contracts Renewed," news release by BIA, Department of Interior, July 25, 1967, Box 74, Folder 17, Fred Harris Papers, Carl Albert Center.

11. Reverend Raymond G. Baines letter to Lyndon B. Johnson, March 8, 1968, Box 121, Folder 1f, Page H. Belcher Papers, Carl Albert Center.

12. Gerard Littman, "Alcoholism, Illness, and Social Pathology among American Indians in Transition," *American Journal of Public Health* 60, no. 9 (September 1970): 171.

13. Alan L. Sorkin, *The Urban American Indian* (Lexington, Mass.: Lexington Books, 1978), 20.

14. Ibid., 21–22.

15. Report on Urban and Rural Non-Reservation Indians, *Task Force Eight: Urban and Rural, Non-Reservation Indian, Final Report to the American Indian Policy Review Commission* (Washington: U.S. Government Printing Office, 1976), 20.

16. Memorandum from Eugene Stewart, President of the Urban Indian Development Association, Box 114, Folder Urban Indians 4 of 4, White House Central Files, Leonard Garment Papers, Richard Nixon Materials Project, National Archives.

17. "Native American Families in the City, American Indian Socialization to Urban Life," Final report by Native American Research Group, Institute for Scientific Analysis, a Division of Scientific Analysis Corporation, San Francisco, October 15, 1975, 36.

18. *Task Force Eight Final Report,* 36.

19. Ibid., 34.

20. Sorkin, *Urban American Indian,* 74.

21. Ibid.

22. Fair Housing Act, 1968, P.L. 90–284, *U.S. Statutes at Large 82,* 81–90.

23. Sorkin, *Urban American Indian,* 68.

24. Ibid., 69.

25. Ibid., 70.

26. Ibid.

27. James Grundlach and Alden E. Roberts, "Native American Indian Migration and Relocation," *Pacific Sociological Review* 21, no. 1, (January 1978): 118.

28. Sorkin, *Urban American Indian,* 144.

29. As amended (Pub. L. 93–203, 87 Stat. 839); (Pub. L. 93–567, 88 Stat. 1845) hereinafter referred to as the "Special Federal Programs and Responsibilities under the Comprehensive Employment and Training Act: Indian Manpower Programs; Allowable Federal Costs." Federal Register, Department of Labor, October 9, 1975, a copy is in Box 35, Folder Messages, Theodore Marrs Papers, Gerald Ford Library, Ann Arbor, Michigan.

30. Sorkin, *Urban American Indian,* 12.

31. "Half of Navajos are under 19 1/2; Average Household 5.6 Persons," *Gallup (New Mexico) Independent,* March 21, 1975, a copy is in Box 35, Folder Indian News Clippings (1), Gerald Ford Library.

32. Sorkin, *Urban American Indian,* 2.

33. These statistics are from a survey that Dr. Dean Chavers conducted with the assistance of several agencies during the mid-1970s.

34. Joane Nagel, Carol Ward, and Timothy Knapp, "The Politics of American Indian Economic Development: The Reservation/Urban Nexus," in *Public Policy Impacts on American Indian Economic Development,* ed. C. Matthew Snipp (Albuquerque, N.Mex.: Native American Studies Institute for Native American Development, 1988), 40.

35. C. Matthew Snip, "Economic Conditions," in *Native America in the Twentieth Century: An Encyclopedia,* ed. Mary B. Davis (New York: Garland, 1994), 177.

36. Indian Employment, Training, and Related Services Demonstration Act, P.L. 102-477, October 23, 1992, U.S. Statutes at Large, Vol. 106, Pt. 3: 2302-2306.

37. Jicarilla Apache Tribe Water Rights Settlement Act, P.L. 102-441, October 23, 1992, U.S. Statutes at Large, Vol. 106: 2237–2242.

38. Three Affiliated Tribes and Standing Rock Sioux Tribe Equitable Compensation Act, P.L. 102-575, October 23, 1992, U.S. Statutes at Large, Vol. 106, Pt. 6: 4731–4739.

39. San Carlos Apache Tribe Water Rights Settlement Act, P.L. 102-575, October 30, 1992, U.S. Statutes at Large, Vol. 106, Pt. 6: 4740–4752.

40. American Indian Agricultural Resource Management Act, P.L. 103-177, December 3, 1993, U.S. Statutes at Large, Vol. 107, Pt. 3: 2011–2023.

41. Indian Self-Determination Contract Reform Act, P.L. 103-413, October 25, 1994, U.S. Statutes at Large, Vol. 108, Pt. 5: 4250–4278.

42. Indian Tribal Economic Development and Contract Encouragement Act, P.L. 106-179, March 14, 2000, U.S. Statutes at Large, Vol. 110, Pt. 1: 36–37.

43. Jerry Fink, "Mankiller Defends Tribe-State Tax Plan," *Tulsa World Sunday,* March 11, 1990.

3

LANGUAGE, INTELLECTUAL LIFE, ORAL TRADITION, AND EDUCATION

Intelligence among American Indians is manifested in various venues relating to tribal customs. For Indian people, the oral tradition has been the primary means for sharing experiences, information, and knowledge. Stories and accounts, including myths, legends, and songs, have rendered the past for the youth to learn about their people and the admired deeds of notable individuals and beings. For certain, the American Indian mind is different from the thinking typical of the mainstream.

Since the postreservation era of the late 1800s, formal education has had a great impact on traditional knowledge. Education has always been used by the federal government as the proposed key to reform poor Indian conditions. Ironically, American Indians avidly accepted the idea well before the turn of the twentieth century. Many native leaders realized the significance of learning the ways of the white man and learned to read and write English. Well into the twentieth century, many Indians became bilingual and bicultural.

ORAL TRADITION

Language is a vehicle that transports the culture of a people. It conveys the values and beliefs of nearly 600 Indian nations via approximately 100 native languages currently spoken. Originally, there were about 300 indigenous languages spoken in about eight language groups, Algonquian,

Athapaskan, Caddoean, Iroquoian, Muskhogean, Penutian, Siouan, and Uto-Aztecan.

In a way, language is the culture of the people as it expresses how indigenous people perceive things and how they feel. Depending on nonwritten languages for most of the first half of the twentieth century, the spoken word is singular means for communication. Currently, there are about 250 known surviving native languages in the United States. Perhaps as many as one-third of American Indians still speak their languages. The Navajo, Iroquois, Inuit (Eskimo), Tohono O'odham, Pima, Apache, and Lakota have the highest number of native speakers.

THE AMERICAN INDIAN MIND

Native Americans, who are close to their tribal traditions, have a certain way of seeing the world and the universe. The native ethos of many diverse tribes views the world and the universe in a similar way. Hence, the American Indian mind is nonlinear in its outlook and understanding of life. It is this native ethos that shows how Indians view things differently from the American mainstream. Thus, a fundamental difference in perception exists between Indians and non-Indians. As a result, the two groups understand things from, simple to complicated, in separate ways. Basically, the Indian mind is more openly inclusive to accept the truth literally, whereas the mind of the mainstream is linear and desires empirical evidence as proof of the truth. The latter is more factual and scientific, whereas the Indian perspective is open to things that cannot necessarily be explained.

Among American Indians the circular method of thought is an inclusive philosophy that focuses on a single point with examples of familiarity to explain the event, place, experience or even a person. This approach enables everyone to understand, and everything is taken into consideration. In this full inclusive manner, the opportunity is increased for harmony and balance in the community with everything outside of the community. With every person or being acknowledging as the central point and if lines from other entries were drawn, the results would be like the spokes of a wheel in a related way. Hence, all participating beings are included via the unity of this shared experience. This makes communication extremely important, especially by way of native languages. While the native ethos and its logic are inclusive, forming a circle, the mainstream Western mind is left to right in a linear fashion.

ORAL TRADITION

Story is the foundation of Native American oral tradition. It is the vessel that transports traditional knowledge from one person to another and often it passes this precious information from one generation to the next one. The purposes of storytelling include sharing information, teaching lessons on morality, defining identity, telling accounts of experiences and events, and even telling prophecies of the future. Story possesses power and it comes alive as an entity of power. When an effective storyteller speaks, he or she transports their listener to the past as the experience of the story absorbs both storyteller and audience. It is as if the past is brought to the present as the listeners can almost see, hear, smell, and touch what is being described.

Within a story is "power." It can be underestimated for its influence and affect on people in general. Such power holds communities together when the same story is shared. The power of story and storytelling binds us together even if we do not realize it, because a story provides a reference point, such as people recalling and telling their experience of learning of the death of John F. Kennedy, or the story of the death of Sitting Bull among the Lakota, or the Cherokee stories about the Phoenix, a great mythical bird rising out of the ashes to become a new creation. Hence, the telling of a well-known story binds Indians together and this is surrealism among Indian people who possess certain stories among their tribal communities. Indians believe such stories since their reality is a combined one of the physical and metaphysical worlds.

The shared experiences of stories told were a means of education among American Indians long ago, and this tradition continues among many to the present. Some stories are meant to be told during certain times of the year, such as winter counts. Told during winter nights, the counts are stories of important events and deeds of men and women. Others are told during certain occasions and in certain situations. Certain stories are meant not to be shared with everyone, but kept within certain audiences if the account involves privileged knowledge.

Stories are accounts of the past and they are an integral fabric weaving families into tribal communities. This permeation of storytelling creates a reality of its own that crosses time such that it transports listeners to a moment in time itself. It is as if time does not really mater. Told and told again, the stories weaved are a cultural imperative: they tell us who we are.

Oral tradition faces the obvious criticism that any story is never told the same way. Essentially, this is true, although it is also true that fundamental parts of a story remain the same, such as people involved, place, and what happened. In this light, the importance of the story is a clear message or lesson in human behavior, especially for young listeners.

Stories are a major part of being Indian. It is literature in oral forums. Mainly elders talk about "what happened" to someone that everyone knew or needs to know. They identify friends, relatives, and foes. They tell about these people and who they were related to and cover why story events happened. The accounts are in forms of myth, legend, parables, and sometimes songs. They inform, arouse emotions, educate, entertain, and make listeners think about the past.

Place or site is germane to story telling, especially in the native language. Place is naturally where the events occurred, yet it becomes a point of reference for the listeners as they envision how such a place looked, smelled, and what colors it was. In this transformative way, the past becomes the present. Places of reference become touchstones of culture and the history of a people, usually about a human experience or how humans can understand a nonhuman experience such as the origin of thunder, snow, or rain. Everything and everyone has a story.

People and/or other beings are central figures in the story. These characters are often a trickster or cultural hero, ghosts, spirits, or even The Creator. Like actors, the characters carry the story, performing deeds or meaningless actions until they are interpreted by the storyteller. Each character has a special role, for the character survives each time the story is told over the years.

Coyote   For many tribes west of the Mississippi, Coyote is the clever trickster, who sometimes outsmarts himself. Other tribes have the Great Hare and others have cultural heroes by specific names. Coyote is popular among many tribes, especially in the West, for his unpredictable behavior. What cannot be explained is the work of Coyote, as this surrealistic being exists among native people and spiritually in other places at the same time. Indians feel an internal bond with Coyote, particularly in understanding the foolish things they may do.

Coyote is the subject of many tribal stories that describe the creation of the world, plants, animals, and people. Coyote stories are also about other experiences that provide lessons in life and information that makes things make sense. In this generic light, Coyote is everywhere and he can be anything. Using Coyote as an example in a story allows people to use the third person and not use specific names that might blame someone or hurt someone's feelings.

Coyote is universal, a metaphor who can be blamed for wrongdoings. Yet, Coyote is powerful and he is a metaphysical being in the role of a clown. Natives respect Coyote, however, for his actions are to learn from and not to do.

THE BOARDING SCHOOL EXPERIENCE

The boarding school experiment began with the origins of eastern schools like Harvard University, the College of William and Mary, and Dartmouth College long ago as small institutions. These Ivy League schools included in their mission the boarding and education of Indian youth. They have since lost some of their original mission, although a small number of Indian students have attended William and Mary. More have graduated from Harvard, and Dartmouth has recruited Indian students actively since the early 1970s. The idea of Indian students living and studying far from home is especially challenging.

The boarding school experiment on a broad scale happened when Captain Richard Pratt opened the doors of Carlisle Indian Industrial School in 1879 in Carlisle, Pennsylvania. The school would become famous through Pratt's efforts to promote it and for its play in sports. With Carlisle, a second main era of boarding schools for Indians occurred. Others soon followed, such as Chilocco, Chemewa, Sherman Institute, and Rainy Mountain.

Church groups introduced mission boarding schools that also strove to convert native souls to Christianity. Several, such as St. Labre Indian School, a Catholic school for the Cheyenne, and Santee Mission School for the Lakota, were operating prior to Carlisle. During the rest of the 1800s and early decades of the 1900s, boarding and mission schools competed for Indian students. Catholic and Protestant missionaries competed against each other trying to find enough Indian children to start a school. Other Christian groups such as United Church of Christ, Lutherans, Mormons, and others began to open schools for Indians.

Richard Pratt, a former military officer, who once fought Indians in the West, became history's Indian   **Richard Pratt** educator during the late nineteenth century. All of this began when he founded Carlisle Indian Industrial School by receiving permission to use some old army barracks. Placed in command of Indian scouts, Pratt learned about Indian characteristics, abilities, values, and something about how they thought. As Pratt's command came to an end, he received orders to escort 72 Cheyenne Indian prisoners to Fort Marion in St. Augustine, Florida. As prisoners of war, Pratt wondered what would happen to the Indians. Becoming convinced that the Indian prisoners could be civilized; he began an educational program to change them. Pratt wanted to continue his Indian educational program and he was given permission to replace the guards of the Indian prisoners with trustworthy Indians. Eventually, the Indian prisoners were released from close confinement. Afterwards, the military assigned Pratt to the Hampton Normal and Agricultural Institute in Virginia, where African Americans were schooled. Twenty-two Indian prisoners went with Pratt to Hampton. Hampton was already on its way to becoming known for its education of former freedmen under General Samuel Armstrong, and Pratt used it as a model for his own school. In the summer of 1870, Pratt traveled to the West and returned with 43 more Indians.[1]

Pratt dreamed of starting his own school for Indians. He believed that they must be far from their homeland or else they would run away. He would cut their connection to their families and communities and change this communal value. First, Pratt needed facilities. The captain finally found success when he befriended Secretary of Interior Carl Schurz. The secretary worked to have special legislation introduced in Congress to transfer some abandoned military barracks at Carlisle to the Department of Interior. Next, Secretary Schurz permitted Pratt to use the barracks for his new school.

Within months, Pratt officially opened the doors of Carlisle Indian Industrial School on November 1, 1879. No sooner had Pratt started Carlisle than criticism arose about his way of educating his Indian students. Pratt believed that Indians had to be completely assimilated into American society. They would no longer be Indians in their traditional manner. Furthermore, Pratt's personality got him into trouble. His forcible drive, stubbornness, and unwillingness to recognize his mistakes caused people to disagree with him and his strict philosophy to destroy the Indianness in his students and give them a new identity. Pratt campaigned for donations but had to respond to his critics. He remained undeterred. While Pratt was scrupulously honest and a churchgoing man, he criticized his critics, calling them stupid and jealous.

Senator Preston B. Plumb from Kansas was an outspoken critic, going so far as to call Pratt a "fraud" and a "swindler."[2] Such charges made against him only made Pratt more determined to see his school succeed. He stuck to what he knew from learning military rigor in the army. Strict routines at Carlisle became commonplace. Pratt even criticized missionaries for being too sensitive to Indian ways. His way seemed the only logical way. He also believed that the Indian Rights Association was wrong for advocating the creation of day schools on reservations. Finally, Pratt's criticism against the Bureau of Indian Affairs (BIA) for its policy to fund the founding of other boarding schools led to his own dismissal by BIA officials in 1904.[3] Pratt's Indian boarding school experiment in Carlisle continued without him into the twentieth century.

In October 1889, Commissioner of Indian Affairs Thomas Morgan announced his plan for a nationwide program to educate American Indian youth. Undoubtedly Morgan was influenced by the various discussion groups, especially the Friends of the Indian, well-meaning reformers. Morgan wanted a standardization of textbooks and similar instruction at Indian schools to bring them in line with the mainstream public school system.[4]

Reading mainstream literature does not interest a lot of American Indians, especially those who are close to traditions and live in their homelands. For them, it is like reading about a foreign country, because daily concerns in the community or on the reservations are the most important things in one's life. By the end of the twentieth century and into the twenty-first, contact with the outside world was increasing by way of the Internet and television. One concern is that such external contact will undermine the traditional cultures of native peoples. Choosing between the mainstream world and one's tribal life has created a dilemma for many native youth.

The impact of English on Indians has been enormous. Speaking English has been the singular external influence to change Native Americans the most. Learning English as a second language is a challenge and trains native speakers to think differently as well. In many cases, learning English requires unlearning the native way of thinking and learning to think like a white person of the mainstream society.

The retention of native languages is a race against cultural disappearance. Nowadays, among many tribes, one-third or less of the community is able to speak the original native language. With each generation, native spoken languages are being lost with tribal councils conducted in English and intertribal communications depending on English as well.

The federal government continues to support Indian boarding schools while much has changed. Boarding schools are no longer a negative experience and as many as four or five generations of Indian families have attended the schools. Learning with other Indians has attracted native youth to attend Sherman Institute, Chemewa School, and other institutions.

The daily routine at Indian boarding schools like Carlisle and others included a half day in reading, writing, arithmetic, and spelling. The remaining half day involved vocational training in manual labor, **Daily Life in Indian Boarding Schools** which actually benefited the school. Carlisle and the other Indian schools tried to be as self-sufficient as possible. Students raised their food, which included dairy and poultry products, and the girls worked in the kitchen and learned homemaking.

Boarding school life was harsh for the children. At many schools like Carlisle, they wore cadet uniforms, marched to class when a bell rang and obeyed teachers' commands. A typical day's schedule followed as:

5:30	Rising bell.
5:30–6:00	Dress and report for athletics.
6:00	Warning bell.
6:00–6:20	Setting-up exercise.
6:20–6:25	Roll call.
6:25	Breakfast bell; raise flag.
6.25–6:30	Line up; march to dinning hall.
6:30–7:00	Breakfast.
7:00–7:25	Care of rooms.
7:15	Sick call; bugle.
7:25	Work bell.
7:25–7:30	Line up; details report.
7:30–8:30	Industrial instruction.
7:30–8:15	Academic division [breaking into grades].
8:15–8:25	Prepare for school.
8:25	School bell or bugle.
8:25–8:30	Line up. March to school building.
8:30	School application industrial division.
10:00–10:15	Recess; five minutes' breathing exercise.

Elementary school class at Carlisle Indian Industrial School. Courtesy of Library of Congress.

11:30   Recall bell; all departments.
11:30–11:45   Recreation; details return to quarters.
11:45   Warning bell.
11:45–11:55   Prepare for dinner.
11:55–12:00   Line up. Inspection. March to dining room.
12:00–12:30   Dinner.

The afternoon was followed by the rest of the rigorous schedule. Every minute of the morning and afternoon was accounted for. The evening meal was scheduled at 5:30 and taps was played at 8:30, putting the students to bed to rise the next morning to start another day.[5]

The teachers allowed only English to be spoken in the schools and punished the students if they spoke their native tongue. Forcing the ways of white civilization on the Indian youths, they were taught to love the American flag and call the United States their homeland. In a letter dated January 1902, Indian affairs commissioner William Jones instructed Indian agents on controlling Indian students:

You are . . . directed to induce your male Indians to cut their hair, and both sexes to stop painting [their faces]. With some of the Indians this will be an easy matter, with others it will require Considerable tact and perseverance . . . to successfully carry out these instructions. . . . The returned students who do not comply and if they become obstreperous about the matter a short confinement in the guardhouse at hard labor, with shorn locks, should furnish a cure. Certainly all the younger men should wear short hair, and it is believed that by tact, perseverance, firmness, and withdrawal of supplies can induce "all" to comply with this order . . . The wearing of citizen's clothing, instead of the Indian costume and blanket, should be encouraged . . . Indian dances and so-called Indian feasts should be prohibited. In many cases these dances and feasts are simply subterfuges to cover degrading acts and to disguise immoral purposes.[6]

Stubborn objectives at reservation and boarding schools prevented young Indians from learning about their people's past. To overcome the criticism from Indian parents, teachers applied propaganda, and taught that the traditional ways of Indians were useless. When these teachings failed, the teachers punished the youth frequently until they properly responded. Indian parents were helpless to do anything, as the government maintained that forced learning would be in the overall best interest of the youth.

At times, mothers had to choose which child to turn over to school authorities by hiding their other children. This was the most difficult decision for an Indian mother, who was confronted by a school official or Indian police to turn over her child. For the unfortunate child, his or her life changed radically. In the words of tribal Yakima historian Leroy B. Selam, his life was never the same.

After the age of six, my Indian world changed entirely. My parents and grandparents were told they would be put in jail if I did not go to school. I was placed in that infamous white man's boarding school, the Chemawa Indian School, a Bureau of Indian Affairs institution. What is it like for a child of any race to be taken away from his parents and relatives at an age when he needs their love and care the most? What thoughts must go through a child's mind—the fears, anxieties, the loneliness, above all. . . . What are these boarding schools like? What are their policies? I would compare these schools to those of a military barracks, to reformatories, to prisons.[7]

Many native people who attended boarding schools in the early decades of the century had their names **Christian Names** changed by school officials from their original Indian names to Christian names. The new Christian names had little meaning to Indian children because they were in a foreign language. Their original names, according to their tribal languages, held a meaning or description of their personality, and often their Indian name changed as they grew older and accomplished important deeds or had some extraordinary experiences.

School official had more than one reason for the name changes. Too often, they could not pronounce Indian names in the native language and "only English" was spoken, thus Indian students assumed white first names. Often, they also took on white last names such as Peter MacDonald, former chairperson of the Navajo Nation whose last name comes from the nursery song "Old MacDonald Had a Farm."

Outing System After students completed training at Pratt's Carlisle Indian Industrial School, they were provided an applied education for three years. The program's so-called outing system involved placing the students with white rural families near the school, and sometimes they were placed in nonagricultural settings further away. The federal government paid the host family $50 a year for the student's medical care and clothing. For the student, he or she learned the agricultural lifestyle from the farmer and his family. Pratt wanted the students trained in vocations and prepared for jobs. Towards its end, Carlisle included the first two years of high school as a part of its curriculum, and some teaching training.[8]

The almost 40-year, extraordinary history of Carlisle ended on September 1, 1918, when the facility became a hospital in World War I. Many male students were old enough to join the army and navy in the war, so the student population was severely depleted even though not all Indians were classified as U.S. citizens. Because the general citizenship act for all Indians would not be passed until 1924, the Indian students at Carlisle were similar to foreign exchange students, as the Indian nations on reservations still maintained a certain degree of sovereignty.

One of the critical problems that school officials faced was coaxing Indian children to enroll in schools. To meet school enrollment quotas, U.S. Army patrols visited reservations and literally kidnapped children. Indian police, who were supervised by Indian agents on reservations, had the same duty.

Quotas If the children misbehaved in school, they were denied permission to visit their families during holidays. Uncooperative parents were sometimes locked in jail, or rations and annuities were withheld by the Indian agent until consent was obtained to give up the children. Finally, in about 1900, the BIA relaxed its rigid policy of separating Indian children from families. Although the schools on some reservations had the same policy of separating Indian families, the number of reservation schools increased and more children were enrolled in public schools near their families. Indian education had undergone the start of an important transformation from boarding schools to day schools. By the end of the nineteenth century, more than 20,000 Indian students attended 148 boarding schools and 225 day schools. The federal tradition of educating Indian children in boarding schools continued for the next 100 years and more. Many of the same problems persisted.

School officials criticized Indian children for "returning to the blanket," a degrading phrase meaning failure to succeed in the mainstream world.

Irregular attendance was a frequent problem, and running away from school was a common practice. Upon reaching home, the students were caught and returned to school, and this pattern occurred periodically with the same child.

High dropout rates were another serious concern. A lack of motivation existed among the students and a general feeling of defeatism was evident among the students and their parents. Even after they graduated, they returned to their old ways, but things had changed. The communities on reservations and values were changing with continuous contact with non-Indians. Rather than using their education to secure a job and integrating into the mainstream society, many Indian youths felt caught between two cultures.

AMERICAN INDIAN STUDIES PROGRAMS

The advent and rise of American Indian studies as a legitimate academic field occurred during the late 1960s amidst the riots and other protests for civil rights and against American involvement in Vietnam. The impetus to create native studies programs derived from a need to learn about the past as each new generation of Indian youth knew less about their heritage. As members of society questioned their identities and pondered their purposes in life, Indian youth looked towards their tribal histories to learn about themselves. With the emergence of ethnic studies in colleges and universities as a result of activism by African Americans and Hispanic Americans, radical Indian youth demanded courses about their people. Initial courses were offered as introductory courses for undergraduates.

In 1968 protesting Indian students at San Francisco State University demanded an American Indian studies program. Ironically, this was not the first attempt at starting a native studies program. In 1914, Senator Robert Owen of Oklahoma introduced a resolution in the U.S. Congress that called for an Indian Studies Department at the University of Oklahoma. Unfortunately, Owen's efforts did not succeed, and another effort at the same university failed in 1937. In 1949 the University of South Dakota started the American Indian Institute. Timing proved to be essential and the time would not come until the 1960s.

Following San Francisco State University, the University of Minnesota and the University of California at Berkeley started Indian studies programs. The University of California at Los Angeles soon followed and these four universities became the models for other schools to follow. For example, a committee on American Indian Affairs was established earlier at the University of Minnesota for a needs assessment to help Indian students. Two years later in 1969, the report from the committee disclosed that no American Indians were on the administrative staff and it recommended scholarships for Indian students, counseling, tutorial, and additional supportive services.

As early as 1967, Professor Arthur Harkins had organized a small American Indian Center at the University of Minnesota. Called the Training Center for Community Programs, the organization worked with the native urban community as one of the pioneers in urban Indian studies. An upward bound program followed as a part of this impetus to work with native people in the Twin Cities. In the fall of 1968, the American Indian Students Association began meeting with the administration at the University of Minnesota to work on creating an American Indian studies program. The momentum was under way when a group of African American students occupied an administration building, a protest that led to the beginning of a Black Studies Program.

In Canada, Trent University of Ontario started the first program for native college students in 1969. Trent and the first three American Indians studies programs became models for more in Canada. Native studies began to increase during the 1970s as programs changed into academic departments. In 1985 an estimated 112 colleges and universities in both the U.S. and Canada had a native program or department. An estimated 23 of these were in Canada.

In general native studies has often been a part of an anthropology department or is sometimes a part of an ethnic studies program or department. Native studies was initially available in the form of a few courses students could take toward completing a degree in another field, but by the mid-1980s, 18 Indian studies programs or departments offered majors for a bachelor's degree and another 40 offered an Indian studies minor.[9]

The Indian Education Act of 1972 enabled educational programs to be offered to American Indians and Alaska Native college students and adults with funding support from the Department of Education. In addition, the BIA offered scholarships to Indian students. Two years later, President Gerald Ford signed a landmark law in the Indian Self-Determination and Education Assistance Act of 1974. This important legislation called for the encouragement of Indians to attend schools and to control more of the academic curriculum. Funding organizations like the Ford Foundation and the Donner Foundation believe in Indian self-determination and they funded Indian educational projects, while others, such as the Rockefeller Foundation, joined in this reform effort.

With the development of further reform in Indian education, Indian intellectualism began to be recognized. Disregarded previously by the mainstream, American Indians have always had their brilliant individuals such as Tecumseh, Sitting Bull, and Chief Joseph of the nineteenth century and Charles Eastman, Carlos Montezuma, Gertrude Bonnin, and Vine Deloria Jr. of the twentieth century. By the mid-1980s, mainstream academia began to bring Indian academia into its curriculum as more than 90 percent of college students enrolled in Indian studies courses.

As the twentieth century drew to an end, only six American Indian studies programs and departments offered graduate degrees. These schools included the University of California, Berkeley; University of Arizona; University of California, Los Angeles; and Montana State University. Harvard University has a graduate program in American Indian education. A bold move was made in 1996 when the American Indian Studies Program at the University of Arizona offered the first doctoral degree program in American Indian Studies. It took seven years for this program to be approved. The program at the university had seven core faculty, who were Native Americans, and there were a total of nineteen faculty participating in the program. This was a historic precedent for American Indian higher education. The University of California at Riverside and at Davis also offers a doctorate in Native American Studies.[10]

POST-MODERN EDUCATION

The educational progress has continued to lag behind the mainstream average, but steady progress has been made. For example, the average level of education ranged from 8.7 to 11.2 years of schooling for all Indians in the 1970s compared to the high school graduate of the mainstream. In order to get a good job, American Indian young people began to realize that they needed a high school diploma and a college degree. A significant number of Indian youth began to attend postsecondary schools during the 1960s. From 1960 to 1970, the number of Indian students in postsecondary schools rose drastically. In 1970 an estimated 8,000 Indian students were in colleges and universities. An estimated 35 percent of those from 18 to 21 years old completed secondary school, and 20 percent of this age group enrolled in universities. Many students of this age group came from low-income families. In the early 1970s, the BIA awarded scholarships of $868 on the average to 3,432 Indian students. Positive results led to an increase to $1,750 per student by 1975. In this year, 1,497 native students graduated from four-year colleges and had received scholarships from the BIA.[11]

Each year more Indian students attend colleges and universities. On the average, the Indian student is older and many have returned to college after being a part of the labor force. In 1976, for public and private degree-granting institutions for a four-year college degree, American Indian/Alaska Native students were 0.5 percent of the total college student population with Asian/Pacific islanders composing 1.7 percent, Hispanic students 2.5 percent, African American students 8.7 percent, and the white majority student at 86.6 percent. In 1980 American Indian/Alaska Native students were still 0.5 percent of the total students attending college. In 1990 this percentage increased to 0.6 percent and in 2002 American Indian/Alaska Native students were 0.9 percent of the total college student population.[12]

American Indians have the highest enrollment at Arizona State University, Northern Arizona University, University of Oklahoma, University of New Mexico, Brigham Young University, and Northeastern State University at Tahlequah, with more than 1,000 students at each of these institutions. During the mid-1980s, about 60 percent of the total Indians enrolled in higher education were attending two-year colleges.

TRIBAL COLLEGES

Following World War II, more Indian students began to attend college. At first a small but steady stream of Indian young people were graduating from high school and began to enter college. Junior and community colleges began to increase throughout the country during the 1960s; for example, Navajo Community College opened its doors during the mid-1960s. At this time, most Indians attended public colleges, especially junior colleges.

At the same time, the increasing number of Indians graduating from high school and wanting to pursue higher education convinced Congress to help tribal communities to start their own colleges, following the example of Navajo Community College. The early tribal colleges are Sinte Gleska College (1970), Oglala Lakota College (1971), DQ University (1972), Tuttle Mountain College (1972), Northwest Indian College (1973), Cheyenne River Community College (1973), Fort Berthold Community College (1973), Standing Rock College (1973), Blackfeet Community College (1974), and Dull Knife Memorial College (1974). Congress passed the Tribally Controlled Community College Act in 1978. With help from nearby colleges and universities, tribal colleges began to emerge as they were able. By the 1990s over 30 tribal colleges in the U.S. and Canada existed.

Carpentry class at Haskell Indian Junior College. Courtesy of Library of Congress.

The Indian higher education effort has resulted in the formation of the American Indian Higher Education Consortium (AIHEC), which holds meetings twice a year to discuss common issues and concerns. In October 1993, Haskell Indian Junior College in Lawrence, Kansas, became Haskell Indian Nations University by offering the bachelor's degree in four programs. DQ University in Davis, California, which originally started in 1972, celebrated 20 years of operation. The only urban Indian college, Native American Educational Services College (NAES), founded in 1974, continues to educate the urban Indians in Chicago with branch campuses in Wisconsin and Montana.

FEDERAL SUPPORT

The federal government has continuously supported Indian education; though during some periods, more generously than during others. The last decade of the twentieth century witnessed an increase in federal assistance for Indian education over previous decades. On March 19, 1992, Congress passed the Morris K. Udall Scholarship and Excellence in National Environmental and Native American Public Policy Act, P.L. 102-259. This was an act to establish a foundation of the same name that encouraged leadership and higher education for native youth.[13]

This year of the five hundredth anniversary of the arrival of Christopher Columbus convinced the Bill Clinton administration to renew the federal government's efforts in assisting Native Americans. Congress also passed the Higher Educational Tribal Grant Authorization Act, P.L. 102-325, on July 23, 1992. This was an act "to make grants to Indian tribes in accordance with the requirements of this part to permit those tribes to provide financial assistance to individual Indian students for the cost of attendance at institutions of higher education."[14] In this same significant year, Congress passed the Critical Needs for Tribal Development Act for federal funding higher education assistance to tribes on July 23, and on the same day, it passed The Institute of American Indian Native Culture and Arts Development Act "to create a board to establish, within the institute, departments for the study of culture and arts and for research and exchange, and a museum." Other acts on the same day include the Tribal Development Student Assistance Revolving Loan Program Act "to establish a revolving loan program to be administered by a tribe or tribal organization for the purposes of increasing the number of college graduates available to work in tribal businesses, tribal government, and tribal services such as schools and hospitals; to conduct research in postsecondary education; and to encourage development, through grants in addition to loans, transitional and follow up services added to encourage persistence in postsecondary education."[15]

On October 26, 1992, Congress passed the Native American Languages Act, P.L. 102-524. This legislative measure amended the Native American

Programs Act of 1974 for the Secretary of Interior to award a grant to any agency or organization that is to assist Native Americans in ensuring the survival and continuing vitality of Native American languages. On the same day, the Native American Educational Assistance Act, P.L. 102-524 was passed. This act called for "the Secretary of the Interior to enter into an agreement with a nonprofit captioning agency engaged in manufacturing and distributing captioning decoders, for the purpose of carrying out a demonstration project to determine the effectiveness of captioned educational materials as an educational tool in schools operated by the Bureau of Indian Affairs."[16]

On May 4, 1994, Congress passed the Alaska Native Art and Culture Development Act, P.L. 108-239. It was an act for "the Secretary of the Interior to make grants for the purpose of supporting programs for Native Hawaiian or Alaska Native culture and arts development to any private, nonprofit organization or institution which primarily serves and represents Native Hawaiians or Alaska Natives."[17]

Four years later, Congress passed two legislative measures pertaining to native history and culture. On October 6, 1998, Congress passed the Sand Creek Massacre National Historic Site Act, P.L. 105-243, "to authorize the Secretary of the Interior to study the suitability and feasibility of designating the Sand Creek Massacre National Historic Site in the State of Colorado as a unit of the National Park System, and for other purposes."[18] About a year later, on December 9, 1999, Congress passed the Fallen Timbers Battlefield and Fort Miami National Historic Site Act, P.L. 106-164, to recognize the historical importance of this battle to Indians and white settlement. This act was "to establish the Fallen Timbers Battlefield and Fort Miami National Historical Site in the State of Ohio."[19]

CONCLUSION

Formal education has brought about a great change among American Indians in the twentieth century. Unfortunately for Indian people, early in the century, it was aimed at the youth who were taken from their families. Ironically, education under the control of Indian themselves has provided the greatest uplift of Indian life. It is the inherent sovereign right to learn that has propelled native people to higher levels of knowledge. With each generation, American Indians exhibited a desire to learn more about the ways of the mainstream and knowledge about the rest of the world. To be educated in another culture results in indigenous cultures being lost. Theoretically, one culture replaces another, but American Indians have learned to use the English language and earned degrees in the mainstream educational system to perpetuate Indian tribal ways.

NOTES

1. Francis Paul Prucha, *The Great Father: The American Indian and the United States Government* (Lincoln: University of Nebraska Press, 1986 [abridged ed.]), 234–35.

2. Ibid., 10.

3. Ibid., 237.

4. Prucha, *The Great Father*, 236.

5. Francis Paul Prucha, *American Indian Policy in Crisis: Christian Reformers and the Indian, 1865–1900* (Norman: University of Oklahoma Press, 1976), 284.

6. Commissioner of Indian Affairs William A. Jones to Indian Agents, January 1902, Report of Commissioner of Indian Affairs Report, September 30, 1902, microfiche, 13–14.

7. Quoted in Jane B. Katz, *Let Me Be a Free Man: A Documentary History of Indian Resistance* (Minneapolis: Lerner Publications Company, 1975), 142.

8. Prucha, *The Great Father*, 238.

9. Ibid.

10. Ibid.

11. Robert Havighurst, "Indian Education since 1960," *The Annals of the American Academy of Political and Social Science* 436 (March 1978): 19.

12. U.S. Department of Education, National Center for Education Statistics, *Digest of Educational Statistics* (Washington, D.C.: U.S. Government Printing Office, 2004), 55.

13. Morris K. Udall Scholarship and Excellence in National Environmental and Native American Public Policy Act, P.L. 102-259, March 19, 1992, U.S. Statutes at Large, Vol. 106, Pt. 1: 78–84.

14. Higher Educational Tribal Grant Authorization Act, P.L. 102-325, July 23, 1992. U.S. Statutes at Large, Vol. 106, Pt. 1: 798–803.

15. "Critical Needs for Tribal Development Act," P.L. 102-325, Pt. C, July 23, 1992, U.S. Statutes at Large, Vol. 106, Pt. 1: 803–805. See also Institute of American Indian Native Culture and Arts Development Act, P.L. 102-325, Pt. D, July 23, 1992, U.S. Statutes at Large, Vol. 106, Pt. 1: 805–809; and the Tribal Development Student Assistance Revolving Loan Program Act, P.L. 102-325, Pt. E, July 23, 1992, U.S. Statutes at Large, Vol. 106, Pt. 1: 809–812.

16. Native American Languages Act, P.L. 102-524, October 26, 1992, U.S. Statutes at Large, Vol. 106, Pt. 4: 3434–3437, and Native American Educational Assistance Act, P.L. 102-524, October 26, 1992, U.S. Statutes at Large, Vol. 106, Pt. 4: 3437.

17. "Alaska Native Art and Culture Development Act," P.L. 108-239, May 4, 1994, U.S. Statutes at Large, Vol. 108, Pt. 1: 606–607.

18. "Sand Creek Massacre National Historic Site Act," P.L. 105-243, October 6, 1998, U.S. Statutes at Large, Vol. 112, Pt. 2: 1579–1580.

19. "Fallen Timbers Battlefield and Fort Miami National Historic Site Act," P.L. 106-164, December 9, 1999, U.S. Statutes at Large, Vol. 113: 1792–1794.

4

MATERIAL LIFE: CLOTHING, FOOD, AUTOMOBILES, AND HOUSING

The material life of American Indians is a combination of items of tribalism mixed with the modernity of the American mainstream. It is this combination of being part of the Indian world and being part of the mainstream that defines contemporary native reality. Material culture is the most visible evidence that shows to everyone what is valued. The clothes, kind of housing, food we eat, and what we drink reflect our values. Hence, it is the ways in which basic needs are addressed that give us important information about the underlying values of native people they have developed during the twentieth century. This transition to ever-increasing interaction with mainstream culture has been a struggle and it is ongoing for many Indian people. This change involves retaining indigenous identity while enjoying the attractions of the American mainstream way of life.

THE ROLE OF NATURAL RESOURCES IN MATERIAL CULTURE

It can be said that we are products of our environments. This is especially true for Native Americans, because their natural environments provided food, clothing, and shelter to them. In fact, the plains Indians found 52 different ways to utilize the buffalo as their main source for food, clothing, and shelter. Hunting was their primary means of economy.

In North America there are 400 species of mammals. There are 340 reptile species north of Mexico and another 90,000 insect species north of the Texas and Mexico border. In addition, there are 230 amphibian species in United States and 700-plus species of birds in the 50 states and Canada. In North

America, there are also 20,000 species of flora and an estimated 92,000 kinds of fauna, making 112,000 total known species.

Common species of animals among American Indians in North America include two subspecies of buffalo, the plains and wood. There are eight species of bear, including the black bear, brown bear, polar, and others. Several subspecies of wolves live on the continent, and in addition, 59 species of eagle, 150 species of antelope, and 38 species of deer that include elk and moose.

American Indians have adapted to what their regions of the country have to offer and their clothes reflect nature and the climate of their home-lands. The West and Southwest are physically demanding areas with limited food sources that force people to adapt, thereby shaping human culture. The Pacific Northwest is plentiful in natural resources due to the weather patterns of plentiful rain, which has permitted native peoples to advance in art and artifact making. The same plentifulness can be said for the Great Lakes area and the eastern woodlands where indigenous peoples advanced considerably in refining their cultures. However, native people of the Southwest have learned to adapt to the climate and environ-ment. Their successful adaptation allowed them to produce impressive artifacts throughout the centuries.

CLOTHING

One of the most obvious expressions of American Indian material cul-ture is "wearing Indian things." So, what is Indian? First of all, American Indians are an adaptive people who have learned to survive by borrowing parts of culture from other people, especially technology and clothing. Actually, this makes them no different from other peoples, but in this sense, "wearing Indian stuff" is being Indian.

Actually, it is looking Indian on the outside. Looking Indian is normally associated with the American West. It is ironic that, in external appearance, Indians have become more like cowboys, while cowboys are wearing Indian things. This can also be said for Indian women looking like cowgirls and vice versa. For example, Indian cowboys wear cowboy boots, jeans, and cowboy hats. Cowboys often wear something Indian, for example, a Zuni-made turquoise and silver ring. Cowgirls might wear a Navajo squash blossom necklace, turquoise earrings, and rings. Indian cowgirls wear jeans, cowgirl boots, and cowgirl hats, and so forth.

Once on opposite sides, now both sides are looking like each other because it is the West as an environment that has influenced the culture of American Indians and non-Indian Westerners. However, the inner identity remains basically the same. The outer manifestation of what Indians look like to both other Indians and non-Indians looks Indian. This is the irony of life and informs us of the great ability of native people to adjust to new surroundings when guided by a personal preference to

Woman's primitive dress. Courtesy of Library of Congress.

do so. Their own decided need for change has produced an impressive external image that dictates that they have willingly crossed the cultural bridge of differences with a significant degree of comfort.

It is also about image. This is what others see when they look at Indians in the West. This public image exudes an Indianness that shows adjustment to the environment and even to people who might be called outsiders. It is also about self-image and how Native Americans are secure in their identity and know who are they are while wearing Indian stuff. This includes wearing something that is not Indian such as Indian cowboys wearing chaps and an Indian motif or design added to them. While appropriating the dress of another culture, Indians add an Indian design that is appealing to them and it seems acceptable. For example, Virgil Ortiz and Donna Karan have established a modern native fashion. Ortiz, a 35-year-old Cochiti Pueblo, has become a brand name for his innovative designs.

An important agent for change among American Indian tribes has been the presence of trading posts on the reservations. The idea of trade is very old among the tribes themselves who had elaborate trading networks throughout North America. Europeans understood the importance of trade to Indians as each European power—Spain, France, Great Britain, and the Netherlands—established trade relations with Indians tribes in the lands that they colonized.

In vying for Indian trade, the United States in its early years negotiated 389 treaties and agreements by the end of the nineteenth century. The earliest factories were actually trade stores where Indians could trade their pelts from trapping beaver, mink, and other small animals of value. During the reservation era of the late 1800s, the federal government authorized trading posts on some 200 reservations throughout Indian Country, especially in the West.

Trading Posts   The trader came into an immensely powerful position of controlling business matters on reservations. Indian customers became dependent upon the trader for any goods that they needed and often they had no money or anything of value to trade. The credit system became common as Indians fell into debt with the trader, who collected jewelry, material items, and promissory notes to pay their accumulated debts. In that way, the trader acted like a bank and a conduit for introducing white material culture and technology to native peoples. Trading posts held a virtual monopoly on reservations and manipulated prices to put Indians at a severe disadvantage. Prices were typically higher than at off-reservations stores. Since many Indians could not read or write, they used their thumbprint or made some other mark, and the trader wrote their name under the print or mark.

This trade indebtedness continued in Indian Country until the 1970s, when tribes began to start their own stores. After the 1970s, tribal stores replaced the trading posts, and Indians shop at border towns or drive to the closest city. Like the trading post, tribal stores have been instrumental in introducing change in material culture to the native communities.

FOOD

Indian food varies by region. Certain tribes prefer the particular types of food that in the past enabled their people to live off the land. American Indians have always been hunters, gathers, fishermen, and agriculturalists and have learned to eat the offerings of the Earth Mother. In the same manner, she offered them fresh water to drink.

Eastern Woodlands   Among the eastern woodlands tribes, corn, beans, and squash—called the "Three Sisters"—have been and remain staple foods. Agriculture has been the cultural norm for centuries, with a heavy dependency on corn that has been incorporated into ceremony. The Busk or Green Corn Dance celebrates the annual harvest of corn and with it, a New Year. To supplement their agricultural crops, eastern Indians hunted deer, bear, and other game animals for food, especially during winters, when snow blanketed the

Indian Trading Post, Navajo Reservation, Arizona. Courtesy of Library of Congress.

croplands. Small game animals included squirrel, rabbit, and opossum. The woodlands were filled with hickory nuts, pecans, blackberries, strawberries, persimmons, and other nuts and berries.

Contemporary woodlands peoples such as the Creeks in Oklahoma prefer sofkie (a stiff drink made from corn), corn soup, fry bread, beef, pork, or chicken. Common among many tribes, fry bread is flour and milk mixed together and fried in oil. Cherokees eat much of the same foods, with strawberries being plentiful in northeastern Oklahoma. Choctaws and Chickasaws have a similar diet and a favorite dessert is blue dumplings made from flour mixed with water and wild grapes. Other favorites include an assortment of fruit pies—apple, peach, cherry and the like. Wild onions cooked with scrambled eggs are a delicacy. Iroquoian and Algonquin groups have always enjoyed corn, corn soup, and stews. Cooked duck, halibut and cod, pumpkin, plums, and cranberries are favorite foods. Tribes of the eastern woodlands have adopted many mainstream foods in the twentieth century, and chicken and beef is a big part of their diets.

In addition to the usual demand for fry bread among many tribes of the Great Lakes region, wild rice is a favorite food. **Great Lakes** Summers mean farming and berry picking—cranberries,

Apache women at campfire cooking dinner in pot. Courtesy of Library of Congress.

blueberries, chokeberries, and raspberries. Wild rice grew in shallow lakes and streams and ripened in mid-August or early September. Historically, villages divided into smaller groups to harvest the rice fields as men poled canoes and women tied the rice in bunches and knocked the rice from the kernels into the boat. The rice was dried on birch-bark sheets or flat rocks. Fall months involved hunting waterfowl and small animals such as ink, otter, muskrat, rabbit, fox, and beaver. They hunted deer and bear mostly during the cold months and iced fished for whitefish. In late March and early April, they tapped trees for maple syrup that had to be boiled until the syrup thickened, then strained and boiled again until it reached a consistent viscosity.

Spring and summer meant fishing for bass, muskie, sturgeon, and walleye. Walleye is a favorite fish for eating among the western Great Lakes Indians. Sturgeon is another favorite among the Great Lakes Indians of Wisconsin and Minnesota in particular.

Hunting has always been an important part of the economy of the Great Lakes Indian groups and continued to be so into the twentieth century. Other elements of the diet of the Great Lakes tribes include fry bread, fruits, corn, beans, and squash.

PLAINS

Basically, native peoples of plains tribes are beef eaters. Their appetite comes from their many years of hunting the buffalo well before the introduction of the horse to their area in the 1700s. After the arrival of the horse, some 28 tribes of the Great Plains made the buffalo a part of their livelihood, although cattle have now replaced the buffalo for most American Indians as native plains people prefer beef for much of their diet. Deer, elk, and antelope were a part of the diet of the old days. Fertile land in the Mississippi and Missouri valleys permitted the Osage, Mandan, Kiowa, and other groups to grow corn, beans, tomatoes, and squash. Squirrel, beaver, muskrat, and rabbit were common dishes and women hunted fowl eggs. Buffalo berries in season were popular as were turtle eggs, and mushrooms were a delicacy.

Today, stews are made, beef is cooked, and beans and rice, potatoes, and dry corn are preferred. People of the plains eat diets similar to tribes in other parts of the country. Fry bread is a food people look forward to eating. The Red Corn family of the Osage has even produced an Indian fry bread mix to make it easier to produce fry bread.

As for tribes living in other regions of the United States, the native peoples of the Southwest incorporated much of the indigenous foods into their diets. Among the 19 pueblo groups in New Mexico and tribes in Arizona, chili peppers are a favorite. Pueblo farmers and the Navajo have learned to irrigate the arid land to make successful chili crops possible. Corn is a staple among these two groups and other tribes of the region. In fact, corn has become a part of many tribal ceremonies for most tribes in the Southwest. **Southwest**

In addition to corn and chili peppers, gourds, garlic, squash, and beans are supplements that go with corn. Pueblo women bake thick adobe bread using potato yeast. Lamb and goat meat is put into stews to simmer in pots with green peppers and hominy. Squash and squash blossoms are the basis of others stews to which other foods are added. The Hopi grow twelve varieties of beans and four types of corn: white, yellow, blue, and red.

Hopi and Pueblo women learned how grow and harvest white corn to grind into meal for making bread. Green chili stew is a favorite dish, as well as tamales. The Navajos or the Diné became superb sheepherders after sheep were introduced to them. The amount of sheep a person has determines his status. Sheepherding was the way of life and the economy of the Navajo until the 1960s, when many tribal members went to live in cities and part of the federal relocation programs. For these people, corn is used in several important ways, even in ceremonies, as cornmeal is sacred to the people. Piñon nuts are often a part of meals. Mutton remains a favorite in Navajo communities today. An apricot drink made with apricots, honey, and water is popular. Also, a peach honey drink made of sliced boiled peaches mixed with sugar and water is common to the Southwestern tribes.

Another common drink is juniper tea, which is made from the young sprigs of juniper mixed with boiling water. Most commonly, people drink coffee and have done so for a long time. Piñon coffee is available, consisting of roasted piñon nuts mixed with arabic coffee beans.

California and Basin

Fry bread is practically universal among American Indians throughout Indian Country. In California, native peoples have always prided themselves on being excellent farmers. The Basin has always been a challenging environment and the tribes of this region have depended upon small game such as rabbit for food, as well as gathering acorns, nuts, and edible plants.

Today, traditional foods are less important to the diet of these people. Their adjustments have been tremendous enabling them to live successfully in a demanding environment as they have diets like most of the rest of the country. Piñon nuts remain a favorite food, and California Indians enjoy a wide variety of nuts, fish, and breads.

Pacific Northwest

In this region that borders the Pacific Ocean and features rivers abundant with fish, especially salmon, fishing has been the basis of the economy for centuries. In addition, the mountains were plentiful with deer, elk, bear, and wild goats. This region of the country is blessed with abundance of flora and fauna, supplying natural foods to the native people. Tender cuts of meat, especially venison, were prepared over fires or sometimes wrapped with fat in strips of cedar bark to be placed on hot stones to cook.

The many tall trees of various types nourished by heavy rainfall and rich earth produced acorns and hazelnuts. From the earth, wild salad greens of sweet-smelling and pungent aroma supplemented the diet, along with huckleberries, blackberries, raspberries, wild strawberries, blackcaps, salal, and salmonberries. Food was of such abundance in the Northwest that it enabled the Kuwaiti and other tribes to give lavish feasts called potlatches that shared wealth of food, drink, and material items with all those who attended. Salmon and other kinds of fish were served as the main course. Items of copper, blankets, wooden boxes, and other cultural things were given away.

Current foods in this area include frilled salmon steaks, eggs scrambled with smoked salmon, smoked salmon soup, poached salmon, and salmon cakes. What the buffalo is to the plains Indians, the salmon is to the tribes of the Pacific Northwest. Salmon is the diet staple, supplemented often with potatoes baked in hot ashes, baked turnips and buckskin bread, and berry fruits for dessert. Broths, soups, and stews are simple meals during cold days to keep the people warm and nourished.

INDIAN CARS

In 1901, Ransom Eli Olds built 425 gasoline automobiles, leading to the mass production of cars. Seven years later, Henry Ford introduced his Model T, which sold for $850, but by 1916 his car cost less than $400. Ford's automobiles enticed buyers, including the Indians who could afford them, as more than half of the cars by 1927 were Fords. For the majority of the Indian population in the early decades, automobiles were unaffordable. People continued to use horses and wagons until after the Depression. Only the oilrich Indians, like the Creeks and Osages, could afford the new invention of the automobile.

In the 1920s, Lucinda Pittman, an oil-rich Creek woman of Muskogee, Oklahoma, wanted a Cadillac, but she did not like black, the color all cars came in at the time. Pittman found a color she liked in a store in Muskogee, and she demanded the Cadillac dealership to paint the car purple. She also had the car upholstered in the same color. Surprised people watched her newly painted Cadillac leave a trail of dust on the roads around Muskogee, Tulsa, and Oklahoma City. Pittman made Cadillac a popular car among oil-rich Indians, thereby the dealership profited from her insisting on a custom paint job. Other colors of pink, crimson, and green automobiles became the trend among wealthy Indians in Oklahoma.

It is interesting that automobile makers have named models after Indians or their tribes. For example, General Motors made Pontiac. Jeep produced the Grand Cherokee. Mazda made the Navajo. Chrysler made the Dakota pickup, a large recreational vehicle is called the Winnebago, and others carry on this commercial tradition of the Indian-named car. One wonders why Indians have been associated with the names of models but there is a commercial rationale for using Indian names. Indian names for vehicles reflect durability, toughness, roughness, and the proud nature of native tribes and a certain tribal leaders such as Pontiac.

HOUSING

Long ago, the people of the Eastern woodlands that extend to the Southeast constructed bark-covered lodges and crude wooden cabins. Because the Indians of the south lived in crude cabins and farmed gardens to raise corn crops and other vegetables, they were called the Five Civilized Tribes—the Cherokee, Chickasaw, Choctaw, Muscogee Creek, and Seminole. Intermarriage between whites and Cherokees, Creeks, and Choctaws occurred regularly and many of the tribal members converted to Christianity.

In the Great Lakes region, native peoples constructed wigwams that began to be replaced by small crude wooden houses by the late nineteenth century. The decades of the twentieth century saw the wooden houses become more elaborate on the reservations and houses after the 1970s were much the same as those of non-Indian neighbors in Minnesota, Wisconsin, and Michigan. In the Eastern woodlands of the eastern Great Lakes, the traditional long house gave way to small wooden houses and then to wooden homes similar to mainstream houses in upstate New York.

In the Plains area, the tipi was the traditional house type of about 28 principal tribes. Consisting of 10 to 12 buffalo hides sewn together to cover about a dozen pine lodge poles, the tipi was easily transportable. On the reservations in the late 1800s, Indian agents compelled the plains Indians to live in small wooden houses and making the change from round lodges to square houses required a major adjustment on the part of mobile Plains Indians in the twentieth century.

In the Northwest, tribes constructed large cedar houses. In an abundant timber region with continuous supplies of food, tribes have been able to advance their culture, especially in art. Cedar houses had elaborate drawings of ravens, killer whales, eagles, and wolves. Modern homes are typical of the region in that the size of a house is proportionate to the

Blackfoot tepee. Courtesy of Library of Congress.

owners' income. They are ranch-style homes made of wood, as timber is in steady supply.

In the Southwest, tribes build adobe pueblos with thick walls. The rectangular houses with flat roofs were like apartments, built on top of each other. This design has remained with modern homes rendering the same historic style. Long ago, the pueblo groups learned to use mud in making adobe walls like a plaster to build walls with roofs consisting of layers of pole-like tree limbs carefully cut with plasters of adobe mud in between.

Early reservation life at the turn of the twenti- **Early Reservation** eth century entailed tremendous cultural adjustment **Housing** for the typical native person during the late nineteenth century on the Plains, living in a four-sided lodge seemed inconceivable. Navajos lived in an octagonal hogan and the sedentary tribes from the eastern woodlands and Pacific Northwest lived in long houses and cabins. Grass lodges on the prairies and adobe walled pueblos in the Southwest exemplified native homes in these regions. It was all a matter of adjustment to nature's environment and learning how live with climate conditions. The thickness of the walls insulated the hogan against heat or cold.

Indian housing went against nature when American Indians began to live in homes like those of non-Indians. The quality of such housing corresponded to the earned income of native families and this has been a major adjustment among Native Americans even after World War II. For example, a somewhat common characteristic of Indian housing is the usage of the temporary shelter of mobile homes. In the 1970s, almost 9 percent of the homes of American Indians were not permanent dwellings, compared with 5 percent of white homes and 2 percent of African American homes.

URBAN HOUSING

Many Indians moved to urban housing following World War II. Apartment living became common among Indians who had applied for the relocation program, with jobs and housing found for them by relocation workers. Without sufficient education and limited or no occupational skills, Indians found themselves working as laborers in cities. Low-paying jobs led to substandard living conditions, including on reservations. For example, in 1970 an estimated 46 percent of all homes on reservations lacked adequate plumbing, while 8 percent of urban Indians had inadequate plumbing. The annual cost of reservation housing was $5,000, compared to $13,500 for urban Indian housing.[1]

As a result, most American Indians going on relocation during the 1950s and 1960s represented the first wave of urban Indians and they were forced to live in inexpensive apartment dwellings due to their limited incomes. In the following decade, many Indian families were able to live in modest homes in cities as their incomes became larger. The emergence of an Indian middle-class enabled professional Indians who were lawyers, doctors, and others to afford better homes, which were usually in non-Indian neighborhoods.

Tribal Housing Once supervised wholly by the federal government, Indian tribes have been working with the federal government to construct housing for their people. The drive to build tribal housing has been under way since the early 1970s, resulting from a post-1960s effort to raise the standard of living for many American Indians. As a part of President Lyndon Johnson's War on Poverty program during the late 1960s, the following decade saw a combined effort of federal programming and tribes working together to build adequate housing on reservations and in the homelands of Indian people.

For example, the Muscogee Creek Indian Housing Authority succeeded in initiating a tribal housing program. Over 375 low-cost homes were built or under construction by 1975. Such housing was not made available to just any tribal member. A Muscogee family had to have a low income and wait its turn on a list for the tribe to construct the house, while the family members participated in workshops about maintaining the home.

In the following years, the Muscogee Creeks developed an elderly housing project that constructed apartment units. Located near the tribal capital in Okmulgee, Oklahoma, the elderly housing provides a residence for easier access to health facilities at the tribal capital complex.

Federal Legislation toward Improved Housing The federal government has worked with tribes with the idea that better jobs will improve housing by leading to an improved economy in Indian Country. This concern was evident in the Bill Clinton administration of the early 1990s. On October 23, 1992, Congress enacted the Indian Employment, Training, and Related Services Demonstration Act, P.L. 102-477. This legislative measure was an act "to demonstrate how Indian tribal governments can integrate the employment, training and related services they provide in order to improve the effectiveness of those services, reduce joblessness in Indian communities and serve tribally-determined goals consistent with the policy of self-determination."[2] Seven days later, Congress passed a law to help four specific groups for back compensation for loss of tribal lands. This was the Three Affiliated Tribes and Standing Rock Sioux Tribe Equitable Compensation Act, P.L. 102-575. This was an act "regarding that Congress declares that the Three Affiliated Tribes are entitled to additional financial compensation for the taking of one hundred and fifty-six thousand acres of their reservation lands, as the site of the Oahe Dam and Reservoir, and that such amounts should be deposited in the Standing Rock Sioux Tribe Economic Recovery Fund."[3]

Specific legislation targeting Indian housing improvement was in the Native American Housing Assistance and Self-Determination Act, P.L. 104-330. Congress passed this law on October 26, 1992. It was an act "to provide Federal assistance for Indian tribes in a manner that recognizes the right of tribal self-governance, and for other purposes."[4] As the twentieth century came to a close, Congress passed another general measure to assist in building tribal economies with the Indian Tribal Economic Development and Contract Encouragement Act, P.L. 106-179. Passed on March 14, 2000, the act was "to encourage Indian economic development, to provide for the disclosure of Indian tribal sovereignty immunity in contracts involving Indian tribes, and for other purposes."[5]

American Indian architects and designers have taken the best of two worlds—that of the Indian and of the mainstream—to express compelling concepts in buildings that reflect an Indian renaissance. Old beauty and new ideas are combined in the designing of museums, cultural centers, and the like, to establish an indigenous presence. Such material culture perpetuates the Indian way of borrowing ideas and whatever else may work to make a better Indian life. Such strategy is found in the following physical structures that are helping to preserve Indian heritage.

American Indian Museums

An Indian renaissance occurred following the 1970s. Some buildings were distinctly designed in a Native American way. One of the earliest was the Native American Center for the Living Arts near Niagara Falls, New York. The center is shaped in the form of a turtle, an important animal to the Iroquois and many other tribes, representing durability and long life. Iroquois tradition maintains that the earth was created on the back of a giant turtle. Consisting of three levels, the giant "turtle" hosts an amphitheater, national Indian art gallery, heritage hall, crafts gallery, restaurant, craft shop, learning center, orientation hall, library offices, storage area, control room, and artist-in-residence quarters.

The Rockwell Museum in Corning, New York, is named for Robert F. Rockwell, Jr., whose collecting efforts led to exhibits of paintings, bronzes, and artifacts of more than 100 artists. The collections range from the early 1800s to the present, including exhibits of Plains and Southwestern tribal artifacts.

The Eiteljorg Museum of American Indians and Western Art in Indianapolis, Indiana, is advertised as only one of two museums east of the Mississippi River to combine collections of Western and Indian artifacts. Ten native culture areas are represented at the Eiteljorg. Artwork of early-twentieth-century artists and contemporary artists is exhibited. The vast collection includes pottery, basketry, wood carvings, and clothing. The Eiteljorg also hosts the Indian Market in June every year. The inside mall area depicts a Western atmosphere with the outside designed in Southwest pueblo character. In this extraordinary way, the Southwest has been brought east of the Mississippi.

NOTES

1. Alan L. Sorkin, *The Urban American Indian* (Lexington, Mass: Lexington Books, 1978), 22–23.

2. Indian Employment, Training, and Related Services Demonstration Act, P.L. 102-477, October 23, 1992, U.S. Statutes at Large, Vol.106, Pt. 3: 2302–2306.

3. "Three Affiliated Tribes and Standing Rock Sioux Tribe Equitable Compensation Act," P.L. 102-575, October 30, 1992, U.S. Statutes at Large, Vol. 106, Pt. 6: 4731–4739.

4. Native American Housing Assistance and Self-Determination Act, P.L. 104-330, October 26, 1992, U.S. Statutes at Large, Vol. 110, Pt. 6: 4016–4052.

5. Indian Tribal Economic Development and Contract Encouragement Act, P.L. 106-179, March 14, 2000, U.S. Statutes at Large, Vol. 110, Pt. 1: 36–37.

6. National Museum of the American Indian Act, P.L. 101-185, November 28, 1989, U.S. Statutes at Large, 103: 1336–1347.

5

POLITICAL LIFE, PROFESSIONAL ORGANIZATION, CITIZENSHIP, MILITARY SERVICE, AND TRIBAL GOVERNMENT

It has been said in Indian Country that there is nothing else like Indian politics. Due to the complex nature of Indian life, American Indian politics exist at several levels from historical times to the present, including within families, clans, or societies, or communities or tribes and their external dealings with the local, state, and federal governments. Indians and their leaders also find themselves negotiating with energy companies and other corporations to preserve their homelands. In law schools throughout mainstream academia, coursework in federal law as it affects American Indians is offered, and it is becoming more complex with each major law passed by Congress and each new Supreme Court decision involving American Indians. At the same time, modern tribal governments with their own systems of tribal laws are having an increasing impact on tribal relations with state and local governments.

ALL THINGS ARE RELATED

Indians who are close to their traditions think inclusively. In the Indian way, all things in the universe are related to each other. In this manner of perspective, native ethos is important for understanding American Indians. Indian people "see" themselves in personal relationships with nature. Because relationships are extremely important, establishing kinship recognition is important. Hence, building positive relationships is important. To be outside of a community is the worst that could happen, especially if one was banished from a camp or community.

Chief Little Wound in council with others. Courtesy of Library of Congress.

NATURAL DEMOCRACY

It is possible for players in a natural democracy to be in relationships to each other. Such a democracy is a network of relationships based on mutual respect in all things. Although all things are created equal, they are different in power and ability. Plants and animals are integral players in this network of nature. Like human beings, they have certain roles. It is important for cooperation to occur among all things involved, because they are all interrelated.

Because relationships are important, social and cultural kinships are significant to people in the community. As mentioned earlier, blood relations are important, but symbolic relations are also pertinent among human beings and all things, including bad and evil things. This sociocultural kinship is the substance that holds the Natural Democracy together.

This kinship of a natural democracy extends to animals and plants. Navajo surgeon Lori Alvord described her father and his special ability to communicate with animals. He understood them. She said, "My father knew them. Crows also seemed to gather in groups or come and stand on a fence post whenever my father was around. Sometimes I'd turn a corner and find my father standing deep in a philosophical discussion with a crow."[1] Sometimes people find it easier to talk to animals, even plants, but it is a fact that we can understand them, if we simply get used to their sounds and how they correspond with their actions. Indian people have studied animals and plants for centuries, and for this reason they have clans named after totem animals such as the wolf, bear, eagle, and so forth.

Social structure knits Indian life together in a tapestry of kinship relations. For native peoples, this is the natural world, in which everything is respected. Understanding this system of nature calls for acceptance and cooperation from all those involved.

ALLIANCES

Alliances are important among Native Americans. Tribal communities have long since discovered that forming alliances with other communities or tribes helps to protect their interests, people, and land. Throughout the history of American Indians, alliances have been struck, whether between two groups or among three or more tribes. The Iroquois League in the Northeast wielded much power during the eighteenth century; the Muscogee Creeks formed a confederacy in the Southeast as did the Three Fires or Three Brothers in the Great Lakes. The Sauk and Fox formed an alliance of two tribes. The Southern Cheyenne and Southern Arapaho have done the same. The Lakota and Northern Cheyenne have always been allies.

In modern Indian history of the twentieth century, the Southeastern tribes have formed an organization, the Five Civilized Tribes in Oklahoma meet annually, the tribes of western Oklahoma have an alliance, and there are others that could be mentioned.

Throughout history, it is known that tribes consisted of bands, camps, or towns. Predetermined meetings usually held once a year called for the small units to meet as a whole, for instance, the ten bands of the Cheyenne met in the summer for the Sun Dance, Lakota groups meet for the same ceremony, and an annual council pulled together all of the towns of the Muscogee Creeks to celebrate the annual Green Corn Ceremony. Other Eastern woodlands tribes, such as the Cherokee, Chickasaw, and Choctaw, met for the same reason (to celebrate the Sun for giving life to all living things) as other tribes that called their people from various communities together to meet annually.

Amidst all of the changes in their history, the Muscogee Creeks in Oklahoma have continued their fundamental political system since their confederacy days in the Southeast hundreds of years ago. As the tribe moved towards self-determination in the 1970s, a large population of 40,000 to 45,000 Creeks lived in eastern Oklahoma in 11 counties containing the Creek Nation after removal.

President Harding with Sioux and Crow chiefs and Indian Commissioner Burke in front of the White House in 1921. Courtesy of Library of Congress.

The Muscogee Creek maintained a system of tribal towns. In this political system, communities or tribal towns sent their delegates to attend monthly meetings at the old capital site of Ocmulgee in present-day Georgia. This is still done following the Creek removal to Indian Territory, and the new Creek capital in Oklahoma is named Okmulgee like the old one. This political system was revised during World War II. In the early 1960s, the Creeks reorganized and held quarterly meetings of 58 tribal town delegates, who met at the old Council House in downtown Okmulgee. In 1979 a new tribal constitution mandated the integration of the towns into eight district counties with each one electing delegates to the reformed National Council.

Many years ago, the ceremonial dance grounds were the focus of each tribal town. This changed in 1900,when the Creek separated the dance grounds from the towns by referring to them as "stomp grounds." They were named after the "Green Corn" or "Busk" ceremonial dances to celebrate the annual harvest of corn. Through the decades of the twentieth century, the number of stomp grounds has declined with modernity claiming the attention of new generations of the Creek people. By 1980, an estimated 20 stomp grounds remained active throughout the Muscogee Creek Nation in Oklahoma.

The towns, called *tvlvns,* continue to play an important role in the politics and daily life of the Creek Nation government; each town is important. The Creeks are unlike most tribes who have a central capital site because their towns provide certain services. Tribal members of the Creek Nation travel to the tribal town for services rendered by the tribe. This communal system allows the distribution of services to the people, although they may have to go to Okmulgee or Okemah for particular health services. Tribal members can offer their opinion to their councilmen representing the districts of towns. A previous constitution of 1867 revised the old Muscogee Council into a bicameral congress consisting of the House of Warriors and a House of Kings. This means of government to represent the people continued until the Curtis Act of 1898 nullified the entire system of the Creek government including its tribal courts. The statehood of Oklahoma helped to dissolve the possible power of the Creek government and other tribal governments until the 1930s. Under the Indian Reorganization Act, the federal government wanted tribes to reorganize their communities and governments.

SOCIETY OF AMERICAN INDIANS

The Society of American Indians (SAI) was formed in Columbus, Ohio, near the campus of Ohio State University in 1911. In spite of the suppression of American Indians, an elite group of Indian achievers arose and joined together. The SAI was the only group of Indians to succeed according to mainstream standards. It represented the first nationally based group of Indian professionals of various areas and tribes. The SAI met for the first time in Columbus, Ohio, during April 1911. The meeting consisted of educated Indians such as Dr. Carlos Montezuma, the Apache physician; Henry Roe Cloud, Winnebago teacher and tribal leader; Thomas Sloan, Omaha lawyer; Arthur C. Parker, Seneca anthropologist; Dr. Charles Eastman, Sioux physician; and his brother, the Reverend John Eastman. Also, members included Laura Cornelius, Oneida social reformer; John M. Oskisson, Cherokee author; Gertrude Bonnin, Sioux writer and musician; and Episcopal priest Sherman Coolidge, Arapaho.

The SAI proclaimed two themes: pan-Indianism, the belief that because Indians share a common destiny they should be guided politically and socially by that destiny; and assimilation, the belief that Indians should adopt the culture and lifestyle of the dominant society while retaining a pride in their racial identity and those values similar to European ones. The SAI spoke out in criticism against the Bureau of Indian Affairs (BIA) and its federal programs, but found SAI members not always in agreement.

The SAI opposed the BIA because its members wanted improved bureau services. It believed that the BIA was doing too good of a job in preserving tribalism and traditional Indian culture. The SAI members themselves were well educated; some were mixed-bloods or of intertribal descent. Many married white partners or members of other tribes; they spoke English fluently and often belonged to Christian churches and other non-Indian organizations. Absorbed in the white man's life, they were engaged in typical occupations of white society.

Called Red Progressives, the SAI started *The Quarterly Journal of the Society of American Indians* in 1913, which was changed to *The American Indian Magazine* in 1916. Under the editorship of Arthur C. Parker, the publication promoted Indian unity and American patriotism. On his own, Carlos Montezuma started the publication *Wassaja,* a monthly that reported progress among Indian people. He opposed any effort to preserve American Indian cultures and wardship status among Indians. The society experienced factionalism when Charles Eastman departed from the group.

Some SAI members, under the leadership of Gertrude Bonnin, organized the National Council of American Indians in 1926. Bonnin was an outspoken Lakota who believed in Indian rights. The group continued to campaign against peyote and called for the dissolving of the Native American Church. Like the SAI, factionalism caused the new council to have problems, which led to its end in the 1930s. In the years before its demise, the society was ineffective in representing Indian affairs before Congress.

POLITICS OF CITIZENSHIP

While intending to help Indians, Secretary of the Interior Franklin Lane and Cato Sells, the new commissioner of Indian affairs, would play instrumental roles that actually harmed Indian progress. Sells had attended Cornell College in his home state of Iowa. He became a progressive Democrat and was appointed Indian commissioner by the Woodrow Wilson administration. This appointment became politically possible when a congressional investigation forced Commissioner Robert Valentine to retire.

Sells created a "competency commission" in 1915 and selected the Montana Flathead reservation as the first case for issuing fee patents or full Indian ownership to allotments. The competency commission declared Indians case by case for whether they were competent or incompetent to run their own business affairs. If "incompetent," a legal guardian was appointed to help the person. The commission consisted of James McLaughlin, an inspector for the Interior Department, and F. A. Thackery, superintendent of the Pima School. In less than two years, other competency commissions were created, issuing fee patents to approximately 50,000 acres of land. Without considering the possible negative repercussions, they persuaded "incompetent" Indians, who lacked business experience and who were illiterate, "to take the medicine with the rest." During an elaborate ritual, each Indian "stepped from a tipi and shot an arrow to signify that he was leaving his Indian way of life. He placed his hands on a plow," indicating the decision to live from then as a "white man" and the Secretary of Interior presented him with a "purse as a reminder that he must save what he earned."[2] This ritual was exercised at the Crow, Shoshone, Coeur d'Alene, Fort Hall, Sisseton, Fort Berthold, and Devil's Lake agencies.

On April 17, 1917, Commissioner Sells pronounced his "Declaration of Policy," which established dealing with Indians on an individual basis rather than as tribal communities. For all allotted tribes, any Indian person of one-half or more white ancestry, every person twenty-one years of age or older who had completed a full course of instruction in a government school, and all other Indians assessed to be "competent" as a "white man" would be granted full authority over his property and money, and would no longer be a ward of the United States. This policy proved devastating for many tribes, such as the Cheyenne and Arapaho. In their case, in all they lost a total of 181,500 acres, or 34.2 percent of all their allotted lands to while opportunists. Including the land sold during the first decade of the century, a grand total of 297,214 acres, or 56.3 percent of all their lands had passed out of their hands and into those of mainstream businessmen, ranchers, individual farmers, lawyers, and oilmen.

GRAFT AND GUARDIANSHIP

Cato Sells's ideological policies and programs did not benefit the Indians. In his view, progress had been made in health conditions, suppression of the liquor traffic, and in improvement of industrial conditions and vocational training in schools. This assessment encouraged Sells to discontinue guardianship of all competent Indians and prepare incompetents so "that they may more speedily achieve competency."[3] From 1913 to 1920, Sells and Lane were responsible for issuing over 20,000 patents, covering one million acres, of which most of the Indians sold and became impoverished.

The failure of "competent" Indians to adequately handle their business affairs compelled the courts to appoint attorneys and "guardians" to supervise the business affairs for the allotees. Some attorneys charged up to 50 percent of the annual royalties received from allotments for managing the legal affairs, and some attorneys held guardianship over 50 to 100 Indian allottees.

INDIANS IN WORLD WAR I

Young Indian men joined the army as the war in Europe grew into a World War. One Indian reservation superintendent stated, "Indian children learn to expect nothing from the future."[4] While many Indian boys joined the service, Indian girls became pregnant to be placed on welfare, which had no real program until the 1930s under the Roosevelt administration.

Socially, Indians had no status or very little. They lived an invisible existence, as mainstream society ostracized them from public facilities. Signs in stores, restaurants, and other public places stated, "No Dogs or Indians Allowed!" Discrimination kept the Indians on the reservations and allotments. Very few were able to succeed, according to the white man's standards. The clash of the white man's ethnocentric culture with the red man's suppressed the livelihood of Indians. Negative stereotypes fostered public contempt of Indian s. Such a hostile attitude bred mutual dislike from some Indians. One Indian killed a schoolteacher, then killed himself. He vowed to "have a white man die with him."[5]

The effects of the Industrial Revolution in Europe during the late nineteenth century launched a period of Progressivism in the United States. A nationwide spirit of reform combined with rapid urban and industrial growth called for a new age that catapulted the United States to the world stage as an industrial power that would be tested in World War I. Some 9,000 to 10,000 American Indians voluntarily fought for the United States in the armed services. Indian communities were moved by feelings of patriotism. The Iroquois declared war on Germany.

Congressman Homer Snyder of New York introduced a citizenship bill for American Indians in 1919. The Act of 1919 stated that all honorably discharged Indian veterans of World War I would be made U.S. citizens. This bill, made into law, was a part of the federal government's goal to make all Indians citizens, in order to speed their assimilation into the mainstream.

U.S. CITIZENSHIP: 1924

In January 1924, Congressman Homer P. Snyder introduced House Resolution 6355, which authorized the secretary of the interior to grant citizenship to all American Indians requesting it. The Senate Committee on Indian Affairs then proposed a blanket citizenship law that amended the House Resolution. On June 2, 1924, President Calvin Coolidge signed the bill into law.

Citizenship did not imply the right to vote, but this was a major reform period for American Indians. The early 1920s represented the height for reform. The Roaring Twenties brought tremendous changes in society and culture for the American people. For example, women had been citizens, as stated in the Fourteenth Amendment, but they lacked voting privileges. The Nineteenth Amendment, passed in 1920, authorized women's suffrage. In brief, attitudes of the general population were changing. Although discrimination against Indians still occurred, the legal restrictions were lessened and landmark legislation meant major reform in the Indian citizenship act of 1924.

The question of whether Indians could be citizens of their own tribes and citizens of the United States was finally resolved—they could be both. The citizenship movement reached its height during the exploitation of Indian allotments. Popular thought determined that Indians could be single property owners and simultaneously hold citizenship rights and responsibilities. The vast cultural differences still remaining deep within the communities disallowed the citizenship movement to be successfully completed in practice. Legally, the Indian population became citizens, but full rights were denied due to the trust status held on their properties—a paternalistic safeguard of Indian rights.

Thrust into confusion, Indians' rights as individuals and as tribes were left to legal interpretation according to each case requiring an answer. This indefinite status meant that Indian rights were inconsistent, and many factors could be involved. Primarily the assimilation policy and pressure to carry out such policy guided the law, but local constituents and key government officials hoped to influence the law. Above all, the only consistency in federal Indian law was its inconsistency.

Indian rights were determined by the white man's interpretation of his law for Indians. This one-sided interpretation has produced many disputes over Indian legal rights, which the courts have had to explain. During the last several years, many tribes have developed their own courts, so that there are potentially two versions of Indian legal rights. This ongoing situation, to be discussed later, seeks to establish two systems of law, each of which should theoretically arrive at the same decision if justice is to prevail.

INDIAN NEW DEAL

In an attempt to find a solution to the economic misery brought on by the Depression, President Franklin Roosevelt and his supporters began to introduce legislation in Congress that changed the style of government in the United States. The federal government began to play a prominent role in people's lives with the beginning of FDR's "New Deal" for America. Indians were included as well in what might be called an Indian New Deal, which affected an indigenous population of 300,000. By way of the Indian New Deal, the federal government changed the course of American Indian history by encouraging tribal communities to remain intact rather than trying to break them up via the previous assimilation policy.

The individual in the federal government in charge of Indian affairs was the newly appointed commissioner of Indian affairs, John Collier, who served from 1933 to 1945. In 1934, Congress passed the Wheeler-Howard bill soon known as the Indian Reorganization Act (IRA), resulting in one of the most important Indian policies in the century. The IRA called for the restoration of tribal communities to form new governments modeled after the U.S. government, while preserving the production of authentic Indian arts and crafts. The act also provided for federal programs to provide a loan fund for the tribes to restart their economies.

The original IRA excluded two groups from its provisions. The Alaska Natives and Oklahoma Indians were deemed fit enough to improve on their own, but this did not happen as expected. In 1936 Congress passed the Alaska Native Reorganization Act and Oklahoma Indian Welfare Act (OIWA). Basically these two measures provided the same IRA provisions to the two groups. For example, the OIWA provided for restructuring tribal governments and funding economic development, including making loans available for land purchases. Furthermore, tribal and Alaska Native community options were included for whether or not these two groups wanted to participate in the Indian New Deal. The OIWA allowed tribal towns and communities to establish cooperative associations. An estimated 40 Oklahoma tribes with a total population of about 140,000 were affected. In response to why Oklahoma Indians had been exempted from the original IRA, Senator Elmer Thomas believed that Oklahoma Indians had made considerable progress beyond their former lives on reservations. With no official reservations in Oklahoma due to the Curtis Act of 1898, federal officials believed that the Indian communities would do well without assistance.

The OIWA provided available credit and land purchases in federal trust to help Oklahoma tribal groups. The overall objective was to develop programs to help these people through the Depression. Of the Five Civilized Tribes (Cherokee, Chickasaw, Choctaw, Creek, and Seminole), the Creeks suffered the least. The Choctaws and Chickasaws owned the most property and natural resources, but they made little use of them. In economic potential, the Seminoles had the fewest jobs, because most of their people received royalties from oil drilled on their allotted lands. With oil money, things were not as bad for them. The Cherokees suffered the most and their communities were dilapidated. Poverty prevailed among the Cherokees of eastern Oklahoma. Living in wooden houses, they managed a living on small farms and sought work in nearby towns.

WORLD WAR II, KOREA, AND VIETNAM

American Indian men have a long history of serving in the armed forces of the United States. In fact, almost one in every four native man over eighteen is in the military service or is a veteran. American Indians have served this country in the highest ratio per population of their ethnic group. As many Indian men served in World War I, native men had also fought for the North and South in the Civil War as well as on the side of the new United States during the American Revolution. An estimated 25,000 men and 700 women served in World War II; 10,000 served in Korea; and 43,000 served in Vietnam. The same high trend has occurred in the Persian Gulf War and in the Iraq conflict.

Jack Montgomery, Oklahoma Cherokee, and Ernest Childers, Oklahoma Creek, earned Congressional Medals of Honor in World War II. Native men earned 71 Air Medals, 51 Silver Stars, 47 Bronze Stars, and 12 Distinguished Flying Crosses. For Oklahoma Indians, 166 Purple Hearts were awarded and 132 were killed in action.

War heroes included Major General Clarence Tinker, an Osage Indian who was one of the first American Indian officers to be honored in World War II. In the battle of Midway, he selected himself to lead a bomber attack on the Japanese navy. His plane was last seen descending rapidly into the ocean. A careful search produced no trace of him or his plane.

Lieutenant Joseph Woody Cochran, a Cherokee from Skedee, Oklahoma, received four medals, the Distinguished Flying Cross, the Air Medal, the Purple Heart, and the Silver Star. Staff Sergeant Frankie Spindler, an Assiniboine killed in action, received the Distinguished Flying Cross, the Air Medal, and the Purple Heart.

In World War II, 28 Navajo code talkers distinguished themselves by delivering coded messages for the U.S. Marines fighting in the Pacific. More were added as the war progressed. Comanche code talkers were used as well, and Choctaw code talkers served in World War I.

One of the six servicemen to raise the flag on Mount Suribachi at Iwo Jima in the famous photographed scene was Private First Class Marine Ira Hayes, a Pima Indian from Arizona. Hayes became an instant public figure when the U.S. government hailed him a hero in an effort to induce Americans to buy more war bonds. In the hands of government officials, Hayes was exploited as the "noble warrior" who devotedly served his country. Billboards and the media touted him as the virtuous American Indian whose integrity remained unquestioned and whose traditional dignity symbolized American ideals and basic values. Unfortunately celebrity status prohibited Hayes from fulfilling a personal quest as a sol-dier in his tribe's warrior tradition. He was removed from combat duty and sent on tours in the states for the purpose of arousing people's spirit of patriotism. Continuous public exposure led to his ruin. The govern-ment had exploited Hayes without realizing the damaging consequences that would befall him.

MODERN TRIBAL/BUSINESS COUNCILS

Many tribes have adopted a council type of forum for political discus-sions about tribal affairs. Some councils are also called business meetings, and small tribes allow all tribal members to attend. Larger tribes hold councils with chapter representatives (such as the Navajo) or district rep-resentatives (such as the Muscogee Creeks in Oklahoma).

In the 1940s, the Muscogee Creeks continued to have a National Council. In council, the Creeks discussed tribal laws and policies, and this is where the true power lay. According to tradition, the council represented the old way of democracy in which all concerns were heard in a positive light. Elders wielded a great amount of influence because everyone respected them. The tribe called for a general council meeting on January 27, 1944, and 24 towns adopted a new constitution and its bylaws. The Principal Chief remained as the executive authority, and the National Council represented the other branch of government. Later, a tribal court developed as the third entity of the government of the Creeks. The Muscogees remained loosely unified as a nation possessing a strong native identity. Rather than a confederation in the twentieth century, the Creeks viewed themselves as a tribal nation consisting of numerous towns with the emphasis on communities.

Representation of the people is a great concern of tribal councils as a modern form of tribal governments. This is a virtue of the old way of government among many tribes like the Iroquois. Among the Seneca, the legislative part, or the Tribal Council, is the most powerful branch of government. The Seneca Nation government is based on an ancient democracy. In fact, most of the U.S. government is based on the democratic style of the Iroquois Nations. The Seneca have a two-tier legislative council with eight from the Alleghany and a second eight from the Cattaraugus. Members of the council are elected for four-year staggered terms. Council members must be at least 21 years old and have been a resident of the reservation for at least one year. In its monthly meetings, the Tribal Council forms new laws, rescinds old ones, establishes programs to serve the people, and decides on funding to support the programs. The council acts in accordance to the Seneca constitution and it is empowered to make treaties with other governments with the approval of three-fourths of the legal voters and three-fourths of the mothers of the tribe.[6] The Seneca also have a systematic court system. The judiciary branch consists of separate Peacemaker, Appellate, and Surrogate Courts.

In the Southwest, the Isleta Pueblo, originally established about 1200, is a group of people of the ancient Tanoan tribe who are descended from Shoshoncan people. The Isleta Pueblo has a 12-member council that constitutes the legislative part of the tribal government. The governor of the pueblo appoints four council members and the president and vice president appoint three members apiece. The council's secretary and treasurer are chosen by the council. Acting according to the Isleta Pueblo constitution, the council is responsible for hiring legal counsel when necessary, managing tribal lands, and negotiating with all types of governments, businesses, and persons. The council also enacts tribal laws, establishes tax rates and collects taxes, appropriates funding to tribal programs, and establishes committees.[7]

The Isleta Pueblo is a tribe formed in accordance with the Indian Reorganization Act (IRA) of 1934. Its council members hold office for two-year terms. Issues are decided by a majority vote of those members present.

In the Pacific Northwest, the Yakima organized as the Confederated Tribes of the Yakima Nation in 1933. They have emphasized self-sufficiency and economic independence since World War II. The Yakima Tribe established a 14-member tribal council at its general council meeting in 1944. Historically the Yakima consisted of 14 bands, each one of which sent a delegate to the tribal council to represent its views and concerns. The tribal council holds meetings monthly to follow the directives of the general council. Every two years, the general council elects seven new members who serve four-year terms to enable a familiarity with tribal business.

Within the tribal council of 14, 3 people are selected to serve on the executive committee as a chairperson, vice chairperson, and secretary-treasurer. Seven committees regulate tribal affairs in their areas: legislative; timber, grazing and economic development; housing, employment and welfare; enrollment; law and order and fish and wildlife; lands; and education and housing. The Tribal Council appoints councilors as a part of the committees who report back to the Tribal Council.[8]

In the West, the Northern and Southern Cheyenne are examples of consensus being important as well as cooperation. At one time, there was only one Cheyenne Tribe that resided on the northern Plains. Every four years, during the summer, the ten bands of the Cheyenne met to hold the Sun Dance and for the Council of Forty-Four to meet. Four selected representatives from each band, meeting with four respected elders from all of the bands, came together in council to make important decisions for the entire tribe. In the mid-1830s, the Cheyenne divided into the Northern and Southern, but the council style of government continued. The Southern Cheyenne joined with the Arapaho when a reservation was assigned to them in the Treaty of Medicine Lodge in 1867. Together they became known as the Southern Cheyenne and Arapaho Tribes of Oklahoma.

SELF-DETERMINATION

The failure of the termination policy, coupled with mounting Indian protests, called for a new federal Indian policy. A new Indian leadership of angry youth and emerging urban Indian communities convinced the federal government that after more than 200 years of paternalistic practices, American Indians could run their own affairs. The Indian Self-Determination and Education Assistance Act of 1975 established the current federal Indian policy with ensuing legislation and federal programs to assist tribal governments and Indian communities and organizations to contract and administer federal services to Indian communities. The act is intended to give Indian communities great control over services and programs that affect their lives and communities.

Under the rubric of self-determination, Congress has passed the Indian Health Care Improvement Act in 1976, authorizing seven years of increased appropriations to improve Indian health standards. In April

1978, Congress passed the American Indian Religious Freedom Act to protect and preserve the inherent right of American Indians to express and exercise their traditions and beliefs. In November 1978, Congress passed the Indian Child Welfare Act, which established a protocol for the adoption of Indian orphans. In order that an Indian orphan not be deprived of his or her cultural heritage the adopting parents were in the following priority order: relatives, tribal members, other Indians, and non-Indians. When placed in non-Indian homes and institutions, many American Indian youths experience confusion over their identity, which is frequently due to the denial of their Indian heritage.

During the 1980s, Congress passed the Indian Tribal Government Tax Status Act, granting tribes many of the federal tax advantages that states already enjoy. Tribes began assuming more autonomy over their communities and economies. In 1988 Congress passed legislation that officially ended the termination policy. During the same year, Congress passed the Indian Gaming Regulatory Act, which placed limitation on bingos on reservations. Afterward, tribes could operate only certain kinds of gambling. With the trust status still in effect, the federal government remains obligated as the guardian of federally recognized tribes, although self-determination will most likely continue as the prevailing federal Indian policy for the rest of the century.

MODERN TRIBAL GOVERNMENTS

The 1960s and 1970s proved to be a critical period for the survival of nativism for many tribal governments. As the people progressed in the areas of housing, health, and economics, tribal members became more acculturated to the ways of the white mainstream. Trying to achieve parity with the general standard of living set in the United States caused external and internal pressures for American Indians as a people and for their tribal governments. Such conditions mandated a need for an effective leadership in tribal governments, encouraging respected local leaders to vie for the executive office.

The Creeks entered the 1980s as one of the leading tribal groups in the United States, along with the Cherokee of Oklahoma, the Cherokee of North Carolina, the Mississippi Choctaw, the Navajo Nation, and others. The struggle between retention of traditions and adopting new governing methods has challenged tribal governments and their leaders.

As an IRA tribe, the government of Isleta is patterned like the U.S. government with executive, legislative (council), and judicial components. Isleta's population in 2000 was more than 4,000, of which about 2,500 are tribal members. A person must be at least 50 percent pure Isleta blood in order to be eligible for membership in the tribe.

There are more than 8,800 members in the Yakima confederation of tribes. More than 13,700 people live on or close to the reservation. All members of

Sign outside of Hopi Reservation stating that land is governed by Hopi Law.

the Yakima over 18 years of age are voting members of the general council. The Yakima tribe employs an estimated 600 full-time positions.

Tribal enterprises include the following business ventures: Heritage Inn Restaurant, Mt. Adams Furniture Factory, Production Orchards, Real Yakima Fruit Stand, Wapato Industrial Park, Yakima Forest Products, Yakima Nation Credit Enterprise, Yakima National Cultural Center, Yakima Nation Land Enterprise, Yakima Nation Legends Casino, and Yakima Nation RV Resort. In addition, the tribe operates a fisheries program with about 40 employees. The Yakima Indian Nation also co-manages, with the state of Washington, fishing of the Columbia and eight other rivers. Salmon remains an important nutritional and symbolic commodity of the Yakima Nation.

Overall, the Yakima manage 1,118,149 acres, which include 600,000 acres of timber and 15,000 acres of cultivated land. In addition, the tribe irrigates 90,000 acres from the Wapato Project and leases farming and grazing acreage. The Yakima Confederation maintains its own police force and tribal court. The Yakima people maintain numerous parts of their heritage, including the Cultural Heritage Center, which hosts numerous tribal projects to uphold traditional arts and crafts, history, language, and literature. Powwows, celebrations, and sports are a part of modern Yakima life today.

For the Southern Cheyenne and Arapaho of Oklahoma, there is no official reservation, although they have a land base in trust status with the federal government. This parcel of 10,202 acres of land in western Oklahoma is governed from the tribal administration offices located in Concho. On the tribal flag are 28 eagle feathers representing the fourteen Cheyenne and fourteen Arapaho councilmen of the Business Committee, as determined in the original tribal constitution. Fourteen stars on the flag represent the Later-Reviewed Council of seven Cheyenne and seven Arapaho. With the Business Council of fourteen, the Tribal Chairman supervised the affairs of 11,627 tribal members of the Southern Cheyenne and Arapaho of Oklahoma.

The Muscogee Creeks have maintained a central focus on tribal towns, and the capital at Okmulgee has expanded in services to tribal members. By the end of the 1950s, the central government began to grow into a bureaucracy. The Creeks created a Business Committee with the Principal Chief serving as the chairman, who, along with six tribal members, supervises the finances of the 16,640 tribal members. Believing in autonomy, the Creeks wanted only what they needed from the American mainstream. In spite of the declining traditions among the people, the Creeks remained native in their outlook with so much modernization occurring around them. Farming and raising stock became the economic means for many Creek families. The Indian Service at the regional BIA office in Muskogee employed Farm Management Supervisor Al Feighny of Holdenville to advise and assist the Creeks and other Five Civilized Tribes. Feighny advised potential Indian farmers on how to obtain loans to purchase seed for crops and equipment.

For the Muscogee Creek, to help settle this issue of selecting its leadership, Congress passed Public Law 91-495 in 1970, stating that the Five Civilized Tribes of Oklahoma would have total authority in electing their tribal leaders. In the mid-1970s, the federal government was at a high point in its financial support of all tribes. The enactment of the Self-Determination and Education Assistance Act of 1975 (P.L. 93-638) provided abundant funding for tribal programs. The legislation stressed tribal control to supervise services for one's own Indian people. The Republican administrations of Richard Nixon and Gerald Ford, and the following Democratic administration of Jimmy Carter, confirmed that Indian self-determination was the primary directive of federal Indian policy. The Creek Nation government prospered and created a large bureaucracy with an estimated 40 to 50 people working in the offices at the tribal complex. The Creeks' self-government and initiative to direct their destiny was substantiated by the federal policy of self-determination.

The federal Indian policy of self-determination has extensively assisted the Creek Nation, while allowing the tribe to take the initiative in developing programs to serve its people. The election of Ronald Reagan as president of the United States in 1980 also issued new challenges to the

Creeks and all tribes. A conservative Reagan administration proposed an immediate $200 million cutback in tribal housing authorities, and the U.S. Office of Management and Budget requested sweeping budget reforms. Federal reductions called for cutting $75.9 million from the BIA's budget, which identified the Reagan Indian policy as being one of cutbacks in federal funding. Self-determination under Reagan became quickly interpreted as limited federal appropriation and streamlined services.

FEDERAL SUPPORT FOR TRIBAL GOVERNMENTS

Whereas the Reaganomics meant cutbacks in federal support for tribes, the following decade was different. As president, Ronald Reagan knew very little about American Indians. President Bill Clinton reached out to the tribes to understand and his administration responded with support. He appointed Ada Deer, a Menominee from Wisconsin, as the first native woman to be assistant secretary of the Department of the Interior. After 500 years of Indian-white contact, 562 federally recognized tribes existed in the United States on 291 reservations, mostly in the West. Another 43 tribes were recognized by state governments and another dozen or more were petitioning the federal government for federal recognition. Some tribes, such as those in Oklahoma, operated with a land base in trust status but were not regarded officially as reservations. As could be predicted, the federal government worked in partnership with the tribes after the withdrawal and cutback years of the 1980s.

On October 23, 1992, Congress enacted the Indian Employment, Training, and Related Services Demonstration Act, known as P.L. 102-477. This was an act "to demonstrate how Indian tribal governments can integrate the employment, training and related services they provide in order to improve the effectiveness of those services, reduce joblessness in Indian communities and serve tribally-determined goals consistent with the policy of self-determination."[9]

One day later, Congress passed the Indian Environmental General Assistance Program Act, P.L. 102-497. This was an act "to provide general assistance grants to Indian tribal governments and intertribal consortia to build capacity to administer environmental regulatory programs that may be delegated by the Environmental Protection Agency on Indian lands; to provide technical assistance from EPA to tribal governments and intertribal consortia and to develop multimedia programs to address environmental issues on Indian lands."[10]

To help the tribes strengthen their judicial systems, Congress passed the Indian Tribal Justice Act, P.L. 103-176, on December 3, 1993. This was an act "to assist in the development of tribal judicial systems, and for other purposes."[11] Working further to help the tribes, Congress passed Indian Self-Determination Contract Reform Act, P.L. 103-413, on October 24, 1994. This was an act to amend the Indian Self-Determination Act " to specify the terms of contracts entered into by the United States and Indian tribal organizations under the Indian Self-Determination and Education Assistance act and to provide for tribal Self-Governance."[12]

CONCLUSION

Tribal governments and Indian organizations have come to realize that in dealing with the outside, the internal organization of their governments, as well as their external organizations, need to be ultra efficient. In order to represent their people and communities in dealing with the outside mainstream world, modern tribal governments have become like business corporations. As a result of the progress of tribal governments, modern alliances or coalitions, shaped by common regional interests, have become a part of Indian politics.

For outsiders, it is important to understand the internal network of Indian communities and tribal governments and how they operate. The tribal leaders have learned to negotiate and operate in two systems of life, theirs and that of the mainstream. The governments are sophisticated in every area of organization, show great consideration for tribal affairs, and protective of their resources.

The political nature of American Indians is that they have an internal order of politics as well as an external order to the rest of Indian Country and the world. They have to maintain a fine balance between the inside politics and outside politics, which is a constant struggle. Change has been good for the tribes, but such a transition always causes some loss of cultural traditions and the like. Even more, it seems that change is accelerating as the tribal governments are forced to develop and make critical decisions at a faster pace.

NOTES

1. Lori Arviso and Elizabeth Cohen van Pelt, *The Scalpel and the Silver Bear* (New York: Bantam Books, 1999), 84.

2. Annual Report of the Commission of Indian Affairs, Cato Sells, October 15, 1917, microfiche, p. 29. Copy in Special Collections, Marquette University, Milwaukee, Wisconsin.

3. Ibid., p. 49.

4. Statement describing conditions of native youth (no author), May 7, 1918, Carlos Montezuma Papers, microfilm, reel 3.

5. Annual Report of the Commission of Indian Affairs, Francis Leupp, September 30, 1907, microfilm, reel 5.

6. Sharon O'Brien, *American Indian Tribal Governments* (Norman: University of Oklahoma Press, 1989), 111.

7. Ibid., 176.

8. Ibid., 190–91.

9. Indian Employment, Training, and Related Services Demonstration Act, P.L. 102-477, October 23, 1992, U.S. Statutes at Large, Vol. 106, Pt. 3: 2302–2306.

10. Indian Environmental General Assistance Program Act, P.L. 102-497, October 24, 1992, U.S. Statutes at Large, Vol. 106, Pt. 4: 3258–3262.

11. Indian Tribal Justice Act, P.L. 103-176, December 3, 1993, U.S. Statutes at Large, Vol. 107, Pt. 3: 2004–2010.

12. Indian Self-Determination Contract Reform Act, P.L. 103-413, October 24, 1994, U.S. Statutes at Large, Vol. 108, Pt. 5: 4250–4278.

6

RECREATIONAL LIFE, OUTDOORS, AND SPORTS

Playing sports in the outdoors has been an integral part of Indian life, especially in the twentieth century. Like most Americans, Indian people were outdoors more as a part of their lifestyle in the first half of the twentieth century. Recreational life and sports played festive roles in Indian life on reservations and in rural areas, thus keeping Indian people healthy. Playing sports helped to bond community members together and this remains the same with many people today. Laughter can be heard anytime Indians are together in recreation or playing sports. For them, sports is about competing for fun, and they place a high value on sportsmanship. American Indians have also competed at the professional and Olympic levels, demonstrating their talents to the rest of the world.

RECREATIONAL LIFE AND INDIAN FAIRS

In 1883 Buffalo Bill Cody started his Wild West Show, which had a permanent impact on Indians on reservations by making the mainstream aware of Indians. As Cody's show became more popular and traveled to the East, other shows like the Miller Brothers had varying influence on public audiences. This billboard approach of advertising a "Wild West" began to attract attention from curious easterners. Simultaneously, Indians, who were now being referred to as American Indians, were starting to hold their own celebrated events as a means to bring more cheerful days to reservations.

With permission from the Indian agency on or near the reservation, tribes began to hold their own entertainments. In the late 1800s, federal officials remained skeptical of Indians being peaceful since Wounded Knee occurred in 1890, even though it was a peaceful group of Minneconjou Sioux who were coming to Pine Ridge to surrender. At the time, Sitting Bull, a great Lakota leader, still led his people as a mighty warrior. The Ghost Dance, which had more tribes dancing and believing that the dead would come alive and the buffalo would return, spread throughout the West. Wounded Knee ended all of this. Basically, white people were still afraid of Indians, yet those in the East were becoming more curious about them.

In 1897 one of the earliest Indian fairs took place, involving Lakota and non-Indians who watched. This six-day fair on the Rosebud Reservation offered such events as Corn and White Buffalo dances and music played by the Rosebud Cornet Band. The fair also included a reading of the Declaration of Independence. Other activities included the fair goers watching bronc and steer riding. A reenactment of the Little Bighorn permitted the Sioux to kill Custer over and over during these days that included July 4.

In 1904 Samuel Reynolds, a federal agent, planned a fair to be held on the Crow reservation in Montana to display the agricultural success of the tribe. By the time that it was over, the fair included horse races and a rodeo.

Ten years later in North Carolina, the Cherokees started their first fair in 1914. This opportunity enabled the Cherokees to exhibit their arts and crafts for sale to visitors, which led to annual fairs that convinced the western Cherokee and other tribes to start holding their own. In fact, the Oklahoma Cherokee hold an fiddle contest as a part of their annual fair in Tahlequah, Oklahoma.

In other parts of Oklahoma, the Sac and Fox hold an annual powwow that started in the 1950s and is now held near their tribal complex in Stroud. The Muscogee Creeks hold an annual fair in Okmulgee with horseshoe pitching, golf and tennis tournaments, a rodeo, and other events.

INDIAN RODEOS

Indian rodeos frequent the western parts of Indian Country. On a regular basis, tribes sponsor rodeos that carried over from the days of the Wild West shows as Indians became cowboys. Sometime during the last quarter of the century, an Indian rodeo circuit began as Indian cowboys began to earn money from bronc riding, calf roping, and so forth. For many of the Plains tribes, the horse is still an important element in their lifestyle as a part of the Indian rodeos.

Noted Indian bronc riders of earlier years include Jackson Sundown, Jim Carpenter, and Henry Bruisedhead. One of many Indian rodeo stars was David Red Boy Schildt, a Blackfeet who was athlete of the year in 1972 at Flandreau Indian School after winning titles in bull riding; he later coached rodeo. Other notable Indian cowboys include Will Rogers, Tom Three Persons, Kenny McLean, Larry Condon, Joe Chase, Peter Fredericks, Leo Camarillo, Tee Woolman, and Howard Hunter.

Young Indian women also participate in rodeos, such as Kim Rhoda Nez (Navajo). As a high school sophomore at Shiprock, New Mexico, in 1991, she won the junior coed all around with first place awards in barrel racing, breakaway, roping, team roping, and goat tying. She entered her first rodeo when she was five years old.

As they became increasingly popular in the late 1960s, small and regional Indian rodeos began to make an effort to avoid scheduling their events on the same dates. Indian rodeoing became more formalized in 1976 when 11 Indian rodeo associations organized to start the Indian National Finals Rodeo, which received sponsorship from Coors, Levi-Strauss, and other companies. The finals are held every year in Albuquerque, New Mexico. Since the Indian rodeo associations formalized, Indian rodeos have increased throughout the West and are held by tribes like the Muscogee Creek at their annual fair every June. Other tribes have annual rodeo as Indians have become cowboys. By the end of the twentieth century, there were more than 150 all-Indian rodeos held, generating one million dollars and more in purses and awards.

SPORTS AT INDIAN SCHOOLS

Sports at Indian schools did not begin deliberately as a part of curriculum. In fact, sports have always been extracurricular activities for Indian male and female students. Early boarding schools like the Cherokee Female Seminary in Indian Territory (Oklahoma) in the late 1800s included archery, for example, but it was more important the women students to learn how to read and write, plus master finer skills of poetry writing, sewing, and the like. Chilocco, Concho, Sherman, Bacone, and other Indian schools throughout Indian Country produced superb athletes of local prominence.

Carlisle Indian Industrial School and Haskell Institute burst onto the national scene when their teams in football and track defeated almost every team around them, including major universities. During the years from the 1890s to 1918, Carlisle captured national headlines in the sports world.

American Indians in mainstream sports began with athletes from boarding schools, perhaps starting with Carlisle in the late 1800s. Richard Pratt, the founder of Carlisle, was not convinced of the importance of sports to education and was also fearful of the potential for student injury. When Indian students began to play football on their own, however, his

Carlisle School Indian football team. Courtesy of Library of Congress.

Mississippi Choctaw boys playing stickball.

view changed. In his testimony before the fourteenth annual meeting of the Lake Mohonk Conference, Pratt said:

The other day a preacher came to see my football boys practice, and a friend of mine heard him talking about the Indian school afterwards, and he said, "If the Government of the United States has nothing better for the Indians to do than to play football, I am going to quit taking up collections in my church for Indian missionary work." If, through football, Indian boys can kick themselves into association and competition with white people, I would give every one a football.[1]

Carlisle began playing football in 1894 and they lost all of their games except for one win against Harrisburg High School. In 1899, Pratt hired Glen "Pop" Warner away from Cornell University as the new football coach. Warner was much impressed with the speed of the Indian players, especially in the open field. He utilized their talent with strategies of the reverse, crouching start, the single wing, double wing, and pulling linemen to block for the running backs. Warner radically changed the game with his new formations and strategies. During these innovative years of the hidden ball play and the like, the forward pass was legalized in 1906.

During the 1920s, Haskell Institute had to build a stadium to seat at least 10,000 people because of its success in football and track. The awareness and success of Indian athletes convinced Haskell to start the American Indian Athletic Hall of Fame. World War I ended the prominence of Carlisle when the school closed when the government needed the former barracks on the campus. The Depression prevented Haskell from returning to its high status in sports. World War II changed Indian Country as more native people left reservations during the relocation years of the 1950s and 1960s to go to cities to find jobs and housing. Ironically, the Indian sports legacy all began not by design, but by chance.

PROFESSIONAL BASEBALL

Several talented Indians have become stars in the major leagues, and others have played at that level who did not become as well known. Perhaps the earliest Indian baseball star was Louis Francis Sockalexis, a Penobscot Indian from Maine. Sockalexis was the main pitcher from 1897 to 1899 for Cleveland, then known as the Cleveland Spiders. Growing up, Sockalexis did very well in track, skating, and baseball. He did not attend a boarding school like most other famed native athletes. Instead he attended Catholic schools and went to college at Notre Dame and Holy Cross. He started to play major league ball in 1897 and hit home runs in his first two times at bat. Sockalexis's talent as a pitcher brought instant fan support in Cleveland and evoked tides of racial slurs from every city that the Spiders played in. Opposing fans tried to upset Sockalexis and make him mad, but that made him throw that much harder. Sports writers across the country began to exploit his Indian background for more game tickets and newspapers. Cleveland became known as the Indian's team. A leg injury stopped his career short, making 1897 his last season. The Cleveland was known as the Spiders and later as the Broncos, then the Blues, then the Naps. In 1915 fan voting in a newspaper contest chose the new name for their city's team, the Indians, to honor the legendary Louis Francis Sockalexis.

Other great Indian baseball players followed Sockalexis, such as Charles Albert "Chief" Bender was a Chippewa Indian from Minnesota. He was a star pitcher for the Philadelphia Athletics from 1903 to 1914, and he appeared in five World Series. Bender was born on May 5, 1884 in Brainerd, Minnesota. He debuted in baseball on April 20, 1903, as a right-hand pitcher for the Philadelphia Athletics and played for them until 1914. He played for the Baltimore Terrapins in the old Federal League in 1915, for the Philadelphia Phillies from 1916 to 1917, and for the Chicago White Sox in 1925. With a great fastball and curveball, Bender developed a slider to win 212 games during his 16-plus years in the major leagues. He pitched a no-hitter in 1910 and had a total of 1,711 strikeouts. He was voted into the Baseball Hall of Fame in 1953.

John Tortes "Chief" Meyers earned recognition on the baseball diamond. A member of the Cahuilla band of the California, he attended Dartmouth College in the early years of the century. He played catcher for the New York Giants from 1908 to 1915 and later with the Brooklyn Dodgers. Meyers played for New York in the National League. He had 351 at bats with a hitting average of .291. Born on July 29, 1880, in Riverside, California, he played from 1909 to 1917. Meyers was a catcher and during the 1911 World Series, he set a record by throwing out 12 base runners in six games.

Allie Pierce "Superchief" Reynolds, a right-hand pitcher, stood six feet tall. He was born February 10, 1917, in Bethany, Oklahoma. In 1939 he signed as an amateur free agent with the Cleveland Indians. Reynolds, a Creek Indian from Oklahoma, was an outstanding athlete. He attended Oklahoma State University on a track scholarship, running the 100- and 200-yard dashes, and he played varsity football for three years. Reynolds pitched in the Major Leagues. He played for the Cleveland Indians and the New York Yankees from 1942 to 1954. He led the American League in strikeouts in 1943 and 1952. Reynolds was voted the national professional athlete of the year in 1951.

In the World Series of 1948, American Indians were victorious when the Milwaukee Braves played the Cleveland Indians. The Indians defeated the Braves, four games to two.

MASCOTS

In professional baseball in the United States, the Cleveland Indians and Atlanta Braves have names that refer to American Indians. In professional hockey, the Chicago Blackhawks are named after the famous Indian leader of the Sauk tribe of the early 1800s. In professional basketball, the Golden State Warriors representing the San Francisco Bay area are named after Americans Indians. In the National Football League, the Kansas City Chiefs and Washington Redskins are named after American Indians. Legal action has been taken against some teams such as the Washington Redskins, when an unsuccessful lawsuit was filed against the team owners in 1992.

Of 185 major colleges and universities, 12 have that refer in some way to Native Americans. These are the Arkansas State University Indians, Central Michigan University Chippewas, Colgate University Red Raiders, Florida State University Seminoles, University of Hawaii Rainbow Warriors, Illinois University Fighting Illini, Northeast Louisiana University Indians, San Diego State University Aztecs, Southeast Missouri State University Indians, Tennessee-Chattanooga University Moccasins, Texas Tech University Red Raiders, and College of William and Mary Tribe.

Several middle schools and high schools have Indian mascot names and there are local Indian efforts to have certain ones changed that depict Indians as savages and others that are derogatory. For example, in the state of Oklahoma, there are 24 schools that use "redskins" or "savages" as their team name or mascot. State Senator Judy Eason McIntyre introduced Senate Bill 567 in 2005 that would prohibit schools from using "redskins" or "savages" as their name or mascot.

One might be curious why schools, colleges, and universities name mascots after American Indians in some way. Possibly, the stereotypes of the "savage," "brave," and "warrior" suggest to people the image of the stout-hearted Indian who is willing to risk his life in war. Plains Indians counted coup, and counting victories in mainstream sports is very similar in its totaling of victories. Schools want a tough mascot, fierce and mean, and Indian images portray these feelings. In order to win, mainstream teams want their opponents to have fear in their hearts during game time.

OLYMPICS

American Indian athletics has produced many talented athletes and some have gone on to participate in the Olympics. At this level of world competition, American Indians have participated since the 1908 Olympics. Furthermore, they have competed only in the summer games. At the Olympics, Indian athletes have done exceedingly well.

In the Olympic games of 1912 in Stockholm, Sweden, the distance runner Louis Tewanima won silver medals in the 5,000- and 10,000-meter races. In the same games, Jim Thorpe (a Sauk and Fox, and Potawatomi) won his gold medals in the pentathlon and decathlon. Louis Tewanim attended Carlisle Indian Industrial School with Jim Thorpe and they ran track together. Tewanim was a Hopi of the Sand clan from Second Mesa.

At Carlisle, Tewanim impressed the legendary coach "Pop" Warner with his running. He and Jim Thorpe were selected for the U.S. Olympic team in 1912 without having to win places on the team. Four years earlier in 1908, Tewanim finished ninth in the marathon. He set a world record for the 10-mile run indoors at Madison Square Garden. In 1954, Tewanima went to New York to be named to the All-Time U.S. Olympic Track and Field Team. In the 1908 Olympics in London, Tom Longboat, an Onondaga Indian from Canada, participated in the marathon. Longboat, a very well-known runner, won the Boston Marathon in 1907. The Boston Marathon is the oldest such race in the United States.

Another Olympian, Ellison "Tarzan" Brown, proved himself on the track field. Of the Narraganset tribe in Rhode Island, Tarzan Brown succeeded at long-distance running, winning the Boston Marathon in 1936 when he was 22 years old. He also ran the marathon at the 1936 Olympics in Berlin, Germany. In 1939, he won the Boston Marathon again, setting a record for the race.

Ben Nighthorse Campbell is another American Indian Olympian. Campbell was born in Auburn, California, on April 13, 1933. He is a mixed-blood Northern Cheyenne and Portuguese. His mother had tuberculosis when Ben and his sister were children. Their father was alcoholic and proved to be undependable. Their mother's illness forced the Campbell children to be put in an orphanage for several months. Undisciplined, young Campbell lived reckless life, making average grades at New England Mills Grammar School in Weimar, California. At Placer High School in Auburn, Ben continued to struggle with his grades. His teachers said he was intelligent but that he lacked goals and discipline. He dropped out of school and things got worse, involving "stealing cars, drinking, fighting. I was one step away from reformatory."[2] Campbell joined the air force and earned a GED in place of a high school diploma. (In 1991, he received permission to participate in the graduation exercise at his old high school.)

As a teenager, Ben Campbell worked one summer in 1940 in a fruit packing plant. He got into a fight with another teenager, a young Japanese, who introduced Ben to judo the hard way. Ben became friends with the young Japanese worker and became committed to judo for the next 15 years. Campbell served in the Korean War from 1951 to 1953 as Airman Second Class and continued to study judo. He returned to California, continued his judo, and enrolled at San Jose State University to earn a bachelor's degree in physical education. Now obsessed with judo, Ben Campbell worked out six hours a day, six days a week. In 1960, he made a decision to study with the best and entered a three-year program at Meiji University in Tokyo as a special research student. In 1963, Campbell won a gold medal at the Pan American games and a place on the U.S. Olympic judo team and was made team captain. During this same time, he injured a knee and tried to compete with his injury. In admiration of Ben's courage, his Olympic teammates chose him to carry the American flag during the closing ceremonies at the 1964 games in Tokyo. With his leg hurting, Ben Campbell said that "My leg hurt like hell, but I wasn't going to let someone else have the flag [to carry]."[3]

Ben Nighthorse Campbell went on to enter the jewelry business, get a pilot's license, and become a rancher. One night during a rainstorm, he could not fly out of his hometown, so he waited out the storm by going downtown to attend a political meeting. By the end of the meeting, he was chosen as the Democratic candidate to run against an incumbent politician for house representative in Colorado and he won. This victory put him on the road to other political victories and he was elected U.S. Senator from Colorado and served on Indian affairs committees in congress until he retired in 2004.

A total of 5,000 Olympians, representing 94 countries, competed in Meiji Stadium in Tokyo in the 1964 games. In track and field, Billy Mills, a Lakota from Pine Ridge, South Dakota, shocked the world on October 14, 1964. The 26-year-old Marine had run track for the University of Kansas. On that day, Mills, a long shot to win, was one of 38 runners in the 10,000 meter race and pulled a major upset by winning the race and setting a new Olympic record of 28:24.4. Mills became the first American to win this event. His story was immortalized in the 1983 movie *Running Brave*, with Robbie Benson cast as Mills.

Mills was born in 1938 on Pine Ridge Reservation. He went to government schools and his success at running track led to an athletic scholarship at the University of Kansas. Mills was on the University of Kansas championship team that won two years in a row and tried out for the Olympic team but did not make it. Frustrated, he joined the Marine Corps, and a friend convinced him to run track again and he won a place on the U.S. Olympic team.

In Alaska, the World Eskimo-Indian Olympics (WEIO) are held each year with native peoples from Alaska and northern Canada attending. Starting in 1961 in Fairbanks, their events include the high kick, seal skinning, and blanket toss, which stress the importance of strength and agility. The high kick requires an athlete to balance sitting on the floor holding his or her foot. With their free hand the athlete springs up to kick a target. The blanket toss involves a team using a blanket to toss one member high into the air. There are just two of the 15 events at the WEIO and women have participated as athletes since the early 1970s.

OUTDOORS

During the 1970s, American Indian Centers began to emerge in large urban Indian areas such as Los Angeles, Seattle, Minneapolis, and Chicago.

These centers hosted activities for native urban people. In Chicago, for example, the American Indian Center began to sponsors activities such as a softball team, powwow club, and a canoe club that competed in races in the eastern half of the U.S., including around Manhattan Island and across Lake Michigan.

Other Indian centers organized activities for Indians in their neighborhoods such as softball and bowling teams. Some urban Indian areas had enough native teams to form leagues or sponsored teams in city leagues. Many activities involved mainstream sports as many native peoples made the transition to urban living through participation in relocation programs.

STICKBALL AND LACROSSE

A traditional game among the Southeastern tribes is stickball. It is also known as the Little Brother of War. It is said that if a town or community lost four games in a row to another town, then it belonged to the victor. The rules are few and simple. Each team has to have the same number of players, and the length of the game is decided ahead of time. Each team has a goal to defend. In case of a tie at the end of the game, one player from each team played against each other until one of them scored a goal. Broken bones were once common, as well as from the two hickory wood ball sticks about three feet long that each player used.

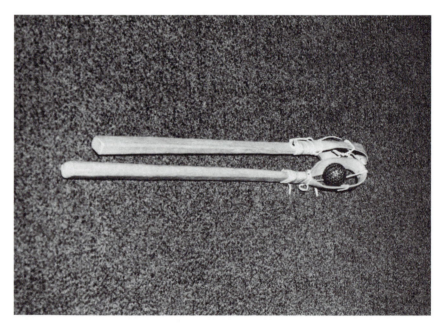

Ball sticks.

Stickball continues to be played today. It is mostly played among members of a stomp ground that used to be a town or community. Stomp grounds are community sites for dancing and taking medicine. During summer months a tournament is played at location such as the Choctaw Fair in Mississippi, with towns in the area competing against each other.

Lacrosse is a popular game played traditionally among the Eastern woodlands tribes including Chippewa, Huron, Miami, Penobscot, Sauk and Fox, Shawnee, Skokomish, and Winnebago. The French named this Indian game lacrosse, meaning "the crook," and it is played with one long stick with a cupped web on the end. A small ball is quickly carried down the field, passed if needed, and thrown into the other side's goal. Canadians adopted the game from Canadian Indians and organized the Montreal Lacrosse Club in 1856. In 1868, Lacrosse was official introduced to the United States. The first U.S. intercollegiate lacrosse association was established in 1882. Lacrosse is nowadays played by 190 colleges and Univeristies in the United States and Canada. Tournaments are held attracting large crowds of student supporters of their teams. The popularity of Lacrosse remains among Northeastern Indians and it has spread to Australia, Canada, and England.

One of the most well known players, though not for his lacrosse playing, was Jay Silverheels. Called Silverheels for his ability to run track, he was also a superb lacrosse player as a member of Canada's national team in 1938. Well known as Tonto in the popular *Lone Ranger* television series of the 1950s, in 1979 Silverheels became the first American Indian to be awarded a star on Hollywood's Walk of Fame.

BOXING, BASKETBALL, AND GOLF

Indians have done well in boxing and basketball. During the 1930s, boxing was popular in boarding schools. Chilocco had probably the best known boxing teams. Indian boxers from Albuquerque, Haskell, Phoenix, and Santa Fe were very good. All of these boarding schools sent boxers to regional and national Amateur Athlete Union (AAU) tournaments.

Oren Lyons, an Onondaga from New York, excelled as an amateur boxer. He boxed in the Army and was talented enough to box in Golden Gloves tournaments. Golden Gloves boxing is the oldest and largest amateur boxing tournament in the world, starting in 1923 in Chicago. He attended Syracuse University and earned All American honors as goal-keeper in lacrosse in 1957 and 1958. After his athletic career, he was a commercial artist for several years in New York City and returned to his reservation where he is a traditional faith keeper.

One known individual, but not for his basketball ability is Peterson Zah, currently special advisor to the President of Arizona State University. Peterson Zah, Navajo or Diné, attended Phoenix Indian School and attended college against his teachers' advice. He went to Arizona State

University on a basketball scholarship and graduated with a bachelor's degree in 1963. In 1981, he was elected to the chairmanship of the Navajo Nation and was elected in 1990 as the first president of the Navajo Nation when this position was created by the tribe.

Basketball is a popular sport on reservations and in urban Indian areas. In fact, there are Indian basketball tournaments and the sport is very popular at Indian boarding schools. James Naismith's decision to move to the Midwest and coach the University of Kansas (KU) Jayhawks also influenced nearby Haskell Indian School. As Haskell fielded a team, KU and the Indian school scrimmaged in the early years and Haskell won some of these games against the up-and-coming powerhouse of men's collegiate basketball.

Golf is very popular among Native Americans, especially those of the middle-class, since it has become an expensive sport. Indian golf tournaments are held regularly as Indians are becoming increasingly drawn to the game. In the early 1970s, Rod Curl, a Wintu Indian from California, made the professional PGA tour. Perhaps his greatest victory on the links occurred in 1974 when he won the Colonial National Open with a four-under-par 276 to beat Jack Nicklaus by one stroke.

Without doubt, Notah Begay was the best American Indian golfer in the twentieth century when he played at the professional level. Begay played golf for Stanford University and has become a positive role model for other Indians following the sport.

CONCLUSION

American Indians have competed at the highest levels in sports, especially in football, baseball, lacrosse, and track. They have succeeded in mainstream sports where athletes are more individualistic, playing for recognition and money. For Indians, sports and business are not compatible because the enjoyment of playing disappears if money and fame are stressed too much.

Many people believe that American Indians are natural athletes and this may very well be true. Being outdoors every day working, hunting, or even just walking made Indians physically fit. Lean bodies and firm muscles developed. Tribal beliefs included the importance of taking care of one's body.

Indians played competitively, but mostly for the fun of the sport, and socialization was important. Playing for individual honors was deemphasized, and sports stressed individual physical development. Today, the most popular games among American Indians are softball, golf, tennis, and bowling with Indian tournaments held in each sport. Playing sports is a major part of Indian life, especially in communities and at tribal fairs. For them, competing with other Indians is more enjoyable than playing in mainstream organizations. Intertribal friendships are made and national organizations have been formed such as the National American Indian Tennis Association.

NOTES

1. *Annual Report of Board of Indian Commissioners 1896*, 49.
2. News article by Hobart Lee in the *Lakota Times*, originally reported in the *Rapid City Journal*, 1948.
3. Ibid.

7

Religious Life, Deities, Creeds, Rituals, and Morality

Indian people who practice their tribal traditions are religious in nature in a true indigenous way. They carry on the traditions and ceremonies of their people of long ago. Such beliefs have persisted with each generation, looking at the universe in a special way that their people have always held. Their perspective involves a complex metaphysical and physical presence in their lives. These longtime honored beliefs are embedded in respect for the earth and the fundamental elements of the universe.

The people's rituals and morals derive from their beliefs and cultural norms. Everyday ways of life are identified and maintained according to the belief system of the people. All of these together constitute the separate realities of each Indian Nation. Although each tribe has experienced change, they retain basics that have endured the twentieth century. It is amazing that a core belief and identity remains while so much change is accepted and occurs around them.

EARLY CHRISTIAN INFLUENCES

Since the beginning of contact between the so-called European Old World and the so-called Indian New World, Christian groups have converted indigenous peoples to Christianity and this continues to be a relentless pursuit. Each country sent its waves of missionaries to work among America's indigenous people. While the list of nations is impressive, the number of Christian groups is more startling. The groups include the Catholic Church, Quakers, Dutch Reformed Church, Baptists, Methodists, Lutherans, and Presbyterians. To destroy the Indian but save his soul has been the ultimate objective of missionaries among Native Americans.

The principal objective is to convert Indians to Christianity. However, Catholic missionaries have not had much success in their work among the Navajo, while Protestants and Mormons have done better. Catholic missionaries have had more success in working with the Lakota on the northern Plains.

By the late nineteenth century, missionary groups had succeeded in reinforcing Christianity among the Indian nations. On the reservations, missionaries appeared and with approval from the federal government, they began to start mission schools. At the start of the twentieth century, an estimated half of Indian youth, or about 21,500, attended schools. Roughly 15 percent attended mission schools and 80 percent were in government boarding schools.

MISSION SCHOOLS

The missionary effort to reform Indian conditions involved educating young American Indians as well. This actually meant teaching vocations to Indian youth and converting them at the same time to Christianity. In this Christian thinking, church and school were inseparable. Mission boarding schools for Indian youth needed funding but they received limited monetary support from the federal government by the end of the 1800s. In 1913, native students increasingly attended government-funded boarding and mission schools, and some youth attended public schools. The majority enrolled in government schools, although 4,804 Indian students attended 69 mission schools. In 1913, 16 of these schools remained under contract for funding from the federal government. Mission schools spent federal monies in the amount of $125 per native student in this year while $165 to $175 was spent in the government boarding schools per Indian student. With the realization of no more federal support, the Catholic Church asked President Theodore Roosevelt to release $58,208 from the Sioux trust fund and he agreed, in spite of protest from the Sioux.[1]

Some mission schools began to close. In 1932, 8 Protestant and 13 Catholic mission boarding schools continued to receive appropriations from the Office of Indian Affairs from tribal funds at $125 per student affecting 540 students at Protestant schools and 1,759 students at Catholic schools. In 1944 the federal appropriation was reduced to $94,250 and by 1950 no more funding was made to mission schools from tribal trust funds. Hereafter, church funds and private donations supported mission schools with Indian students.[2]

Re-enactment of Christian missionary with Indian women. Courtesy of Library of Congress.

Early federal policy in the twentieth century advocated religious instruction in government schools and stressed providing Christian boarding schools for native students. A directive from the Bureau of Indian Affairs (BIA) in 1910 established two hours every day for religious instruction. It also recommended Sunday school classes on campuses and a general assembly of religious exercises. Commissioner of Indian Affairs John Collier, who was appointed in 1932, recognized a monopoly of certain religious churches having schools in Indian Country, especially Catholic and Protestant schools. He cancelled the mandatory religious assemblies in government schools to discourage the religious monopoly, stating that American Indian youth had the constitutional right to freedom of religion, and he ordered that schools must permit the observance of all religions and this included traditional Indian religions.

After World War II, mission schools continued to operate with less external support from donations and especially from the federal government. Furthermore, the years of termination as the federal Indian policy in the 1950s and 1960s involved a withdrawal of the government from Indian affairs, including federal funding. The 1970s called for a change in federal Indian policy to self-determination in tribal communities and the mission schools responded to support the government, even to the decline of their own interests. The mission schools began to change to day schools and Indian school boards began to be elected for the first time as more mission schools closed. Others transformed into tribally controlled schools. For example, the BIA reported that 5 percent of the Indian student population attended mission schools for the 1986–87 school year.

In 1993 only 5 Catholic mission schools in South Dakota remained open and another Catholic school was in North Dakota; more such schools operated in the Southwest. In New Mexico, 16 mission schools operated with the support of Baptists, Catholics, and several other Christian denominations. The negative impact of Christian missionary and education efforts on native cultural and tribal identity has led to several official apologies to native peoples of America. These apologies have been offered in the State of the United States Catholic Bishops on American Indians in 1977; the Thanksgiving Day, 1987, apology from nine Protestant and Catholic denominations in the Northwest; and an apology in Juneau citing historic wrongs to Indians and Alaska Natives in 1987. In 1991, many churches made statements against the Columbian Quincentennial celebrations and renewed their support of Indian issues.

MORMON INDIAN STUDENT PLACEMENT PROGRAM

The Mormon Church initiated the Indian Student Placement Program of the Church of Latter-Day Saints in 1947. The church formalized the goals of the program in 1954: (1) to place Indian students in Mormon foster homes; (2) to secure a public school education for them; and (3) to train them in Mormon beliefs and lifestyle.

The parents of the Indian student were asked to sign a voluntary form consenting to have their child placed in the program. Program officials discouraged the parents from visiting the first year of a student's participation, because the program was intended to be an immersion in the Mormon Church. Originally Indian children at the age of six were placed in the program, but this was raised to the age of eight. From 1954 to 1976, 38,260 native children were placed with Mormon families. During the mid-1970s, the Congress responded to help all native youth since it was estimated that about one-fourth of all Indian children were in some federal institution and the Indian Child Welfare Act was passed in 1978. The act was a culturally sensitive measure of Congress to try to ensure that Indian children would be given the opportunity to grow up with the knowledge of their people and cultural ways. First, relatives would be given the chance to adopt the Indian child. Tribal members of the same tribe as the child would be next to adopt the child and then non-Indians would have their chance for adoption. Mormon lobbyists worked hard to have their Indian student program exempted from the legislation in order to continue converting and educating native youth.

Over the years, the placement program came under criticism for damaging the native identity of the Indian students. Studies reported the children in the program felt anxiety and stress about their tribal identity. By the late 1980s, George Patrick Lee became the first Native American to rise through the ranks of the Mormon Church to membership on the Quorum of Seventy. His criticism of the Indian Student Placement Program for its destructive effect on native students' identities led to his excommunication.

NATIVE BELIEF AND SPIRITUALITY

To see is to believe in the native way and those people who are close to their tribal ways see things in a certain manner. Even more, they think and view the world and universe from a native ethos based on certain tribal ways. Their reality is a combination of the physical and the metaphysical world. Generally these people have been raised in this ethos since childhood, and it is characterized by circularity and visuality instead of the linear way of the Western world.

To understand this particular ethos, it is important to realize the significance of "relationships." For example, among the Muscogee Creek in Oklahoma, relations include the known and the unknown, such that all things are a part of the universe. It is believed that there is a continuum of energy at the heart of the universe and this exists everywhere in a spiritual energy called *boea fikcha* or *puyvfekcv*. All things should be respected, for they possess this energy. With such potential, all things are capable of releasing their spiritual energy.

By attempting to understand relationships between all things, an Indian way of "seeing" has developed according to different tribal beliefs. It is the connections that are important as Indians also believe that being connected to your people and homeland is essential. In the traditional Indian world, realizing one's surroundings, both good and bad, is important and respecting them is also emphasized. This is Indian thinking and the basis of tribal ethos.

VISIONS AND VISION QUESTS

Native people who are close to their traditions believe that dreams are a part of reality as the subconscious and conscious form one whole that is real. Dreams are taken seriously as signs and messages that may connect to the metaphysical deity and the other side of life. In this way, precious insight into the metaphysical side becomes knowledge for us on earth on the physical side.

Native peoples have always sought visions as a means to see the other side of life, if given the opportunity. In a humble way, Plains tribal members typically go to a hill where they chant, pray, plea, or sing for a vision so that they might be blessed with this gift of insight that will help them in a particular way. A vision is the human body's experience of the metaphysics of another kind of existence. Among the Pawnee, a grand council of all animals called *Nahurac* remains always in session in a cave near or under a mountain, perhaps located near the Missouri River. The council of animals observes the Indians on earth. If a man or woman is in dire need of help and with humility asks for a vision, then the council sends one of its animals to appear to the vision quester to give something of its own power or insight to guide the person in a decision or for the rest of their life.[3]

Spirits exist among native peoples and this belief continues into the twentieth century. The many Chippewa (Ojibwa) groups throughout Michigan, Wisconsin, and Minnesota believe in spirits called "manitous." Each tribe has its own names for spirits, such as the previously mentioned Muscogee Creek *boea fikcha* or *puyufekcv*. On the Plains, the Lakota refer to the spirit as *wakan,* usually translated as "holy." For example, to say that someone is *wakan* is to mean that they are spiritual. In Cheyenne The Creator is *Heammowihio.*

Spirituality among American Indians is human-metaphysical feeling that touches the soul of native people and their community. It is what binds Indian people together like a shared experience. This commonality exists within tribes, yet is powerful enough to cross tribal boundaries and embrace people.

It is like an invisible smoke that engulfs a person or many people in a gathering and gives them a sense of belonging. Being connected to one's family, clan/society, and community or town is most important, but when ceremonies are held, dances occur, or a song is sung, then spirituality exists, seemingly coming from nowhere as if it was always there and it is awakened. This is the spirituality "within." It emerges and permeates a group of people, having the same affect on all of them. It is as if they all share the same feelings and thoughts and as if they are one being that is alive. Such spirituality within is momentary and may last as long as a song or dance lasts and may come to a stop when the people disperse. It comes and goes, and the longer that it lingers, the closer the people feel to each other in a sacred way.

Spiritual "other" is that which is within a metaphysical being. It is always spiritual and the sacredness is eternal, not fleeting like the spiritual within. It is always of this nature and it lives forever. If a medicine person becomes of such spiritual other, then they become spiritual forever. Their name exudes this manner, and memories about them are sacred for they are powerful in a good way and have lived a metaphysical existence for a good part of their lives. These people are few, but more than we realize for they are gifted and they have been directed to live a certain kind of life with special routines and responsibilities. Spirituality is stored metaphysical energy and these special people are able to tap into this energy to help others and perform medicine tasks beyond the abilities of normal individuals.

In native reality, many people see visions, ghosts, and spirits. One might first question this, but it is not unlike characters in the Old Testament of the Bible who saw angels, and many people are reported to have seen Jesus in spiritual form in the New Testament. Angels are real aberrations that appeared in the Old Testament. Throughout history, people have said that they have seen them. Whether this is acceptable or not, it is certain that people need to believe in such aberrations like angels to have hope and belief in a greater power than themselves, especially when they are in despair. Similarly, many American Indians believe in ghosts and spirits while Christian Indians believe in angels and the Holy Ghost.

MEDICINE MAKERS

Medicine makers are special individuals who have been given talents from a greater power than humankind. Black Elk of the Lakota, who was born in the 1800s and lived into the twentieth century, was such a person. Philip Deer, a Muscogee Creek, was a spiritual leader for the American Indian Movement during the late 1960s and 1970s. Sanapia, a Comanche eagle doctor, was another gifted person who helped to heal the sick among her people. Severt Young Bear of the Lakota and Left Handed of the Navajo are among the many medicine makers of the twentieth century who have been written about. Some medicine people prefer not to be recognized, for their responsibilities of helping others are numerous. Less attention enables them to be more effective in their healings with fewer distractions. At the same time, they need opportunities to restore their energy and power.

These special people have powers at various levels and they have different kinds of powers. Some are curers, others are more powerful healers, some are visionaries, and some are prophets. But it is known that they have been given certain powers and these gifts can be taken away. They were given such gifts to serve and to take care of others who need help battling illness, direction in life, and protection from evil.

INDIAN CHRISTIAN BELIEFS

For many American Indians, Christianity has certain fundamental elements that are very similar to native beliefs. God is a singular deity and for many tribes there is one recognized Creator. In the Old Testament of the Bible, God was active in creating the world, and the Creating Spirit or Manitou was also active in creating a world for native people. For this singular force, the Lakota name is *Wakantanka;* in Muscogee Creek, *Hesaketvmese;* in Ojibwa, *Kitchi Manitou;* among the Iroquois, *Orenda;* and so forth.

Siletz, and Klamath in Oregon, and Smith River and Hoopa Valley in northern California. By the end of the twentieth century, the Indian Shaker Church had an estimated 20 congregations and about 4,000 members.

NATIVE AMERICAN CHURCH

In the Southwest, a buttonlike spineless cactus known as peyote, with a mescaline active ingredient, is found mostly in northern Mexico and the lower Rio Grande valley of southern Texas. Its powerful hallucinogenic effects enable indigenous people in Mexico, especially the Apaches, to develop a systemic belief based on the usage of peyote. At the start of the 1870s, the Lipan Apaches introduced peyote to the Comanche and Kowa. By the 1880s, Apaches in Indian Territory received dried peyote by railroad shipments coming from Laredo, Texas.

Two ceremonial versions—in the East, using an enclosed room and in the West, using a tipi—developed, with the incorporation of Christianity including gourd rattles, fire, smoke, and all-night ceremonies as converts walked the Peyote Road with renewed life, better health, and a faith in a Supreme Power. The Peyote Road is a commitment to practice the Native American Church (NAC) in this combination of Christianity and native beliefs. By 1915 the peyote religion expanded to Colorado, Iowa, Kansas, Nebraska, Minnesota, Montana, New Mexico, South Dakota, Utah, and Wyoming. In February 1915, about 54 Omaha Indians of Nebraska petitioned Commissioner of Indian Affairs Cato Sells for the legal right to include peyote ceremonies as part of their religious practice. Several members of the tribe stated that the new religion saved them from alcoholism and bettered their lives. In 1916, James Mooney, a respected ethnologist working for the federal government in Washington, testified in support of the peyote religion stopping alcoholism. Two years later, the peyote religion became incorporated as the Native American Church (NAC) in Oklahoma. In El Reno, Oklahoma, a religious association formed under the laws of the State of Oklahoma and the religion of the Native American Church continues to be practiced.

CHURCH REFORMERS

As a part of the reform movement to help native peoples during the late reservation era from the 1840s to the 1880s, missionary groups established churches on tribal lands. Their two-fold efforts included introducing Christianity and education to the indigenous peoples. White reformers believed that they could introduce a better life to impoverished American Indians.

Making Medicine, a Cheyenne leader, became a deacon in the Episcopal Church after the Red River War of 1874–1875. This war marked the end of the way of life for the Cheyenne, Kiowa, and Comanche. On the northern plains, Sitting Bull led Lakota people into the Roman Catholic Church. Fall, another influential Lakota leader, led his Lakota band into the Episcopal Church. Geronimo and Naiche led their Chiricahua Apache band to join the Dutch Reformed church, now the Reformed Church of America, while they were prisoners of war at Fort Sill in Indian Territory. In 1874 evangelists of the Society of Friends or Quakers approached the Osage Agency in Indian Territory and began to open schools. In 1877 the Methodists operated 22 missions throughout the United States. As Indian Territory prepared to become the State of Oklahoma, the Indian Mission Conference served the Indian people until 1906, when it joined the Oklahoma Conference of the Methodist religion. Years later, it was revived to serve Indian people in the state in 1918 and supported missionary work among 28 different Indian nations. In 1972 the Indian Mission Conference changed its name to the Oklahoma Indian Mission Conference and in 1980 it became a voting member of the United Methodist General Conference. By 1990, the Indian Mission Conference had 94 churches in Oklahoma, 5 in Kansas, and 2 in Texas with total membership in the Methodist church of about 8,000.

SWEATS AND SMOKE

Sweats have always been a part of Plains Indians' way of life. Sweats are performed as a purification ceremony, which has also developed in a therapeutic direction in the late twentieth century. Sweats are performed without a religious purpose for Indians and non-Indians who feel that undergoing this experience will help their health and general well-being. Sweats are held to introduce people to the idea and practice of purification and there are ceremonial sweats that are for religious reasons and selected individuals. A concave shaped structure of poles and blankets or hides are used with heated large rocks carefully moved into the lodge's center. A medicine person pours water over the hot rocks at intervals while leading the ceremony.

The importance of smoke is cleansing and purifying oneself. Like the Eucharist, it is the spirit of Jesus as some people say who believe both in Christianity and the traditional ways of their tribes. Burning sweet grass or cedar and smoking tobacco is a visual means of seeing the spiritual and the goodness in it. In a traditional manner, smoking tobacco is a means of communicating with a great power that has created everything and is responsible for all things. Ceremonial smoke pays respect to the powers of nature and the creator. In some situations, smoke is used in praying or singing to the great powers and the creator.

INDIAN CHRISTIAN CHURCHES

Christianity has a long history of contact with the indigenous people of North America, with the Spanish introducing Catholicism in the Southwest and California, the French Jesuits doing missionary work in the Great Lakes, and other groups like the Dutch Reformed Church, Baptist, Methodist, and Lutheran working among Indian groups. These efforts have amounted to regional areas where certain Christian dominations have been successful.

In every urban Indian area, there is usually an Indian Baptist church and an Indian Methodist church. Sometimes, the Baptist church is named the First Indian Baptist Church and there may be other ones. These are significant to the lives of modern native people who have been converted to Christianity, which includes many Indian people in rural areas and on reservations.

In 1950 a survey by a Christian missionary named 36 Protestant denominations in Indian Country with 39,200 members. Protestant missions boasted some 140,000 Indian converts. By the 1990s, perhaps as many as several hundred ordained Christian ministers spread the Gospel. By 1974, 452 parishes with a total staff of 177 missionaries represented the United Presbyterian, Protestant Episcopal, United Methodist, American Baptist, United Church, and Christian Reformed.

INDIAN RENAISSANCE

During the 1960s, many Indians began to raise questions about non-Indian religious beliefs and the impact of Christianity on the native population. Vine Deloria Jr., a Standing Rock Sioux and activist turned scholar, wanted to become a Lutheran minister. His questioning of the impact of Christianity on Indian people led him to write several books on Indian–white relations, notably *God Is Red* (1973). Other Indian authored books about individual Indians and their religious experiences began to appear, including Lame Deer of the Lakota, Sanapia of the Comanche, and others.

Other native spiritual leaders include Thomas Banyacya, a Hopi who was called by his people to spread the prophecy of his tribe to help the world. Part of this prophecy was that technology would lead humankind away from harmony with nature. Oren Lyons, the Haudenaasaunee Faith Keeper of the Six Nations of the Iroquois, continues to teach non-Iroquois about the importance of his people's spiritual beliefs.

The Church of Jesus Christ of Latter-Day Saints has been active in recruiting Indian converts on the Navajo Reservation and in Oklahoma. In 1980 a United Methodist survey estimated that about 15 percent of American Indians were Christian. An estimated 25 percent of First Nations peoples in Canada professed to be Anglican. An estimated 85 percent of the Inuit claim to be Anglican. The Aleut and Tlingit of Alaska represent the largest numbers of Native Russian Orthodox members.

By the 1990s, 28 Christian Indian organizations existed in the United States and 8 existed in Canada. This was the impact of more than a dozen Christian denominations that proselytized throughout Indian Country for more than 500 years.

INDIAN PREACHERS OF CHRISTIANITY

Native peoples have embraced Christianity to the extent of becoming well-known ministers and preachers. Among the earliest notables who advocated Christianity is Black Elk, the renowned visionary of the Oglala Lakota who converted to Catholicism. He became locally famous as a Catechist and led other Lakota to Catholicism in South Dakota.

Just as the mainstream has popular evangelists such as Billy Graham and Oral Roberts, American Indian congregations have their own well-known native ministers and preachers. They are extremely articulate and relate personal experiences to people's lives in a hypnotically appealing way. While some are more well known than others, the following are examples of the talented clergymen who can relate to people.

In Oklahoma since the 1950s, notable Indian preachers include the nationally known Richard Pickup, a Cherokee Baptist from Salina who travels throughout the United States to spread the word of God. An early preacher turned evangelist is Ernie Best, a Cherokee from Stidham, Oklahoma. Others who are very popular and in big demand include Likke McIntosh, a Creek from the Eufaula area, and Johnny Lay, another Creek from the same area. They preach to large crowds of Indians and non-Indians in Baptist churches or other denominational audiences. As large revivals are planned, well-known Indian preachers travel throughout Indian Country to preach, with some branching out to non-Indian church groups.

The rise of native preachers of Christianity who command large audiences would seem to be the ultimate of native polytheism. This fact stirs the imagination to envision Christian Indians everywhere, but it would be safe to guess that only about one-fourth to one-third of American Indians are practicing Christians.

INDIAN HYMNS AND GOSPEL SINGING

Singing is a central part of many cultures and it is the same for American Indians. As native people turned to Christianity, they adopted and composed Christian hymns. In the early stages of the introduction of Christianity to Indian people, hymns were introduced in the English language. Native Americans sang these songs without knowing what they meant until they learned English. Early English-speaking Indians began to translate these hymns into their tribal languages and missionaries also realized that translation could assist in converting more Indians to Christianity. "Amazing Grace" is perhaps one of the most common hymns among Protestant Indians.

As more Christian hymns were translated, hymnals in tribal language became more common, which in turn was a factor in increased numbers of native people learning to read their own language. As Indian language hymnals appeared in the backs of pews in the church, native peoples began to compose Christian hymns in their native languages. One belief is that Indians did not write these songs, but they were inspired by God and the spirituality of Christianity. One Kiowa in Oklahoma said, "When this Christianity came into our area, they [Kiowa] were so dedicated to this Christianity that these songs [came to them]. They don't compose these songs. They come to them through the Spirit. That's the reason they're so beautiful."[4]

Sharing these hymns in Sunday morning and evening worship services has given Native Americans a long history of gospel singing. Singers grouped into duets, trios, or quartets and accompanied by musical instruments or a cappella have become a part of doing the Lord's work as it is commonly said. People will drive considerable distances to attend a nightly gospel singing. Some singing groups have become popular enough to have recorded record albums in the 1970s, cassettes in the 1980s, and CDs in the 1990s.

AMERICAN INDIAN RELIGIOUS FREEDOM ACT

During the Indian activist years of the 1960s and early 1970s, the nation saw much concern among Indian leaders over issues involving Indian rights and culture. The Jimmy Carter administration responded with the American Indian Religious Freedom Act of 1978. The 95th Congress entertained a joint resolution, S.J. Res. 102, "To insure that the politics and procedures of various Federal agencies, as they may impact upon the exercise of traditional Indian religious practices, are brought into compliance with the constitutional injunction that Congress shall make no laws abridging the free exercise of religion." Signed by President Carter into law, the American Indian Religious Freedom Act, also known as AIRFA, did not achieve much beyond stating that American Indians had religious freedom. AIRFA did little to protect native cultures, ceremonies, sacred sites, and the return of sacred artifacts to Indian tribes.

In 1990, the Native American Grave Protection and Repatriation Act (NAGPRA) was passed to address the burning issue of repatriation of Indian artifacts and human remains. As a result, many items have been returned by museums and private collections to Indian tribes. One of many examples is the Sand Creek site returned to Cheyenne and Arapaho tribes in 2002. Sand Creek is the infamous place where Colonel John Chivington and 700 U.S. volunteer soldiers killed 500 Cheyenne and Arapaho camped along the banks of Big Sandy Creek in southeastern Colorado on November 29, 1864.

Since the American Indian Religious Freedom Act, other important legislation has been passed that supports Indian religious rights. On May 4, 1994, the Alaska Native Art and Culture Development Act became Public

Law 108-239. This legislation is an act for the secretary of the interior to make grants for the purpose of supporting programs for Native Hawaiian or Alaska Native culture and arts development to any private, nonprofit organization or institution that primarily serves and represents Native Hawaiians or Alaska Natives.[5]

The desecration of sacred sites and burial sites may seem to be actions that are far removed from the daily lives of American Indians, but they are not. To watch mountain climbers scale Devil's Tower in Wyoming for recreation and to be Cheyenne or Lakota is to feel a pain thoughtlessly inflicted upon you. To find out that a farmer has plowed up your tribe's ancient burial site and hauled away parts of your ancestors with no regret is painful disrespect that will never be forgotten.

CONCLUSION

It has been said that we are what we believe. The same can be said for Indian people who still believe in the old ways. These people might be called the "traditionalists," for they carry on the old ways and place their souls in the tribal beliefs that have rendered identity and a special way of believing and seeing the world and universe through a native ethos.

Christian Indians are native peoples who have been converted from the old tribal ways to Christianity. They are also Indians who have grown up in a Christian home and have never known anything else except this way of believing in God.

There are those people who have formed their own beliefs that combine some form of tribal traditions and Christianity, such as the Native American Church and Indian Shaker religion. Like most of native culture in the twentieth century that combines the Indian and mainstream ways, native believers in this combination have increased in number, especially in the Native American Church. This may seem unusual, perhaps even extraordinary, but it is no different than Protestants or Mormons developing their own form of Christianity.

Simultaneously, the same people can believe in new ways by selecting certain values from the modern world. By the end of the twentieth century, traditional native beliefs declined seriously as tribal languages and value systems gave way to mainstream ways. At the same time, many Indian people have combined old ways of the tribes with Christianity and live comfortably in combining religious beliefs.

NOTES

1. Margaret Connell Szasz, "Educational Policy," in Mary B. Davis, ed., *Native Americans in the Twentieth Century: An Encyclopedia* (New York: Garland Publishing, 1994), 182.

2. Ibid.

3. Joseph Epes Brown, *The Spiritual Legacy of the American Indian* (New York: Crossroad, 1988), 124.

4. Luke Eric Lassiter, Clyde Ellis, and Ralph Kotay, *The Jesus Road: Kiowas, Christianity, and Indian Hymns* (Lincoln: University of Nebraska Press, 2002), 81, originally quoted by authors during recorded conversation, Ralph Kotay's Kiowa hymn class, Anadarko, Oklahoma, January 25, 1994, see note 12, p. 132 in *The Jesus Road*.

5. American Indian Religious Freedom Act, P.L. 95-341, August 11, 1978, U.S. Statutes at Large, 92: 469; Alaska Native Art and Culture Development Act, P.L. 108-239, May 4, 1994, U.S. Statutes at Large, Vol. 108, Pt. 1: 606–607.

8

ART, ARTIFACTS, MUSIC, AND ENTERTAINMENT

The art and music of American Indians is derived from the earth and their many diverse cultures. In fact, the people and their communities are products of their natural environments of their original homelands. Rhythms of the earth and patterns of life in nature influenced the creation of native art. Beauty is everywhere. The native mind has observed the movements of nature and its beauty for centuries with great appreciation.

The history of native art can be divided into four time periods: prehistoric, colonial, historic, and contemporary. Briefly, the prehistoric period recorded the earliest drawings and sketches of native peoples in the Americas on the walls of caves and on flat rocks in open areas. These ancient pictroglyphs served as history, stories, knowledge, and art for other peoples dating from about 25,000 B.C. to A.D. 1500. The number of pictroglyphs cannot be estimated, numbering in the hundreds, if not thousands throughout North America. Well-known pictroglyph sites are at Nanimo on Vancouver Island, British Columbia; at Writing-on-Stone Provincial Park in southern Alberta; at Jeffers Site in Minnesota; and at Petroglyphs Provincial park Near Peterborough, Ontario. Vivid pictographs are located in the homeland of Chumash Indians of southern California as well as in upper New York State and in the Southwest, particularly in New Mexico and Arizona.

The colonial period of native arts dates roughly from A.D. 1500 to 1750. Symbolism in native arts is recognizable and native colonial art could also be considered as "contact" or "encounter" art. This native artwork addresses the first encounters and contact with other peoples like the

Spanish, French, and British and expresses the native people's initial impressions of seeing strangers for the first time and the stories surrounding these incredible events. Iroquoian wampum belts are both art and historical records of the time as European powers colonized much of Indian Country. Beautiful pottery in the Southwest of the Pueblo communities document early life among their people. In addition, there are some 400 different kinds of Kachina dolls that represent various deities such as those for rain, corn, and the like, in Pueblo society.

The historic period from 1750 to 1900 describes the continual contact between tribes and non-Indians, with individual experiences reflected in hide paintings, carvings, and beading works. War is a major them in the art and artifacts of this period, which depict individual experiences and accounts of Indian–white history. In an extraordinary effort, artists of this period transported their cultures with them to new homes when the federal government negotiated nearly 100 treaties to remove them to new homelands to concentrated areas in the West during the 1820s to the 1870s. This remarkable transporting of families and belongings also transferred art, music, and artifacts with the people to new homelands called reservations.

Artists of the contemporary period in the twentieth century have had the opportunity to be more liberal in their artwork. Their work is highly interpretive and it remains free from immense pressures placed on them like the removals of the previous century or war fought for survival.

ART

American Indian art is obviously different from that of the Western world of art. Indian arts began to be recognized when Jesse Walter Fewkes commissioned a group of Hopi artists for a publication called "Hopi Kachinas, Drawn by Native Artists." This compilation was published in the *21st Annual Report of the Bureau of American Ethnology, 1899–1900,* in 1903. In 1902, Kenneth Chapman collected drawings by Apie Bega, a Navajo in western New Mexico, for the Museum of New Mexico. Boarding schools also had begun to encourage native students to draw and paint. Zuni art pieces are at the Denver Art Museum with dates of 1905. Hopi students at Sherman Institute in California created artworks in 1908. Between 1909 and 1912, Cochiti Pueblo in New Mexico sold art. In the fall of 1910, Alfredo Montoya of San Ildefonso sold drawings of ceremonial dancers now housed at the Museum of New Mexico. Alfonso Roybal of San Ildefonso sold paintings of his own in 1917. Crescencio Martinez of the same pueblo community painted a series of paintings about winter and summer ceremonies for Edgar B. Hewett, Director of the School of American Research and the Museum of New Mexico.

With each new generation, talent in arts passes forward to young hands and minds. Ceremonial art and contemporary art began to be produced at a steady rate, demonstrating the amalgamation of the past and the present being intertwined. In the Pacific Northwest, carvings of totem poles and wooden boxes continued. For example, Kwakiutl artist Tony Hunt Jr. produced art since the 1980s that retained the old art style of his people. Early twentieth-century artists include Charles Edensaw (Haida) and Willie Seweed and Mungo Martin, who are both Kwakiutl. Bob Davidson is another Haida artist who carves totem poles.

Contemporary artwork done by Northwest native artists focused on traditional coastal style and iconography. This is possibly due to the culture being so steeped in tradition and refinement of detail. In the 1970s and 1980s, the imagination and creativity of the artists led to new interpretation. Their influences of interpretation derive from both the native world and mainstream world.

In the Southwest, Western art began to influence native art as early as about 1910 until 1960. The Southwestern primitive or traditional pueblo style developed under the influence of Dorothy Dunn of Chicago, a non-Indian who pioneered teaching art at the Santa Fe Indian School and who had similar influence as James Houston did in Canada. The Southwest style focused on ceremonial dances, domestic activities, and hunting scenes in a flat, two-dimensional illustrated artwork. Houston has brought world attention to Inuit art since the 1960s.

In Plains Indian art, a similar two-dimensional style was influenced and promoted by Oscar Jacobson, another non- **Kiowa Six** Indian artist. Subjects in this style include romanticized images of hunting buffalo and other large animals and warriors in ceremonial dances. Notable Plains and Southwest artists include Archie Blackowl (Cheyenne), Rance Hood (Comanche) Jerry Ingram (Choctaw), Harrison Begay (Navajo), Gilbert Atencio (San Ildefonso), and many others. But where did this begin? It is not for certain, but about 1918, Susie Peters, a government field agent to the Kiowa tribe in Oklahoma who came equipped with crayons and paints, discovered six promising Kiowa kids with artistic talent. She introduced her group of protégés to Professor Oscar B. Jacobson, the head of the department of art at the University of Oklahoma. After a series of workshops, the so-called Kiowa Six painted in a tradition that has been called the "renaissance of southern Plains painting." The Kiowa Six are Spencer Asah, James Auchiah, Jack Hokeak, Stephen Mopope, Lois Smoky, and Monroe Tsatoke. Jacobson successfully promoted the artwork of the six Kiowa artists in museums and at universities in the United States and internationally. In 1929 a limited edition collection of their work, titled *Kiowa Art,* was published in France.

The Kiowa Six brought attention to the talents of young Indian artists in Oklahoma. Among the earliest painters **Oklahoma** are Acce Blue Eagle, Creek (1907–1959); Woody Crumbo, Creek-Potawatomi (1912–1989); and Richard West Sr., Cheyenne (1912–). These artists worked during years before World War II and afterwards when the public gave scant notice to Indian art. Most people of the mainstream did not know Bacone College existed, much less that it used to be a boarding school. Acce Blue Eagle became the first head of the Indian art department at Bacone near Muskogee, Oklahoma. Woody Crumbo succeeded Blue Eagle from 1938 to 1941. Dick West was the head of the department from 1947 to 1970. In later times, Ruth Balock Jones, Delaware-Shawnee, a former art student, returned to Bacone to head the department. Bacone enrolled students from more than 25 tribes in Oklahoma and many groups far away, allowing an abundant number of artists to develop their skills.

Notable artists who attended Bacone include Terry Saul, Choctaw-Chickasaw; Solomon McCombs, Creek; Joan Hill, Creek-Cherokee; Virginia Stroud, Cherokee-Creek; and David Williams, Kiowa-Kiowa Apache-Tonkawa. The tradition of Bacone Indian artists continues. Some individuals paint traditional scenes of their tribes. Other artists are influenced by the mainstream and paint about relations between Indians and the modern world in America.

Other Oklahoma Indian artists of fame include Archive Blackowl, Cheyenne, and Fred Beaver, Creek, who painted during the 1930s and 1940s. In the 1950s and 1960s, Doc Tate Navaquaya, Comanche, and Bert Seabourn, Cherokee, are renown talents of Indian art.

Woodland Style Norval Morrisseau (Ojibwa) was influenced by tradition when he began painting in the 1960s. His work inspired others who became recognized as Woodland School or Legend Painters. Focusing on systems of woodland animal and tribal images, these artists include Car Ray, Roy Thomas, Josh Kakegamic, Saul Williams, and Blake Debassige. An Odawa artist, Daphne Odjig, was a part of the Woodland School tradition. She taught the next generation this tradition while combining native style with modern influences. Her work and influence spans the second half of the twentieth century.

Native Indian artists of various styles and subjects are T. C. Cannon (Caddo/Kiowa), Harry Fonseca (Maidu), Richard Glazer Danay (Mohawk), R. C. Gorman (Navajo), Oscar How (Sioux), Peter Jemison (Seneca), Frank LaPena (Wintu-Nomtipom), George Longfish (Seneca-Tuscarora), George Morrison (Ojibwa), Jaune Quick-to-See Smith (Cree-Shoshoni), and Fritz Scholder.

Like artists of other regions, artists of the woodlands paint in the traditions of their peoples much like a pictorial history.

Style Trends After the 1930s, the style of most Indian art continued in a flat two dimensional manner. No shading was involved as artists painted figures running, jumping, and so on. Color helped to illustrate motion and the subject was culturally real, depicting life in the nineteenth century and customs. This style, called primitive, prevailed in Indian art, focusing on tribal life.

Building on the realism of this period, the works of Blackbear Bosin (Kiowa-Comanche), Oscar Howe (Dakota), Rafael Medina (Zia), and Jerome Tiger (Creek-Seminole) began to paint with drama and emotion. Their mystical impressionism illustrated subjects rather than the detailed ceremonies or acts of war. For example, Oscar Howe and Blackbear Bosin painted ceremonies focusing on parts of them, but not actually representing them in a big-picture way. Medina painted close-up scenes of sacred clowns called "koshare" at a pueblo dance, but not the ceremony. Jerome Tiger's works are statements about oppression, suffering, and despair in his illustrations of the Trail of Tears when his people endured their removal from traditional homelands in the Southeast. Symbolism, spirituality, and surrealism identify this trend.

ART MUSEUMS

Santa Fe Indian School

On a spring day in 1932, several Indian artists of the Southwest and one Plains artist, Jack Hokeah from Oklahoma, began painting murals in the dining room at Santa Fe Indian School. The artists expressed their talents in beautiful scenes. These murals led to the creating a studio for art at the school. Dorothy Dunn, the founder of this effort, wanted to preserve and promote the native talent that she witnessed. With the doors opened to welcome young Indian artists, as many as 300 students found themselves at Santa Fe Indian School. Dorothy Dunn's supervision of this early effort lasted until 1937, but the momentum continued to establish the school for budding young Indian artists. The impressive results yielded well-known Southwestern artists like Narciso Abeyta, Navajo; Harrison Begay, Navajo; Allen Houser, Apache; Gerald Nailor, Navajo; Oscar Howe, Sioux; Quincy Tahoma, Navajo; Andy Tsinajinnie, Navajo; and Pablita Velarde, Santa Clara Pueblo. Early famed artists of the school are Gilbert Atencio, San Ildefonso; Joe Herrera, San Ildefonso; and Ben Quintana, Cochiti; and others.

The Eiteljorg Museum of American Indian and Western Art

In Indianapolis, the Eiteljorg is one of the outstanding places to see Native American and Western art. Starting from the collective efforts of industrialist Harrison Eiteljorg (1903-1997) in 1989, the museum has one of the finest Indian collections east of the Mississippi with more than 3,400 items. The Eiteljorg sponsors a series of fellowships and workshops for native artists. The Eiteljorg is one of two museums east of the Mississippi that contains both American Indian and Western art. One of the goals of the Eiteljorg is to bring Indian art into the art world.

The Gilcrease Museum

The Gilcrease in Tulsa, Oklahoma, is another excellent place to view Indian art. It has one of the largest collections of Indian arts and artifacts. Gilcrease highlights native art of Oklahoma Indians, representing more than two dozen tribes. Founded in 1943, the museum was a part of the private collection of Thomas Gilcrease (1890–1962) who was part Creek Indian. His land allotment had oil under it and he proved to be a successful businessman. In 1955 the Gilcrease Museum opened in Tulsa, Oklahoma.

The Five Civilized Tribes Museum   The Five Civilized Tribes Museum in Muskogee, Oklahoma, houses a small but excellent collection of arts, artifacts, and history of the Cherokee, Chickasaw, Choctaw, Creek, and Seminole. The talent shown by the artists' exhibits is in the fine details of native art. Some examples are the wood sculptors of Woody Crumbo and artwork of Jerome Tiger. The museum highlights art portraying the Trail of Tears and cultural scenes. The museum had humble beginnings in 1875 when it was built by the U.S. government as the Five Civilized Tribes Superintendency at Muskagee. The city of Muskagee owned the building and it was opened in 1966 as the Five Civilized Tribes Museum.

ART FAIRS

Heard Museum   The Heard Museum in Phoenix, Arizona, holds an annual Indian art fair every year that attracts national attention. While the fair is Southwest oriented, artists from around the country compete for prizes and are able to sell a high volume of their work to appreciative buyers. Dwight B. and Maie Bartlett Heard founded the private museum in 1929. The Heards were business people and collectors of American Indian artwork, pottery, and textiles. The Heard collection focuses on the Southwest Indian cultures during the nineteenth and twentieth centuries. In addition, the museum has a 24,000 volume library and 50,000 photographic archives.

Santa Fe   Santa Fe hosts the annual Santa Fe Indian Market, and important fair at which Indian artists exhibit and sell their artwork, with an emphasis on art and pottery of the Southwest. Held annually in August, the Indian Market exhibits impressive handmade Indian art. Santa Fe is a historical trading site for American Indians and Mexicans. Today, it continues to be on the national circuit for Indian art fairs and native artists and buyers come from far away to attend.

Red Earth   Every year in Oklahoma City, Red Earth occurs as a celebration of art, artifacts, and native culture. It hosts one of the largest powwows in Indian Country, drawing large crowds to view and purchase native art. Red Earth began in 1978 with the founding of the Center of the American Indian. Red Earth became an annual event when a group of influential Oklahomans and tribal leaders formed the Red Earth American Indian Cultural Festival in 1987.

There are other Indian art fairs and the above mentioned are some of the more well known ones.

POWWOWS

Dancing is a part of the Circle of Life that American Indians celebrate in various ways and throughout the seasons of the years. Powwows are one the primary means with great contemporary symbolism involved. Powwows are social dances for all tribes, especially plains, to gather and dance with competitions for traditional and fancy dancing. The drum at the center of the dance serves as the heartbeat for all people in attendance, even those who are not dancing, as they become one people during this shared experience. The dancers move clockwise to the beat of the drumming as each sound touches everyone there.

Indian elder Ed McGaa (Oglala Sioux) stated that

Powwow dancing is social dancing. It is not religious dancing on a par with the Sun Dance. I danced for sheer enjoyment in my early days as a pow wow dancer. The steady drum beat kept us in rhythm as we danced around in a circle. Women and men often danced together but seldom as partners. You were allowed your own freedom of movement as your body seemed to pulsate to the drum beats. I would dance in the afternoon and long into the night, whirling, spinning and keeping my feet in time to the drumming. Bells were attached to our ankles over furred padding. The bells added to the sound of the drums. At a young age, I did not seem to tire. The flow of the rhythm seemed to add to your energy.[1]

Powwow dancers at Red Earth, Oklahoma City, in 1980s.

Powwows continue to play a major role in the pan-Indian way of socialization. Friends and relatives come together who have not seen each other for some time, or they see each other on a nearly regular basis at powwows. Naturally, new friends are made as well. The origin of pow-wows is not clearly known, but one likely explanation is that intertribal dancing and songs began to occur on a regular basis during the mid to late nineteenth century, especially on the Plains. Some studies suggest that powwows originated from the grass dances of the Omaha tribe, while powwows also emerged during the Wild West shows of the late 1800s into the twentieth century. Another possibility is that the modern powwow developed from Plains Indian cultures, evolving into a southern Plains style, central Plains type, and northern Plains style.[2] It would be safe to suggest that the powwow has several sources and has merged into a modern phenomenon of the twentieth century.

Every weekend, powwows are held indoors and outdoors all across Indian country, on reservations and in urban Indian communities. Some annual powwows have become well-known stops on the cir-cuit in urban areas, including the Chicago Powwow at the Navy Pier, which has been going on for more than 50 years; the Denver Powwow, an event that grows in attendance every year and is on the calendar of every dancer on the powwow circuit, and the Stanford University Powwow. Oklahoma City's annual Red Earth celebration attracts more than 1,200 powwow dancers. The Gathering of Nations meets annually in Albuquerque, New Mexico, to celebrate life and ceremony of many tribes coming together.

GOURD DANCING AND FORTY-NINES

Gourd dancing and forty-nines are often associated with powwows. Southern Plains Indians will gourd dance prior to a powwow or some-times in an urban area. The gourd dancers represent warrior societies of the southern Plains tribes. Wearing certain style clothing, they use special rattles and feathered fans. The vocal range of the singing is lower than powwow singing and the dancing is much slower compared to the vigor-ous powwow dancing.

Forty-nine dances are typically held by young Indians following powwows. Various sources account for the number 49, but the most likely explanation is a burlesque show with a California gold-rush theme that toured Kiowa country in the 1920s. A popular lyric was bor-rowed by the Kiowa, "see the girls of '49, see the '49 girls." Kiowa men sung about their women, using the lyric in semitraditional war-journey songs. These '49 songs became widely used by other tribes in addition to the Kiowa during late-hour social dances after powwows. Powwows are social and often last all night long. The dances and lyrics of songs are about love, heartbreak, blues, and Indian problems. Drums are used when available, but any flat surface is used when necessary that will provide a resonant sound.

RELIGIOUS MUSIC

As American Indians adopted Christianity, they also adopted hymns and gospel music. As missionaries worked with native groups, protestants discovered that Indians were receptive to music in the church. Missionaries translated hymns into native languages in the early nineteenth century and Christian Indians began translating and composing their own words to the melodies of Christian hymns. This led to the Christian converts creating new songs for their churches as they had already started translating hymns into native languages during the 1800s.

Gospel singing had become common in Indian churches in the early decades of the twentieth century as "sings" became a part of Christian life. Sings became special affairs at churches, sometimes as a part of revivals, drawing soloists, duets, trios, and quartets who traveled from far away to participate. By the late 1980s, Indian Christian music began to appear on albums, cassettes, and CDs. Most groups sang to the accompaniment of a piano, guitar, bass fiddle, organ, or other type of instrument. In the 1990s, soundtracks, synthesizers, and electronic keyboards began appearing in the arrangements.

Choirs in churches have been popular and so has nonreligious school group singing. Across the nation, choirs gaining attention with their singing have made recordings, including Bacone College in Oklahoma, Brigham Young University in Utah, Fort Lewis College in Colorado, the Institute of American Indian Art, and Santa Fe Indian School in New Mexico.

CONTEMPORARY MUSIC

American Indian musicians have a long history of traditional music and an impressive one in Western type of venues. Native musicians perform ballads, blues, classical, jazz, country, punk, rock, rap, and new age. Using imaginative ways, they combine traditional music with mainstream rhythms and instruments. Native musicians include Tom Bee, Robby Bee, Joe Manuel, Cody Bearpaw, Eddie Johnson, Brian Johnson, Jimi Poyer, Arliene Nofchissey Williams, Vincent Craig, and Chief Dan George. Other artists are Frank Montano, Tomas Obomsawin, A. Paul Ortega, Sharon Burch, Jim Pepper, Buddy Red Blow, Joanne Shenandoah, Bill Miller, Gene T, Buffy Sainte-Marie, Bruce Hamana, Floyd Westerman, Louis Ballard, Brent Michael Davids, Billy Thunderkloud, and John Trudell.

A few of the many Indian bands are Sand Creek, Winterhawk, Borderline, El Cochise, Joe Montana and the Roadrunners, Rockin' Rebels, Wingate Valley Boys, Burt Lambert and the Northern Express, the

Fenders, Undecided Takers, the Navajo Sundowners, Zuni Midnighters, Apache Spirit, Redbone, and XIT.

In the late 1960s, Tom Bee formed the band XIT. They were one of the first Indian groups to combine traditional sound with rock-n-roll. Their protest style music led to two-album contracts with the Motown label, and they have played concerts in various parts of the world. Tom Bee was a Grammy award winner in 2001. On May 20, 2000, XIT celebrated its thirtieth anniversary at Mystic Lake Casino in Prior Lake, Minnesota.

Redbone, the rock band, took its name from an old Cajun word meaning "half breed." Two brothers, Patrick and Lolly Vegas (Yaqui) selected the band's name and they wrote songs that were recorded by Aretha Franklin, the Righteous Brothers, and Bobbie Gentry. In the early 1970s, their band's first hit, "Maggie," sold three million copies of their album "Witch Queen of New Orleans." This led to their next big hit, "Come and Get Your Love."

FIDDLES, GUITARS, AND FLUTES

Indian fiddlers and guitar players are many and they meet to show off their talents at local concerts or just get together to jam. Every year, the Cherokee National Holiday hosts a national Indian fiddler's contest in Tahlequah, Oklahoma. Other such events are held where Native Americans come to listen, meet friends, and make new ones. One can imagine listening to Indian blues on the rez or at an urban bar as life experiences become the words of songs and tunes in an Indian modern way.

The flute has been a popular instrument among American Indians for as long as anyone can remember. Flute playing became more popular after World War II. This revival of the flute owes much to Doc Tate Nevaquaya, a Comanche from Oklahoma. He was also a first-year recipient of a National Heritage fellowship from the National Endowment for the Arts. He taught several young men the old songs and played non-Indians songs as well. Flute players have found success as concert artists, including Kevin Locke, R. Carlos Nakai, Edward Wapp, Jr., John Rainer, Jr., Gordon Bird, Fernando Cellicion, Robert Tree Cody, Herman Edwards, Daniel C. Hill, Frank Montano, Cornel Pewewardy, D. M. Rico, Stan Snake, Douglas Spotted Eagle, Robert Two Hawks, Woodrow Haney, and Tom Ware.

PERFORMING ARTS

Native Americans have excelled in many of the fine art performance fields. Symphony conductors and opera singers are as yet nonexistent among American Indians. Special training, mentorship, and years of expensive lessons are not among the resources for the majority of Native Americans. Yet, American Indians have had a true star in the Fine Arts.

Maria Tallchief, Osage, reached international acclaim as a prima ballerina. Born in 1925, she began studying ballet and taking music lessons at the age of four. At eight years old, her family moved to Beverly Hills so that she could receive expert training. At fifteen years old, Maria Talllchief performed her first solo at the Hollywood Bowl. She debuted as the first American ballerina to perform with the Paris Opera Ballet and became America's first prima ballerina. Three other native women from Oklahoma achieved fame as ballerinas during the 1920s and 1930s. They are Rosella Hightower, Marjorie Tallchief, and Yvonne Chateau. Others included Moscelyne Larkin, Melissa Hale, and Gail Gregory.

Te Ata, Chickasaw storyteller, has earned fame among Indian and non-Indian audiences. The late Te Ata was born on December 3, 1895, in Oklahoma. As a girl, she spent hours listening to her father tell stories about their people, myths, and legends. Te Ata was a splendid storyteller who mesmerized President Franklin and Eleanor Roosevelt and their audience at the White House on April 22, 1933. Te Ata shared American Indian folklore with America beginning in the 1920s through the postwar years. She stunned her audiences with her multiple voices characterizing people, birds, and other animals in her host of stories that involved drama, pathos, native humor, and life. Her one-woman storytelling performances delighted audiences and helped them learn to appreciate the oral tradition of Native Americans.

FEDERAL SUPPORT

A number of federal legislative efforts have attempted to preserve indigenous cultures in America. This endeavor began in the early 1930s when John Collier was appointed commissioner of Indian affairs. Although federal policy outlawed the Sun Dance for the Plains Indians, Collier worked to preserve the production of Indian artifacts by Indian artists. He had a deep appreciation for the Taos Pueblo Indians of the Southwest and saw the cultural value of their way of life. On August 27, 1935, Congress enacted the Indian Arts and Crafts Board Act in order to establish a board of five commissioners to promote the economics of Native Americans by the development of arts and crafts for marketing.[3]

Further federal legislative efforts to preserve Indian artwork would not occur significantly until the 1970s when sacred sites were returned to certain tribes by the Richard Nixon administration. The return of Taos Blue Lake and Mount Adams to the Taos Pueblo Indians and the Yakima tribe in Washington, respectively, set a significant precedent of modern federal protection and respect for Indian religious and ceremonial artwork. Another major legislative effort was the American Indian Religious Freedom Act passed during the Jimmy Carter administration. Because much of Indian artwork is about ceremonials, native artists and craftspeople have been able to confidently produce items, although looters have robbed artifacts from sacred and burial sites.

On July 23, 1992, Congress enacted the Institute of American Indian Native Culture and Arts Development Act, known as P.L. 102-325. This act amended the American Indian, Alaska Native, and Native Hawaiian Culture and Art Development Act "to create a board to establish, within the institute, departments for the study of culture and arts and for research and exchange, and a museum." Like the Indian arts and crafts board act passed much earlier, opportunists saw Indian arts and crafts as a means to make money, and this legislation placed further restrictions to authenticate such items made by Indian people.[4] Within months, Congress passed another measure in an effort to help preserve indigenous cultures and languages. The timing proved perfect with the 500-year anniversary of the arrival of Christopher Columbus which led to the enormous loss of native populations, cultures, and languages. On October 26, 1992, Congress passed the Native American Languages Act, P.L. 102-524. This act amended the Native American Programs Act of 1974 "for the Secretary of Interior to award a grant to any agency or organization that is to assist Native Americans in ensuring the survival and continuing vitality of Native American languages."[5]

In less than two years, Congress passed the Alaska Native Art and Culture Development Act, P.L. 108-239, on May 4, 1994. This was "an act for the Secretary of the Interior to make grants for the purpose of supporting programs for Native Hawaiian or Alaska Native culture and arts development to any private, nonprofit organization or institution which primarily serves and represents Native Hawaiians or Alaska Natives."[6] Unguarded historic artifacts made by Indians were at risk as private collectors and opportunists acquired items to sell. Furthermore, native peoples needed federal protection of their artwork and craftwork as they continued to retain their indigenous cultures with so many modern changes occurring within their communities.

ARTIFACTS

For people who are curious about Indian artifacts and where collections of them are located, there are several notable sites. There are national museums like the Field Museum in Chicago and the Denver Museum of Nature and Science in Colorado that house impressive collections of Indian artifacts, and there are some places that specialize in Native American objects only.

The Heard Museum in Phoenix, Arizona, is one of the outstanding places to see native artifacts on public display. The museum was started in the 1920s by Dwight and Maie Heard, early entrepreneurs in Arizona who collected native art and artifacts and decided to share their private collection with the public.

The National Museum of the American Indian (NMAI) of the Smithsonian Institution in Washington, DC, opened in 2004, becoming

Basketry of the Mission Indians. Courtesy of Library of Congress.

the greatest public exhibition of native art and artifacts in the western hemisphere. The endeavor became possible with the passage of the National Museum of the American Indian Act, heavily supported by Senator Daniel Inouye (D-HI) and enacted on November 28, 1989, as Public Law 101-185.[7] Under the direction of Rick West, more than 80,000 native art pieces and artifacts are available for display. At the turn of the twentieth century, George Gustav Heye, a wealthy New Yorker, formed the Heye Foundation and the Museum of the American Indian in New York City. Thousands of masterworks of wood and stone carvings, including masks from the Northwest Coast; quilled hides, clothing, and war bonnets from the Plains; and pottery and basketry from the Southwest; with artifacts from the Great Lakes, and Eastern woodlands represented Indian America. The museum's collections included archaeological items from the Caribbean; ceramics from Costa Rica, central Mexico, and Peru as well as from the Olmic and Maya groups; and textiles from the Andean cultures and featherwork from the Amazonian peoples.

With plans in place, the museum pieces began to be relocated from New York to Suitland, Maryland for preparation for exhibition at the new national museum. The result has been a spectacularly museum designed in the shape of a Mesa of the Southwest of four flours on the National Mall in Washington, D.C.

The forthcoming Oklahoma Indian Cultural Center promises to be a premier site to view Indian artifacts and cultural history using advanced technology. The idea behind this approach is the artifacts have stories, lives of their own, and these are shared with visitors of this cultural center based in Oklahoma City, Oklahoma. It is scheduled to open in 2007.

There are over 150 tribal museums that have American Indians on staff at all levels. Tribal museums are appearing with growing frequency among the 562 federally recognized tribes, each of which would to have such a museum and many tribes have their own. As more of these institutions are being built, workers will continue to require expert training to handle and catalog artifacts.

Perhaps the grandest tribal museum is the Pequot Museum in Connecticut, which was constructed in the early 1990s. It cost the Pequot tribe about $192 million and it is impressively large with an enhancing native design.

Other tribes have constructed tribal museums, but on a lower scale, and some of them are cultural centers, such as the All Pueblo Cultural Center in Albuquerque, New Mexico, that sells artwork by local artists and beadwork and silverwork produced by pueblo artists.

In a collective manner, the Five Civilized Tribes Museum in Muskogee, Oklahoma, has a fine collection of wood carving, paintings, and artifacts produced by historical and contemporary artists. The Cherokee, Chickasaw, Choctaw, Creek, and Seminole Tribes have had a number of fine artists like Wood Crumb and Jerome Tiger, whose works are displayed at the museum.

CONCLUSION

American Indian art is coming to be appreciated on a par with world art. Great strides have been over the last two decades. Critics believe that Indian art is not of the equality of European Impressionism and other kinds of western art. It is certainly not of the Western world, but this is one of its striking qualities. It has its own identity. Much of Indian art is about experiences that the artist has committed to share with others. It is through art that a visual tapestry can be told of the history of individual, tribal, and collective Indian experiences. It is most apparent if the viewer of Indian art knows the linear history of Indian people that coincides with this visual history recorded on canvas or in other media.

Whether the professional art world accepts Indian art or not, native artists continue express their inherent sovereignty of cultural expression. Once paid little or no attention by the non-Indian world, the works on native artists are now in expensive non-Indian collections in the United States and around the world. In this manner, historic Indian artworks have become artifacts themselves. Yet, it may be best to realize that each

Indian art piece holds a story via the native oral tradition and accounts need to be retold about each item.

NOTES

1. Ed McGaa, *Native Wisdom: Perceptions of the Natural Way* (Minneapolis: Four Directions Publishing, 1995), 29.

2. Susan Applegate Krouse, "A Window into the Indian Culture: The Powwow as Performance," unpublished Ph.D. dissertation, University of Wisconsin–Milwaukee, Department of Anthropology, 1991, 33–34.

3. Indian Arts and Crafts Board Act, August 27, 1935, *U.S. Statutes at Large,* Vol. 49: 891–93.

4. Institute of American Indian Native Culture and Arts Development Act, P.L. 102-325, July 23, 1992, *U.S. Statutes at Large,* Vol. 106, Pt. 1: 805–809.

5. Native American Languages Act, P.L. 102-524, October 26, 1992, *U.S. Statutes at Large,* Vol. 106, Pt. 4: 3434–3437.

6. Alaska Native Art and Culture Development Act, P.L. 108-239, May 4, 1994, *U.S. Statutes at Large,* Vol. 108, Pt. 1: 606–607.

7. National Museum of American Indian Act, P.L. 101-185, November 28, 1989, *U.S. Statutes at Large,* Vol. 103: 1336–47.

9

AMERICAN INDIANS IN LITERATURE AND MEDIA

Images of Indians have mystified mainstream America and the rest of the world because of human curiosity and intrigue about the glorious past of Indian people. The stereotyped images of the savage, warrior, or natural man have been the focus of books, European literature, American textbooks, mascots, and early and modern films. In the world, the people of Germany, Japan, and England have been keenly interested in American Indians. In the United States, Indians have been portrayed in literature and film as the bad guy, sidekick, documentary subject, and relic of the past.

Generally, American Indians have been misinterpreted and stereotyped in literature and the media. They have not been the main characters of films and have had more focus in literature that has been written and produced by non-Indians. This is easily understood because of market purposes that the target audience is white Americans in general and they are not ready for Indian men and women to be the main characters. Furthermore, Indian men and women characters have been mostly played by non-Indians until the 1990s with the rise of prominent Indian actors and actresses.

EARLY PORTRAYAL OF THE INDIAN

Writers with biased opinions and little accurate information about American Indians and their rich cultures constructed their own versions of the "Indian." The idea of the Indian and frontier developed simultaneously during the earliest American writings such as novelist James Fenimore Cooper's *Last of the Mohicans* (1826) and other titles. In this light, the Indian was a part of the frontier.

Dime novels about the West continued the saga of frontiersmen struggling, facing Indian attacks, and conquering the West. As the United States finalized its borders after the Civil War, the frontier and the West became the focus of writers and readers. Outlaws became heroes, such as Billy the Kid and Jesse James and Doc Holiday. In contrast, Indians remained as the bad guys. For Indians, unfortunately, an interested American public was primed to believe fiction more than fact. The facts were often distorted, and like fiction, presented only one view about Native Americans—the negative interpretation. Although non-Indians lacked in-depth knowledge about American Indians, they have written about Indian identity.[1]

IMAGES OF INDIANS IN EUROPEAN LITERATURE

The appeal of the American West and Native Americans drew the attention of the curious as a result of the writings of Karl May, a German author, who never visited the American West until late in his life. May was a novelist, who lived from 1842 to 1912. He started with a book called *The Treasure of Silver Lake* and added to his repertoire of other subjects about the West. In his novels about Indians, the main character was an Apache warrior named Winnetou, who was accompanied by a fair-haired companion, "Old Shatterhand." German studios filmed 11 of May's tales set in early America.

German children grew up and continue to hear the stories of Winnetou and other native characters developed from the imagination of Karl May. Fascinated by these stories, they wondered about "real Indians." May's novels spread throughout Germany and Europe among readers who were curious about America. In Europe, more fiction about Indians and the true identity is written than objective scholarship. The same pattern is true for England, Finland, Japan, and other countries with a growing interest in American Indians.

INDIANS IN AMERICAN TEXTBOOKS

The portrayal of Native Americans in American history textbooks at all levels of education is an embarrassment to Native Americans. Outdated, biased information is still used to teach school children, therefore perpetuating the same old negative stereotypes. Why does such a modern industrialized society allow such insensitivity to continue? Indian people protest, but this effort is not enough to bring about a more accurate portrayal of Native Americans. More Native Americans and supporters, advocates in the publishing industry, and persons at all political levels need to correct this wrong. As early as 1970, at least one book by Indian writers, Rupert Costo and Jeanette Henry, *Textbooks and the American Indian,* attempted to address the incorrect portrayal of Indians in textbooks.[2] The book has had little impact on the textbook industry.

On the average, Native Americans usually capture the attention of two chapters, perhaps three chapters, in American history survey textbooks. The first chapter typically describes a lost Christopher Columbus "discovering" America and meeting Indians. The other chapter usually involves Plains Indian wars with Americans winning the West. A possible third chapter may include information about the militant activities during the late 1960s and early 1970s of the American Indian Movement (AIM), which was founded in the summer of 1968 in Minneapolis, Minnesota. Revised textbooks might include in their final chapters discussions of the spiraling profits made by tribes from the Indian gaming industry. All of this proves that American Indians are not regarded by textbook publishers as being central to U.S. history.

MASCOTS AND SPORTS TEAM NAMES

Fans of the Atlanta Braves cheer their baseball team on by using a hand motion called the tomahawk chop. In a different stadium, different sport, a different city, fans cheer for the Washington Redskins professional football team. In another city, a different stadium, different sport, fans cheer for the Chicago Blackhawks professional hockey team. The Kansas City Chiefs football team and the Cleveland Indians baseball team are among the other professional teams named after Native Americans. Television advertisements promote the native mascots to a buying pubic of loyal fans.

At the college level and in the high school ranks, numerous teams are named after Indians in admiration or working the angle of using Indians for stereotyped ferocity. Almost one-fifth of the major colleges and universities are named after Indians. In general, the Indian mascot controversies involving professional, college, and high school teams in all sports have provoked opinions from most native peoples. The feeling is an uncomfortable disagreement with teams abusing Indian logos where American Indians are made fun of. For example, the motion of the tomahawk chop at the Atlanta Braves baseball games, the child-level warrior sounds made by people, and the obnoxious Indian grinning face of the Cleveland Indians emblem. Indian mascots running or riding onto sports fields screaming war cries reminds Indian people of all of the negative stereotypes ever said and written about them.

INDIANS IN EARLY FILMS

American Indians have been the subjects of countless books and movies written and produced by non-Indians. More than 30,000 books and nearly 1,000 movies have been written and produced about American Indians. Furthermore, Indians have not been the main character in these books and movies. In fact, Indian people have been exploited for commercial reasons and for the advancement of the personal careers of non-Indians. Before 1975, there were more non-Indians playing as Indians in movies about Indians.

Hollywood has helped to perpetuate positive and negative (mostly the latter) stereotypes in an estimated 823 films made between 1907 and 1995, with perhaps a more realistic count of about 1,000 films portraying Indians by the end of this century. To the American public, Indian is an image that does not necessarily represent a people, but an enemy that had to be defeated in history and on the movie or television screen. As a result, there are more than 30 negative stereotypes about Indians such as savage, lazy Indian, and wagon burner.

Early films about American Indians were imbued with white racial prejudice. One of the first films about Indians was *Sioux Ghost Dance* (1894), produced by (Thomas) Edison Studios as a series of short documentary clips. This was a silent film showing Sioux Indians in full regalia of a breechcloth and feathers on their heads and beating on drums.[3] Although it might be suspected that Hollywood was the origin of early filmmaking about Indians, many of the first films about Native Americans were made in New Jersey.[4]

Edison Studios produced the first film on Pocahontas in 1908. *Pocahontas* is the story of John Rolfe of early Virginia Colony and his marriage in 1614 to Pocahontas, the daughter of Powhatan, leader of a powerful Indian group of tidewater Indians. In 1907 the Independent Motion Picture Company released *Hiawatha,* based on the well-known 1855 poem by Henry Wadsworth Longfellow. Early film pioneer D. W. Griffith reworked James Fenimore Cooper's Leatherstocking Tales, a group of five novels that includes *The Last of the Mohicans* (1826), into the film *Leather Stocking* in 1909. Griffith directed *Ramona* in 1910, based on the Helen Hunt Jackson novel of the same name from 1888, which was a biographical account of a Southern California Indian woman and her struggle to survive. Griffith made several dozen early Western films that included Native Americans, such as *The Battle at Elderbush Gulch* in 1914, where a non-Indian kills the son of a Sioux leader and the Indians terrorize a community of settlers. Other Griffith films included *The Redman and the Child* (1908), *The Mended Lute* in 1909, and *A Squaw's Love* (1911).[5]

Films about Indians between 1910 and 1915 were more serious about Indian life. *The Squaw* in 1914 and *The Red Woman* in 1917 represent this genre.[6] During the early years, it is interesting that the Indian woman begins to appeal to film makers with the general developing movement to make films about Native Americans.[7]

PREJUDICE IN FILMS

Perhaps the best illustration of racial prejudice against Indians was in *They Died with Their Boots On* (1941). This depiction of the Little Bighorn presented George Custer (Errol Flynn) as the hero and the Indians as crazed with savagery. This historically inaccurate movie made Custer into an American hero. The film became one of the most notorious anti-Indian films ever, and unfortunately appeared to the public during war in Europe and prior to the bombing of Pearl Harbor.[8] American needs heroes and Hollywood has recast history making fiction more appealing than fact.

Unfortunately, *They Died with Their Boots On* placed American Indians on the other side as the enemy and showed native peoples slaughtering George Custer without cause. In this light, the movie made Custer into a hero that the public needed at the time of the outbreak of World War II in Europe. Very shortly, toward the end of 1941, the United States found itself in the war and in need of heroes throughout this period.

In addition to the unfair treatment of Indians in film, the term "Indian Country" has been used extensively by the U.S. military. It was a common term used in the Vietnam War during the 1960s, even by Indian soldiers themselves who were compelled to understand that Indian Country over there was where the Vietcong might be. Naturally, American Indian soldiers saw themselves as Americans while being called by non-Indian servicemen "Chief," "Hey Indian," or some other derogatory name. Such prejudice and racism in the modern half of the twentieth century found roots in early films perpetuating stereotypic beliefs that Indians were savages and the enemy.

INDIAN WOMEN IN FILMS

In the film industry in Hollywood, Indian women do not exist as main characters, except in a few films. Even then, a non-Indian woman typically has played the role of the Indian woman. This trend would continue until the last decade of the century.

Hollywood exploited the Indian woman. She was a dark, beautiful, and sensual princess of the forest with an undying love for a white man. Or, the white male hero would pursue the dark princess and win her heart after achieving some heroic deed.

The theme of Indian women being sacrificed was clear in the film *The Indian Squaw's Sacrifice* (1910). The plot involves Noweeta, an Indian woman, who nurses a wounded white man back to health, marries him, and has his baby. He falls in love with a white woman and leaves Noweeta, who becomes heartbroken and goes into the woods to die to free her husband to marry the white woman. The same theme with variation was depicted in *The Kentuckian* (1908) and in Cecil DeMille's *The Squaw Man* (1914), a film remade several times due to its popularity, but unfortunately reinforcing with each generation of viewers that it is acceptable for Indian women to have little importance in society.[9] In this perspective, the Indian woman is the loser, she is portrayed as having her spirit broken, leaving her people, or being willing to sacrifice her life.

The young Indian woman also decides to leave her beloved white man and still loves him as demonstrated in *The Far Horizons* (1955) when Sacagawea leaves Captain William Clark because she does not fit into his civilized society. In *Captain John Smith and Pocahontas* (1953), the beautiful Indian woman, Pocahontas, does not marry Smith but stays behind to help maintain peace between her people and the whites, then marries another white man.[10] This became a trend of the Indian women not marrying the white hero or she dies soon after the marriage, so that she never lives happily thereafter with the white man hero. When the Indian woman in film does not marry the white man hero, she then marries him in other movies, but she dies. In *Broken Arrow* (1950), Sonseeshray, a beautiful Apache woman, rejects the Apache man she is promised to in order to marry the white hero, but she is killed in the end. Running Deer rejected Black Eagle in *A Man Called Horse* (1970) in order to marry the Englishman, but then she is killed by Shoshones. The message is that mixed racial marriages do not work, and this is also illustrated in *Dances With Wolves* (1990) when the Lakota woman falls in love with the white hero, but she is actually a white captive. If the mixed marriage does work in films, then the Indian-white couple lives far from white society in the wilderness, as shown in *The Red Woman* (1917), *The Big Sky* (1952), and *Black Robe* (1991).[11]

Until an Indian woman has earned celebrity status in mainstream America, native women will continue to suffer in their film roles as backdrop characters. This is like sitting at the back of the bus. Mainstream filmmakers are pressured to make films about mainstream personalities in plots that involve mainstream stories.

INDIANS IN MODERN FILMS AND SHOWS

Early films about Indians in black and white perpetuated the "cowboy and Indian" imagery. However, it was always the cavalry riding to the rescue to chase away or defeat Plains Indian warriors. This "John Wayne" history continued throughout the early decades of the twentieth century as urban Indians and reservation Indians saw themselves as the "bad guys." This typical theme in Western films involving Indians encountered a change in the movie *Broken Arrow* (1950). In it, the character of Tom Jeffords (James Stewart), an Indian scout and supervisor of the U.S. Mail in Arizona, and Cochise (Jeff Chandler), leader of the Chiricahua Apaches, talk peace. White vigilantes kill Jeffords's Indian bride, and Cochise has to convince Jeffords that Indians and whites will not have a lasting peace during their lifetimes.[12] Since the *Vanishing American* (1925), *Broken Arrow* presented a sympathetic view for Native Americans, although these movies played to smaller audiences. American guilt fell to feeling sorry for the victimized Indian who could not help himself. Living in mainstream America was too much pressure for the poor Indian according to this view of the sympathizers. Similar movies followed, such as *Jim Thorpe, All American* (1951), *Seminole* (1953), and *Broken Lance* (1954). *Broken Arrow* represented a turning point in aged stereotypes and prejudice against Indians as noted by Oliver LaFarge of the Association on American Indian Affairs, who endorsed the movie. He wrote, "'Broken Arrow' also points out to Hollywood that stereotypes can be discarded and that both Indians and whites emerge as human beings: cruel, frightened, courageous, kindly."[13]

After World War II and in the postmodern years, the television industry carried on the negative visual imagery of Indians with *The Lone Ranger, Davy Crockett,* and frequent a Indian presence on Western serials such as *Bonanza*, and *Roy Rogers*.

In movies during the protest years of the late 1960s and early 1970s, political themes found their way into films about Native Americans. *Little Big Man* (1970) and *Soldier Blue* (1970) depicted the American practice of genocide against Indians, reflecting the biased attitudes of producers and directors about Vietnam and prejudice against minorities.[14] Indians were used as themes of injustice, wrongdoing, and human mistreatment. Soldiers in Vietnam referred to the enemy territory as "Indian Country."

Since the 1970s, a few independent films broke from typical images of the hostile Savage and the friendly Noble Red Man and portrayed contemporary Native Americans as fictional characters significant in and of themselves, not only as contrasts to the white heroes, as is always the case in the Westerns. In *House Made of Dawn* (1972), *Three Warriors* (1972), *Spirit of the Wind* (1979), *Harold of Orange* (1984), *Journey to Spirit Island* (1988) and *Powwow Highway* (1988), main native characters, played by Native American actors, experienced a renaissance in strength and identity when semitraditional values and cultural ways were relived in the films. Although the films and their Indian characters covered a large variety of roles and subjects, including contemporary themes on reservations, Indian viewers learned about their ways of life and themselves. Acting roles involving elders, families, dreams, trickster stories, and warrior rituals also taught the mainstream about Indian people and their ways with a worthy level of respect.[15]

Television series in the 1990s paid only slight attention to Native Americans and often presented distortions. The series *Dr. Quinn, Medicine Woman* featured one named Indian, "Cloud Dancing," even though the other Indians of his tribe, the Cheyenne, have no names. Another program, *Renegade,* with actor Lorenzo Lamas, has an Indian sidekick named Bobby Sixkiller (a Cherokee name). The popular serial placed in Dallas, Texas, *Walker, Texas Ranger,* starring actor Chuck Norris, depicted his Cherokee background, although much of the Indian portrayal is Plains Indian and powwow dancing, which is alien to Cherokee tradition.

In television sitcoms, Native Americans have never been the main stars, as production companies wanted to produce shows with main characters reflecting the mainstream white American population. Due to the majority white television audience wanting to see itself, and because viewing numbers influenced the television ratings, production companies were under pressure to employ white actors and actresses. But there certainly are Indian actors and actresses. These include Graham Greene and Rodney Grant (both of *Dances With Wolves* fame) and Floyd Westernman, who has appeared frequently on television and in films.

During the late 1960s, one ridiculous sitcom, *F Troop*, portrayed a military fort in the West with all kinds of silly dealings made with the nearby Indian tribe. In this case, the show made fun of both the U.S. military and the Plains Indian tribe. Neither side wanted to go to war, and the commander of the fort was afraid to ride a horse, feeling inferior to a cowgirl type white settler who loved him.

In the early 1960s, an Indian cartoon character appeared on television in the afternoons. He was Powwow, the Indian boy, and his counterpart was a little Indian girl cartoon figure named Powwee. This unsophisticated show made the little Indian boy and girl appear to be cute and simple.

For a while during the 1970s, many newspapers carried the comic strip "Tumbleweeds." This was supposed to be a humorous depiction about Plains Indians and the U.S. Cavalry, with one of the Indian cartoon characters always seeming to screw things up, and the others of this make-believe Indian tribe then look at him with expressions that seemed to say, "Well, you did it again!"

For most of the films "about" or "including" Indians, Native Americans were the enemy. Cast as the "bad guys" in spaghetti Westerns, they were defeated on the cinema screen over and over. Even when Native Americans were seemingly the main focus of a film, a non-Indian portrayed them. One such example is the casting of Chuck Connors (of *The Rifleman* fame) to play the infamous Apache leader in the movie *Geronimo*. Originally producers wanted Connors to wear brown contacts to hide his blue-grey eyes. This did not work because his blue-grey eyes were appealing to the camera, and he made the film without the contacts.

Generally Indians have been used as props for other actors. They are rarely the main stars, and if they are, non-Indians would play the parts. Indian characters were in 1970s films such as *Soldier Blue* (1970), *Little Big Man* (1971), and *One Flew over the Cuckoo's Nest* (1975). These Indian actors, however, where individual targets and somehow did not fit into the white American mainstream of life. The 1969 production of *Tell Them Willie Boy Is Here,* starring Robert Blake posing as a Paiute Indian and Katharine Ross as his Indian girlfriend , illustrated the Indian plight of not fitting into the white man's world at the same time as the rise of Red Power and Indian activism in the late 1960s and early 1970s. In the end of the movie, Willie Boy is hunted down by the white sheriff, Coop (Robert

Redford), and they both aim to shoot each other, but unknown to the sheriff, Willie Boy's gun has no bullets.

The Indian epic *Little Big Man* (1970) starred Dustin Hoffman as a white captive of the Cheyenne formerly known as Jack Crabb. More accuracy about Plains Indian culture was displayed, although the complexity of visions and how Jack Crabb learned much from the Cheyenne was not translated to the viewers. The humor in the film and its charm caused a commercial success. Such humor becomes the appeal instead of the understanding of Cheyenne ways and their tribal values. The massacre of the Cheyenne at Sand Creek as shown in *Little Big Man* and the Indian massacres of *Soldier Blue* (1970) paralleled the U.S. military's campaign to destroy non-whites as they did in Vietnam, declaring enemy territory to be "Indian Country."

THE SIDEKICK

Indians became the sidekick, such as the character of Tonto, played by Jay Silverheels (1912–1980), in the *Lone Ranger*.[16] Silverheels, a Mohawk, brought much attention to Native Americans, but he represented the stoic stereotype Indian, and he never upstaged the Lone Ranger. Few people know that the first Tonto was played by Chief Thundercloud, a full-blood Cherokee, who also played in *Geronimo* in 1939.[17] Tonto's lines were few, and every other phrase was "Kimo sabe," which no one never knew what this meant unless they were a semi-historian of the Lone Ranger, who was a former Texas Ranger, and left for dead by vigilantes. The Lone Ranger was named Kimo sabe (bright scout) by the Indians, and he was nursed back to health by Tonto. Then Tonto helps the Lone Ranger to heal the white stallion, Silver.[18] Many Indians have given their own humorous interpretations of what kimo sabe meant to them. For example, the Lone Ranger might say, "Tonto, we're in trouble. We are surrounded by Indians." Tonto then grunted, and replied "Kimo sabe," translated to mean, "What do you mean WE, White Man!"

As a sidekick, the Indian companion to the white hero always stands to the side or to the back. Camera angles and film shooting techniques place the white hero as the center of attention, sometimes placing him on higher ground or more in the foreground. For example, Tonto never upstaged the Lone Ranger, and in *The Last of the Mohicans* (1936), Chingachgook and Uncas appeared on either side or slightly behind Hawkeye.[19]

INDIAN LEADING ROLE FILMS

Indian lead-role films did not include Indian actors in the lead role, such as Trevor Howard playing Windwalker in the movie called *Windwalker* (1980). The cult film of *Powwow Highway* (1988) featured an Indian, Gary Farmer (Mohawk), playing the star, but the film was distributed to a very limited audience.[20]

The Hollywood Indian demeaned real Indians. For example, in movies,

The prototype of the Hollywood Indian was treacherous, vicious, cruel, lazy, stupid, dirty, speaking in ughs, and grunts, and often quite drunk. An alienated, impressionable audience swarmed in to see Billy Jack do his leg work and defy the establishment. It may be of some interest to note, that, since Billy never mentions his tribe, he apparently does not know where he belongs, and is, therefore, undeniably illegitimate.[21]

Films during the 1990s continued to portray Indians, but with an increased appreciation for Indian culture, although Indians were still used as props and were never the leading actors or actresses. Recent films *Dances with Wolves* (1990), *Squanto* (1994), *The Last of the Mohicans* (1993), *Lakota Woman* (1994), *Hawkeye* (1994), and *The Broken Chain* (1994) have caused a renaissance of interest in Native Americans; an estimated 75 films have been made since the 1960s. Documentaries and videos about Native Americans and other educational films increase this number to 175 to 200 productions.

Documentaries and videos are being produced with increasing frequency, but they have gone too far in portraying a "noble savage" who is a teary-eyed environmentalist, as did one television commercial that featured the late Iron Eyes Cody.[22]

ACTORS AND SCREENWRITERS

Will Sampson, a Creek Indian from Oklahoma, made his debut in *One Flew over the Cuckoo's Nest*. This successful movie led to other parts for Sampson. Jay Silverheels has been mentioned. Other native actors include Adam Beach, born in Ashern, Manitoba, Canada on November 11, 1972. He is Saulteax and was raised on the Dog Creek Indian Reservation in Manitoba until he was eight years old when his parents died. A small role in Graham Greene's *Lost in the Barrens* in 1990 for television led to a major role in Disney's *Squanto: A Warrior's Tale* in 1994. He played the role of Victor Joseph in Chris Eyre's *Smoke Signals* in 1998 and costarred with Nicolas Cage in *Windtalkers*, a movie about the Navajo code talkers in World War II. Beach also played Jim Chee in PBS's movies made from Tony Hillerman's novels, *Skinwalkers* (2002), *Coyote Waits* (2003), and *A Thief of Time* (2003).

Graham Greene is a veteran actor of television shows and movies. Born on June 22, 1952, on the Six Nations Indian Reserve in Brantford, Ontario, Canada, Graham Greene is a full-blood Oneida and lives in Toronto. He started his theatrical career as a sound engineer and made his debut as an actor on the London stage. He first big hit was playing the character Kicking Bird in the film *Dances with Wolves* in 1990. His performance earned him a nomination for an Oscar for Best Supporting Actor. He appeared in more than 30 films in the next ten years, including *Die Hard with a Vengeance* in 1995 and *Wolf Lake* in 2001.

Russell Means is an American Indian Movement (AIM) activist turned actor. He was born on November 10, 1939, on the Pine Ridge Indian Reservation in South Dakota. He was the first national director of the AIM and became one of its national spokespeople. He appeared in *The Last of the Mohicans* in 1992 and *Natural Born Killers* in 199, and was the voice of Powhatan in *Pocahontas* in 1995.

West Studi, a full-blood Cherokee, was born on December 17, 1947, at Nofire Hollow, Oklahoma. He grew up speaking Cherokee and learned English while going to school. A veteran of Vietnam, he was a reporter for the *Cherokee Advocate* and became an activist in the AIM and was at the occupation of Wounded Knee, South Dakota, in 1973. He became interested in acting while performing with the American Indian Theatre Company in Tulsa and moved to Los Angeles, where he got a small role in Kevin Costner's *Dances with Wolves* in 1990. This part led to his playing Magua in *The Last of the Mohicans* in 1992. Three years later, he played a role in *Heat* and another part in *Mystery Men* in 1999. Studi played the part of Joe Leaphorn in PBS's productions of Tony Hillerman's novels, *Skinwalkers* in 2002, *Coyote Waits* in 2003, and *A Thief of Time* in 2003. West Studi's next role was Opechancanough in *The New World* in 2005.

Sherman Alexie is a gifted writer of poetry, short stories, and novels who has also written movie scripts. Alexie was born on October 7, 1966, on the Spokane Indian reservation in Wellpinit, Washington. He is Coeur d'Alene and wrote poetry first before writing the successful novels *The Business of Fancydancing* in 1991 and *The Lone Ranger and Tonto Fistfight in Heaven* in 1993, which became the foundation for *Smoke Signals,* the movie, in 1998. Alexie's other novels include *Reservation Blues* in 1995, *Indian Killer* in 1996, *The Toughest Indian in the World* in 2000, and *Ten Little Indians* in 2003.

Chris Eyre is a talented filmmaker. He was born in 1969 on the Warm Springs Indian Reservation in Oregon. He is Cheyenne and Arapaho. He made short films with successful reception from audiences and earned a master's degree at New York University. He produced *Smoke Signals* in 1998 and a documentary, *Doe Boy,* in 2001. He has also produced *Skins* in 2002, *Skinwalkers* in 2002, and *A Thief of Time* in 2003.

COMMERCIALS AND ADVERTISING

Unfortunately, Indians have been exploited in commercials and advertising since even before the invention of the television. Early advertising has used figures of American Indians as advertising to sell products. Baking powder with a general image of a chief on the front, "Big Chief" writing tablets for grade school students, and chewing tobacco are among the many commercial products that use Indians for their own benefit. It is certainly evident that Indians are not the recipients of the profits of these commercial items, nor have the companies consulted with Indian groups for their views.

American Indians have benefited the corporate because business companies have appropriated negative images. The commercial world has used Indian images to sell toys, food products, tobacco products, motorcycles, automobile tires, and automobiles as previously mentioned in another chapter. The list goes on to include the U.S. military naming attack helicopters after an Indian tribe (Apache) and a native leader (Black Hawk), although the government is not in the business of selling these war items. Nonetheless, businesses have benefited from this exploitation of Indians without the Indians benefiting at all from these ventures.

OUTDOOR DRAMAS

In Oklahoma, the Cherokee Nation sponsors the *Trail of Tears* outdoor drama from Thursday to Sunday during the summer. This drama has been in production since the 1970s and is performed at the Tsa La Gi Amphitheater in Tahlequah.

In Ohio, the outdoor drama *Tecumseh* is held from June 9 through September 2. It is performed at the Sugarloaf Mountain near Chillicothe, Ohio, and there are tours backstage. An Indian Museum is also at the site and the Ohio Historical Society assists in displaying prehistoric Indian artifacts from the Scioto Valley. The two-hour drama portrays the efforts of Tecumseh, the noted Shawnee leader who organized a massive Indian army consisting of various tribes with the influence of his mystical brother, the Shawnee Prophet, as Tecumseh led an alliance of numerous tribes to stop white settlers from taking Indian land in the War of 1812.

Near Xenia, Ohio, the *Blue Jacket* outdoor drama is performed during the summer months. Blue Jack, a Shawnee leader, is portrayed as a native patriot to save his people against the advancement of white settlers coming into the Ohio Country during the early 1790s, resulting in the famed Battle of Fallen Timbers.

Another favorite outdoor drama is *Unto These Hills*. This drama depicts the removal of the Cherokee people from North Carolina in a beautiful setting of the Smokey Mountains. The summer months are when this impressive drama is shone.

CONCLUSION

There is no doubt that American Indians have been exploited by the media in movies, literature, and other forms. Unfortunately, it has been for the entertainment of non-Indians. Furthermore, it has been for the personal gain of non-Indians. Some of this exploitation has also been for satisfying the simple curiosity of others who want to know more about Indians and their cultural ways of life. In fact, that is what this book is about. However, the last ten or twenty years of the twentieth century have experienced a change with the rise of Indian authors, Indian-produced movies, and non-Indians who want to see Indians as the main characters and have done something about it. It is encouraging that this sincere effort to tell the full story of American Indians as the main actors and characters is a reform attempt to tell the truth about Indian people. Much has to be done and it is critical because media and literature are the two main venues for people to learn about American Indians.

NOTES

1. Writings about American Indian identity include Stan Steiner, *The New Indians* (New York: Dell Publishing Company, 1968); Joseph H. Cash and Herbert T. Hoover, eds., *To Be an Indian: An Oral History* (St. Paul: Minnesota Historical Society Press, 1995); Hazel W. Hertzberg, *The Search for an American Indian Identity: Modern Pan-Indian Movements* (Syracuse: Syracuse University Press, 1971); T.ºC. McLuhan, *Touch the Earth: A Self-Portrait of Indian Existence* (New York: Outerbridge and Dienstfrey, 1971); Murray L. Wax, *Indian Americans: Unity and Diversity* (Englewood Cliffs, NJ: Prentice Hall, 1971); D'Arcy McNickle, *Native American Tribalism: Indian Survivals and Renewals* (New York: Oxford University Press, 1973); Dennis Tedlock and Barbara Tedlock, *Teachings from the American Earth: Indian Religion and Philosophy* (New York: Liverlight Publishing, 1975); William W. Savage Jr., ed., *Indian Life: Transforming an American Myth* (Norman: University of Oklahoma Press, 1976); Robert F. Berkhofer Jr., *The White Man's Indian: Images of the American Indian from Columbus to the Present* (New York: Alfred A. Knopf, 1979); Leonard Dinnerstein, Roger L. Nichols, and David M. Reimers, *Natives and Strangers: Blacks, Indians, and Immigrants in America* (New York: Oxford University Press, 1979); Richard Drinnon, *Facing West: The Metaphysics of Indian Hating and Empire Building* (Minneapolis: University of Minnesota Press, 1980); Brian W. Dippie, *The Vanishing American: White Attitudes and U.S. Indian Policy* (Middleton, CT: Wesleyan University Press, 1985); Peter Matthiessen, *Indian Country* (New York: Viking Press, 1985); Francis Pail Prucha, *The Indians in American Society: From the Revolution to Present* (Berkeley: University of California Press, 1985); Clifford E. Trafzer, ed., *American Indian Identity: Today's Changing Perspectives* (Sacramento: Sierra Oaks Publishing Company, 1985); Stephen Cornell, *The Return of the Native: American Indian Political Resurgence* (New York: Oxford University Press, 1988); Roy Harvey Pearce, *Savagism and Civilization: A Study of the Indian and the American Mind* (Baltimore: Johns Hopkins University Press, 1988); James A. Clifton, ed., *Being and Becoming Indian: Biographical Studies of North American Frontiers* (Chicago: Dorsey Press, 1989); James A. Clifton, ed., *The Invented Indian: Cultural Fictions and Government Policies* (New Brunswick: Transaction Publishers, 1990); Laurence M. Hauptman, *Tribes and Tribulations: Misconceptions about American Indians and Their Histories* (Albuquerque: University of New Mexico Press, 1995); Patricia Penn Hilden, *When Nickels Were Indians: An Urban, Mixed-Blood Story* (Washington, DC: Smithsonian Institution Press, 1995); Fergus M. Bordwich, *Killing the White Man's Indian: Reinventing Native Americans at the End of the Twentieth Century* (New York: Doubleday, 1996); Joane Nagel, *American Indian Ethnic Renewal: Red Power and the Resurgence of Identity and Culture* (New York: Oxford University Press, 1996). For Indians portrayed in literature, see Scott B. Vickers, *Native American Identities: From Stereotype to Archetype in Art and Literature* (Albuquerque: University of New Mexico Press, 1998).

2. Rupert Costo and Jeanette Henry, *Textbooks and the American Indian* (San Francisco: American Indian Historical Society Press, 1970).

3. Alesis and Appleford, "Indians in Film and Media," 768.

4. John E. O'Connor, *The Hollywood Indian: Stereotypes of Native Americans in Film* (Trenton: New Jersey State Museum, 1980), xii.

5. Alesis and Appleford, "Indians in Film and Media," 768.

6. Ibid.

7. Writings about Native Americans in the media of film include Michael Hilger, *From Savage to Nobleman: Images of Native Americans in Film* (Lanham, MD: The Scarecrow Press, 1995); John E. O'Connor, *The Hollywood Indian: Stereotypes of Native Americans in Film* (Trenton, NJ: New Jersey State Museum, 1980); G. M. Bataille and C. L. P. Silet, ed., *The Pretend Indians: Images of Native Americans in the Movies* (Ames, Iowa State University Press, 1980); and Mark A. Rolo, ed., *The American Indian and the Media* (New York: The National Conference for Community and Justice, 1991). Other books include Ralph E. Friar and Natasha A. Friar, *The Only Good Indian . . . : The Hollywood Gospel* (New York: Drama Book Specialist/Publishers, 1972). See also, James R. Smith, "Native American Images and the Broadcast Media," *American Indian Culture and Research Journal*, 5, no. 1 (1981): 81–92.

8. O'Connor, *Hollywood Indian*, 39.

9. Hilger, *Savage to Nobleman*, 3.

10. Ibid., 4.

11. Ibid.

12. O'Connor, *Hollywood Indian*, 49.

13. Ibid., 54.

14. Ibid., 13.

15. Hilger, *Savage to Nobleman*, 253.

16. Indians have remained as the background or marginal person in Hollywood films, because members of the paying public want to see themselves in the roles of the main stars of the stories on the screen, whether film or television. The Indian as the marginal person is written about in William T. Pilkington and Don Graham, *Western Movies* (Albuquerque: University of New Mexico Press, 1979); J. A. Place, *The Western Films of John Ford* (New York: Citadel, 1974); David Rothel, *Who Was That Masked Man? The Story of the Lone Ranger* (New York: Barnes, 1976); and Jean Jacques Sandoux, *Racism in Western Film from D. W. Griffith to John Ford: Indians and Blacks* (New York: Revisionist Press, 1980).

17. O'Connor, *Hollywood Indian*, 10.

18. Hilger, *Savage to Nobleman*, 5.

19. Ibid., 11–12.

20. Alesis and Appleford, "Indians in Film and Media," 771.

21. Rita Keshina, "The Role of American Indians in Motion Pictures," *American Indian Culture and Research Journal* 1, no. 2 (1974): 26.

22. Literature on Indians as the principal actor or actress in film include Judith Logsdon, "The Princess and the Squaw: Images of American Indian Women in Cinema Rouge," *Women's Studies Librarian* (Summer 1992) University of Wisconsin System, 13–17; Gretchen M. Bataille and Charles L. P. Silet, "A Checklist of Published Materials on the Popular Images of the Indian in the American Film," *Journal of Popular Film* 5 (1976): 171–82; Dan Georgakas, "They Have Not Spoken: American Indians in Film," *Film Quarterly* 25 (1972): 26–32; Robert Larkins,

"Hollywood and the Indian," *Focus on Film* 2 (1970): 44–53; John W. Turner, "Little Big Man, the Novel and the Film: A Study of Narrative Structure," *Literature/Film Quarterly* 5 (1977): 154–63; and Rita Keshena, "The Role of American Indians in Motion Pictures," *American Indian Culture and Research Journal* 1, no. 2. (1974): 25–28. Indians viewing themselves in film include the works of Kathleen M. Sands and Allison Sekaquaptewa Lewis, "Seeing with a Native Eye: A Hopi Film on Hopi," *American Indian Quarterly* 14, no. 4. (Fall 1990): 387–96.

10

NATURE, ENVIRONMENT, HOME SPACES, AND RESOURCES

The reality of American Indians who are close to their traditions is one of understanding relationships. It is knowing the earth while learning about rivers, valleys, mountains, hills, meadows, and all of the names of the flora and fauna of one's home space. It is also finding beauty to nurture one's soul especially in time of need for spiritual strength. This is the natural world of American Indians.

In a different light, 14 reservations received 96 percent of all timber revenues in the 1960s. As late 1955, 90 percent of $30 million in total Indian mineral revenues were received by six reservations and a few in Oklahoma. In 1980 with 278 reservations total, only 42 had enough natural resources to be members in the Council of Energy Resource Tribes (CERT). In the 1970s, the energy crisis pressured tribes with natural resources into situations of what to do with them. In the old ways, the earth held many meanings for Native Americans. The natural world of American Indians was at risk.

SACRED PLACES

On this earth, many places exists that Native Americans fear and respect. Such places are sacred grounds to Indian people. Indian people know where such sites exist as their ancestors have known them for centuries, and such places are good and bad. In either case, they are empowered and their power is respected by Indian people.

Fear is a common response to such empowered, sacred places. For such power is greater than human beings, according to native beliefs.

The Devils Tower. Courtesy of Library of Congress.

The extent of such power is unknown since American Indians can only learn what powers can be manifested. Energy is emitted from empowered places of the sacred in physical energy displayed like a thunderstorm, earth tremor, foggy area, or unexplainable lights. The other type of energy is spiritual, with unseen activity that affects those in the area. With sacred places in action, it can be assumed that such sacred grounds have greater power than human beings.

Throughout Indian America, there are hundreds of places sacred to American Indians. Many of these important sites have become known to non-Indians who hold little regard for native beliefs. As a result, a common practice of non-Indians desecrating Indian sacred places occurs everyday. For example, if you visited Devil's Tower in Wyoming, known as Bear's Lodge to several tribes, you will see non-Indians climbing Devil's Tower without regard to tribal beliefs that this is a sacred site to them. From the

Indian perspective, it would be like someone climbing the cathedral at the Vatican, and it could be anticipated what would happen next.

As a part of sacred places, Indian artifacts and burial sites have been desecrated in gross numbers. Even with the federal laws passed to protect American Indian remains and sites such as the Antiquities Act of 1906; the National Historic Preservation Act (NHPA) of 1966 with amendments in 1992; and the American Indian Religious Freedom Act (ARIFA) of 1978 have had little success in helping Indians. In addition, the Archaeological Resources Protection Act (ARPA) of 1979 with amendment in 1989; the Native American Graves Protection and Repatriation Act (NAGPRA) of 1990; and President Bill Clinton's Executive Order No. 13007 of May 1996 set out to protect tribal lands, but American Indian artifacts, sacred places and burial sites continue to be exploited.

Disrespect has also been practiced by scholars and museums. In 1988 the American Association of Museums reported to the Senate Select Committee on Indian Affairs that 163 museums possessed 43,306 skeletal remains of American Indians.[1] Through repatriation, many of these human remains were returned to the tribes.

Respect is important for sacred grounds and powerful places. It is one of the most important values among native peoples. In studying the relationship of a sacred place with the people, it is obvious that Indians believed that these places could exercise a great deal of power. Within all due respect, Indian people are fearful of such powerful places.

Power is an act of potential energy that can have positive and negative effects, which American Indians have learned to respect. They have countless experiences with powerful sites that might be called haunted or considered to be dangerous places where unfortunate incidents occurred and continue to happen. So, then why are such places in Indian Country, sites that might be analogous to the Bermuda Triangle, the dangerous events of which even scientists cannot explain?

Throughout the United States and Canada, hundreds of sacred sites exist. They are in many forms of landscape and of water. Natural sacred places to native people special to the understanding and learning about life and the universe include the Black Hills, Blue Lake of the Taos, Mackinac Island, Mount Rainer, Mount Taylor, and Bear Butte.[2] Other sacred places to indigenous peoples include Uinta in Utah, Tucumcari in New Mexico, and the Four Corners area of the Southwest that held special meaning for the Hopi, the Diné (Navajo), and early Spanish peoples.[3]

Such sacred grounds of the American Indian deserve respect from all people, not just from Native Americans. These grounds and tribal artifacts are powerful for the reasons only nature really knows, and they have exhibited such power that can be dangerous to human beings. Harm comes in many ways, and the lack of acknowledgement of such power exhibits the ignorance and insensitivity of anyone who believes this is being superstitious.

Certain places are important and they are personal. Some people might call them sacred sites, but it is noted that they are empowered and they can bestow this gift to human beings. At the same time, there are natural sacred places or sites that are common to many people for they are very powerful. Such places of power include, the Black Hills, Blue Lake of the Taos, Serpent Mound, Mackinac Island, Mount Adams, Mount Rainier, Mount Taylor, and Bear Butte.[4] Other sacred places to Indian people include Mount Taylor in Arizona, Uinta in Utah, Ocmulgee Mounds in Georgia, Tucumcari in New Mexico, and the Four Corners area of the Southwest that held special meaning for the Hopi and the Dene (Navajo).[5] There are hundreds, even thousands, of such places, and they are uncountable at any given time for their sacredness changes with the seasons, times of day, and personal accounts.

Sacred places have power and important knowledge. They are doors of opportunity to the other side of life—the metaphysical. Indigenous people have observed them and sought to understand the relationships with them in the natural world. It is as if the natural world speaks a language that has been neglected, and human beings have not listened except for a few of us. By observing and listening and watching for certain signs, the American Indian mind can communicate with nature.

NATURAL RESOURCES

Since the late nineteenth century, American Indians have had to deal with opportunists wanting the natural resources from their lands. The choice lands were taken by white settlers and Indians were left with useless lands. Native peoples were left with unappealing lands that became reservations. Ironically, reservation lands possess enormous amounts of coal, oil, gas, uranium, and water. Water is the most precious resource of all.

Increasing demands for natural resources have forced tribal leaders to contend with the two areas of economics and law. As the number of automobiles on highways and traffic builds up in cities after World War II, tribes have been compelled to obtain expertise in these two areas. This has placed an enormous among of pressure on tribal leaders in dealing with energy companies, the federal government, and their own people. With advice from business councils, lawyers, and CERT, they must act in the best interest of their tribe. Native leaders must comply with the business practices of the mainstream society and capitalism. Thus, tribal leaders have had to become knowledgeable in economics and law.

Daily contact with the mainstream has severely undermined native cultures. With each tribal generation, the cultural meaning of Mother Earth becomes less significant to young Native Americans. Simultaneously, young Indians striving to become educated, wanting good paying jobs, modern health care, better homes, and a better life have been drawn closer to the American mainstream. Cultures change with time, but the increasing demand for natural resources has acted as a catalyst in bringing about change throughout Indian Country. The Indian desire for progress is a regression of tribal ways at the cost of preserving the earth as they once knew it. Should tribes mine their natural resources for money to fund needed programs to help their people? This is a common dilemma in Indian Country.

Some tribes have become keepers of energy natural resources, or "energy tribes," and they face difficult situations in attempting to preserve their natural resources. Each tribe with such resources has had to evaluate its potential in resources and consider the possibilities of harvesting their resources for revenue to pay for programs to help their people. In some instances, tribes have become almost like capitalistic corporations. These energy tribes have undergone considerable change, especially since the 1970s. Although all tribes do not participate directly in the American mainstream, the energy tribes and their leaders have to compete with the mainstream if they are going to successfully defend their natural resources.

The energy tribes have found themselves in courts and lobbying for certain legislation in Congress. What might be gained and lost in the courts seriously affects them. Legislation establishes certain conditions or changes them and defines the rules or regulations for tribes and their resources, and previous court cases have set legal precedent that must be understood. Most important, the federal government has taken a position of leaving the tribes to manage their own affairs with less federal intervention as the trustee. Currently the federal policy of Indian self-determination shifts the responsibility of the government's responsibilities to the tribes, although it is still the trustee for tribes.

In 1982 Congress took an important step to help tribes when it passed the Indian Mineral Development Act, P.L. 97-382, sometimes referred to as the Melcher law. Senator John Melcher of Montana introduced the bill to permit the tribes to negotiate their own mineral contracts and to participate as part owners in the mining development on their tribal lands. Tribes like the Blackfeet have negotiated part ownership with energy companies with clauses in agreements to assume full ownership at later times.

OIL

Oil and coal have had negative effects on the lives of American Indians. So much exploitation has occurred, and for one tribe it has happened more than once. In the early 1920s, the Osage of Oklahoma experienced the "Reign of Terror" when an opportunist named William H. Hale plotted the murder of members of the Kyle family and others involved with the Osage family. Starting with the killing of Henry Roan, Hale hired assassins to murder the Kyles in an evil plot to gain control of their headrights over land allotments that had oil. The Osage Tribe was the richest tribe due to huge oil deposits under their lands in northeast Oklahoma. Trains carried oilmen, wildcatters, and their geologists to the auctions held at Pawhuska. Beneath a famous tree, called the "million dollar elm," Colonel Ellsworth Walter auctioned oil leases to oil barons like Bill Skelly, E. W. Marland, Frank Phillips, G. F. Getty, whose son, J. Paul Getty, sat on wooden bleachers in the shade. The oilmen stayed at Pawhuska's new hotels along with others wanting to get into the oil business. Pawhuska, Oklahoma, became known as the "Osage Monte Carlo."

In this case, more than a dozen murders occurred involving the Kyle family. Following a three-year investigation, the federal government connected the killings to William K. Hale, who proclaimed himself as "King of the Osages." One federal agent posed as a cattle buyer from Texas, another became an insurance salesman, and a third agent pretended to be a medicine man on the reservation. The murders happened in the most horrendous ways—bullets in the head, shotgun blast murders, poison, and even nitroglycerin was used to kill one family, blowing up most of their house. Osage families strung electric lights around their yards and armed themselves for protection.

In the early 1980s, the U.S. government intruded again into the affairs of the Osages. In this situation, oil and water did not mix. Flooding was a problem in northeastern Oklahoma. The Army Corps of Engineers planned to build dams and reservoirs for flood control. However, this action threatened to flood up to 83, 000 acres of oil-rich land belonging to the Osages. In another project, the National Park Service wanted to obtain another 97,000 acres for the Tallgrass Prairie National Park. Since the 1970s, the Army Corps of Engineers constructed dams and reservoirs that have submerged 45,000 acres of land.[6]

The conflict over water and oil interests forced the Osages to file a suit in 1976. It was too late. The federal court ruled that the Osage still owned the oil under the reservoirs and that the United States had no authority to condemn the Osage land for construction. However, the court's ruling halted the Army Corp's Candy Lake project and threatened the future of the Skiatook Lake project where the dam was already built, costing $44 million. If additional federal construction continued, the Osage alleged that they would lose 436 oil and gas wells, amounting to more than $1 million a year.

Far to the north in Alaska, the Alaska Native Settlement Act of 1971 involved 40 million of acres of lands returned by the Richard Nixon administration, plus $940 millions from the Alaska oil discovery on the Northern Slope. Since then, the Alaska natives have had serious problems. Oil royalties brought overwhelming windfalls of wealth to the Alaska natives such that many could not handle it like the Creeks and Osages in Oklahoma during the 1920s. In 1989 the Exxon Valdez ran aground, spilling millions of gallons of crude oil. In 1997 the Alaska native groups were in a law suit against Exxon because of the incident since it was their oil.[7]

On January 12, 1981, the *Los Angeles Times* reported that oil had been stolen from the Wind River Reservation in Wyoming. This allegation was only a small part of larger oil theft and fraud on federal and Indian lands amounting to between $3 billion and $5 billion. Furthermore, more oil and gas operations were involved in as many as 12 states.[8] Oil was thought to have been stolen two ways, by removal of waste oil (diverting good oil) from waste oil pits and by removal of production oil from on-site storage tanks. Because oil production is calculated from measuring amounts based on sales of crude, theft via diversion is done prior to sales. On-site security is the only means to monitor such fraud, but this is costly and time consuming. Arrests and convictions were reported for oil thefts in Oklahoma, New Mexico, and California; although most crimes occurred on private lands, this activity convinced the Assiniboine tribe of the Fort Peck Reservation to investigate for oil theft on their reservation in Montana. Fortunately, no theft was officially confirmed at Fort Peck.

In 1979 the General Accounting Office (GAO) of the federal government reported that energy companies underpaid tribes by as much as 7 to 10 percent each year. For example, the GAO reported that hundreds of millions of dollars may be going uncollected annually. In response, the government established the Linowes Commission to monitor illegal activities with an emergency fund to audit royalty payments for reimbursing states and tribes. The states and tribes responded that the federal government should pay for its own royalty management responsibility.[9]

In 1980 energy tribes with oil totaled 45 Indian nations. The Bureau of Indian Affairs (BIA) estimated that the energy tribes earned a combined $169,011,012.96 from oil and gas production on 5.3 million acres of tribal lands. In the 1980s Indian reservations in 12 states were responsible for almost all of the Indian oil business. The leading oil producing tribes included the Osage of Oklahoma; the Navajo of Arizona, New Mexico, and Utah; the Shoshone and Arapaho of Wyoming; the Micaville Apache of New Mexico; and the Uintah and Ouray Utes of Utah. Oklahoma remained as the leading oil-producing state on Indian lands, with current oil production occurring on a total of 21 separate tribal lands, yielding a total income of $70,266,407.33 in 1980. Wyoming was second leading productive state with an income of $17.3 million in 1980, and New Mexico was third with an income of $17.1 million involving six tribes.[10]

TIMBER, COAL, AND URANIUM

Thick stands of timber are another natural resource for certain tribes. Such woodlands are a part of the culture of these timber tribes and they were free of problems until the late nineteenth century. Almost one-fourth of reservations have forests, estimated at 13,000,000 acres. Before developing gaming in the 1980s, about 60 tribes earned 25 to 100 percent of the tribal incomes from timber operations. A Tribal Timber Consortium contained 130 tribes as members.

Certain timber-rich tribes are the Klamath, the Menominees in Wisconsin, and various Chippewa bands in the Western Great Lakes region. They experienced enormous losses of timber during the 1960s and they have tried to protect their remaining resource in the following decades of the twentieth century. Many other tribes found themselves in the same situation. As of January, 1981, 104 tribes had a total market of 5.8 million acres of timber. This amount of timber is estimated to mean an income of $89.9 million. As an example of the inherent value of timber, for all forest lands in the Southeast between 1955 and 1985, the U.S. Forest Service reported that approximately 42 hectares or 30 to 50 percent had disappeared to illegal cutting.[11]

An estimated one-third of the coal west of the Mississippi River rests under tribal lands on reservations. Energy companies have intensely mined coal, particularly in the last three decades of the twentieth century. The Council of Energy Resource Tribes (CERT) was formed to help energy tribes. For example, with one-third to one-half or more of the estimated reserves of uranium in the United States located in the Four Corners area alone, CERT has an enormous responsibility of protecting Indian interest in the Southwest.[12]

WATER: THE MOST PRECIOUS RESOURCE

In 1908, the most important court case involving Indian water rights resulted in a very important victory for American Indian tribes. Known as the *Winter's* Doctrine, Judge Joseph McKenna ruled in the U.S. Supreme Court that Gros Ventre and Assiniboine Indians on the Fort Belknap Reservation in Montana had "reserve right" to sufficient water from the Milk River to develop their lands. Previously, white ranchers had dammed the river upstream, thus preventing water to flow onto the reservation.[13]

Water is essential to all things that are alive. For example, land without water is useless, as proved in the Pueblo lands controversy of the 1920s when white opportunists illegally claimed Pueblo irrigated lands. The tribes in the Southwest, and in other parts of Indian country, who have sufficient water tables will have to protect their water rights in the courts. Since the *Winters* decision established the Indians's "reserve right" in 1908. Tribal groups are facing a steadily growing power in the influence of state governments to challenge Indian water supplies as indicated in the *Arizona v. California* water case in 1963.[14] Although the court determined that five reservations had the right to water on the lower Colorado River, the case raised the issue of "practicably irrigable acres" involving future federal and tribal water cases. The State of Arizona sued California to determine its water rights in an effort to provide water for the Central Arizona Project canal to irrigate areas in the state. In the process of the decision, the Supreme Court reaffirmed the Winter's Doctrine and for the first time, quantified Indian water rights, which has set a precedent for future Indian water cases.

Tribes, especially in the Southwest, felt the pressure even earlier for this resource when Congress passed the McCarran amendment in 1953. The law vested state courts with jurisdiction to determine water rights comprehensively, if the water usage was a part of the larger usage like national forests, wildlife refuges, and types of national recreation areas.[15] Congress intended the McCarran amendment to end piecemeal federal adjudication of water rights by granting this privilege to the states, but it did not mention Indian water rights as being subject to state court jurisdiction.

The legal war for water had already begun. By 1982 there were 48 lawsuits on Indian water rights in ten Western states. Tribal leaders in Arizona, Utah, Washington, and California entered a new political period of protecting

Woman collecting water from stream in the southwest. Courtesy of Library of Congress.

water rights for their peoples. In 11 states, a total of 97 irrigation projects were being developed, producing crops worth more than $178 million.[16]

During the early 1980s, 68 percent of the groundwater in the country was used for agricultural irrigation, with approximately 90 percent of the irrigated lands existing in 17 western states. After 85 percent of the water consumed in the West went to irrigated croplands, the remaining 15 percent was divided among domestic, municipal, and industrial uses. By 1990 the United States used more than four million hectares for raising crops, an estimated fifth of the nation's irrigated areas. Using such amounts during the early 1980s dropped the water levels lower in Texas, California, Kansas, and Nebraska, four primary food-producing areas. In Texas, as an example, the water tables fell about 15 centimeters (six inches) per year beneath 1.54 million hectares, or 72 percent of the state's total irrigated area, amounting to 30 percent between 1974 and 1987.

In 1989 the U.S. Supreme Court began to reexamine Indian reserve water rights when it agreed to review a 1988 Wyoming Supreme Court decision. The case had awarded extensive federal reserved water rights to the Shoshone and Northern Arapaho tribes on Wyoming's Wind River Reservation, establishing that the tribes had 477,000 acre feet of water for agricultural purposes, but none for industrial or municipal usage. The state of Wyoming and the tribes appealed the decision. The Supreme Court rejected the state's petition to deny the tribes any reserved water rights but agreed to review the quantification of those rights based on the "irrigable" standard.[17]

The federal government has tried to help preserve water areas on the Zuni reservation in the Southwest. Congress passed Zuni River Watershed Act, P.L. 102-338, on August 11, 1992. This measure was "an act to formulate a plan for the management of natural and cultural resources on the Zuni Indian Reservation, on the lands of the Ramah Band of the Navajo Tribe of Indians, and the Navajo Nation, and in other areas within the Zuni River watershed and upstream from the Zuni Indian Reservation."[18]

As a part of the water claims, Congress has passed legislation to help specific tribes. For example, Congress passed the Jicarilla Apache Tribe Water Rights Settlement Act, P.L. 102-441, on October 23, 1992. This was an "act for the settlement of the water rights claims of the Jicarilla Apache Tribe against the State of New Mexico, the United States and other parties."[19] Another Apache group received similar help from the federal government. Congress passed the San Carlos Apache Tribe Water Rights Settlement Act, P.L. 102-575, on October 30, 1992. This was an "act regarding that Congress declares that the Secretary of the Interior will authorize the actions and appropriations necessary for the United States to fulfill its legal and trust obligations to the Tribe as provided in the Agreement's provisions of this law."[20]

In regard to the situation at Rocky Boy Reservation, Congress passed the Chippewa Cree Tribe of the Rocky Boy's Reservation Indian

Reserved Water Rights Settlement and Water Supply Enhancement Act, P.L. 106-163, on December 9, 1999. This was an "act to provide for the settlement of the water rights claims of the Chippewa Cree Tribe of the Rocky Boy's Reservation, and for other proposes."[21]

Water is the source of human sustenance and unfortunate conflict. Because the money involved is not as apparent as that represented in energy negotiations for oil and coal, water does not arouse immediate concern. That more conflicts over water are approaching is already evident in some parts of the country. The by-products of water, such as geothermal energy and hydroelectricity, are important, but they are secondary to human needs.

Water can be used as power. For example, the Warm Springs Confederated Tribes in Oregon have developed the only Indian-owned hydroelectric project in the country. Planned in June 1978, the tribe received a grant of $86,000 from the Department of Energy for a feasibility study to develop the hydropower plant at the Pelton Reregulating Dam, built during the mid-1950s in Oregon. The $30 million project, completed with financing of $10 million in tribal funds, $15 million raised by a state bond issue, and a $5 million federal loan, is expected to produce annual net revenues of approximately $4 million to the Warm Springs Tribes.

To help repair dams on tribal lands, Congress passed the Indian Dams Safety Act, P.L. 103-302, on August 23, 1994. This is an "act to maintain and include a repair program within the Bureau of Indian Affairs to maintain identified dams on Indian land that if they failed would present a threat to human life."[22]

INDIVIDUALS

Overall, American Indians as individuals have not ventured into the mining of natural resources to own their own companies. There is one exception in the case of the Pourier family. Pat and Opal Pourier of Pine Ridge, South Dakota, owned the first Indian-owned gas company, which they purchased in 1973 from Amoco, for whom Pat Pourier drove for three years. The Pouriers renamed their new company the Lakota Gas Company and operated it with the help of their 12 children. In 1982 they had 1,500 accounts after the early years proved difficult with a lot of experience gained from struggling to stay in business. Pat and Opal cited good bookkeeping, careful crediting, and having enough capital for the first year of operation as being key to their success.[23]

NUCLEAR ENERGY

One serious problem affecting one tribe is the nearby location of a nuclear energy plant to tribal land. The Yakima tribe in Washington have petitioned thorough the Columbia River Intertribal Fish Commission

(CRIFC) of Portland, Oregon, to the Nuclear Regulatory Commission (NRC) to intervene regarding two Washington state nuclear power plants. Originally five nuclear power plants of the Skagit-Hanford Project were planned, but two were halted during funding debates. The Yakimas protested that the plants were too close to the reservation and that radiological, chemical, and thermal pollution of the air and water would contaminate the Columbia River Basin, affecting their fisheries. The Yakima are the first tribe in the United States to pass a tribal resolution to prohibit the transport of nuclear waste, residues, fuels and by-products by land, rail, air, or water across reservations.[24]

In another related affair, Browning-Ferris Industries (BFI) of Houston, Texas, one of the largest waste disposal firms in the United States, started a campaign to locate toxic chemical disposal sites on tribal lands. In 1982 BFI negotiated with the Fort Mohave Reservation on the Colorado River and contacted the Chemehuevi and Hualapai in Arizona, the Duckwater Shoshone in Nevada, Paiute reservations in southern Utah, Eastern Cherokees in North Carolina, and possibly the Winnebago of Nebraska, and it also attempted to locate a site on Muscogee Creek lands in Oklahoma. The Houston business firm approached the tribes explaining that the federal cutbacks to tribes would hurt their revenue and that arrangement for such sites on their lands could help tribal economies. The tribes reported that slick promotional materials were used to convince them to agree to chemical waste being deposited on their lands.[25]

URANIUM

Mining has come back to harm Native Americans when radiation from uranium contaminated Indian miners and drinking water where they lived. Among the Lakota in the Black Hills where more than 25 mining companies are active, uranium mining has caused Lakota workers to be exposed to radiation. The Pine Ridge Reservation has experienced related health hazards since the 1970s.[26]

Tribes with uranium are in a situation of learning more about this natural resource. To make matters worse, the state of New Mexico released a 216-page report on February 4, 1982, stating that the BIA lacked staffing and technical skills to properly advise and represent Indian people in negotiations involving energy affairs.[27] Almost half of all of the uranium in the United States is on tribal lands. In 1989 the Havasupai who live in Nataract Canyon of the Grand Canyon faced the possibility of a 17-acre mining operation for uranium at Red Butte near the south rim of the Grand Canyon. Unfortunately this area is near the original site of the Havasupai's historical territory, and it is a sacred area. "The preparation of the mine which is being [developed] now wounds the earth at a sacred and vital place. A mine will kill it," said Havasupai leaders.[28]

In New Mexico on the Navajo Reservation, Navajo miners worked deep below the Colorado Plateau to extract soft, yellow uranium for three decades. In their effort to supply the uranium needed for American nuclear warheads during the Cold War, the Navajo mining veterans have been affected with radiation. More than 2,700 Navajo miners and their relatives have registered with the tribe's Office of Navajo Uranium Workers. Of this number, only 242 applied for compensation under the Radiation Exposure Compensation Act of 1990. Unfortunately, the "old-timers" among the Navajo miners did not save any check stubs or other documents to prove that they worked the uranium mines.

ENVIRONMENT AND ALTERNATIVES

Of the 291 Indian reservations, 93 have the potential to use wind as an energy source. Located primarily in the West, reservations in California, New Mexico, Nevada, Utah, Wyoming, Arizona, Montana, and North and South Dakota have the possibility to develop electric generators powered by the wind. In the upper Midwest, reservations in Minnesota and Wisconsin have the same hopeful situations.

To help environmental management and tribes, Congress passed the Indian Environmental General Assistance Program Act, P.L. 102-497, on October 24, 1992. This was an "act to provide general assistance grants to Indian tribal governments and intertribal consortia to build capacity to administer environmental regulatory programs that may be delegated by the Environmental Protection Agency on Indian lands; to provide technical assistance from EPA to tribal governments and intertribal consortia and to develop multimedia programs to address environmental issues on Indian lands."[29] On October 22, 1994, Congress passed the Indian Lands Open Dump Cleanup Act, P.L. 103-399. This was an "act to clean up open dumps on Indians lands (affecting at least 600 open dumps on Indian and Alaska Native lands)."[30]

The federal government is supportive in helping tribes to study renewable sources of energy to protect the environment. The Warm Springs Tribes in Oregon are collaborating with Pacific Gas and Electric for the operation of a hydroelectric project on the reservation.

The Skull Valley Band of Goshute Indians in Nevada have completed a feasibility study on developing a solar-driven generator to produce electricity to meet the needs of the reservation and tribal community center as well as to create jobs and generate excess power to sell off the reservation.

CONCLUSION

The last decade of the twentieth century was a period of environmental concern among Americans and other citizens of the world. Global warming is a common subject of international conferences. The rapid decline of the rain forests in South American at the expense of agricultural development is vigorously debated. Redwood trees populated an estimated two million acres in California a mere 200 years ago; today, this area has shrunk to 85,000 acres of virgin redwood forest, with 65,000 acres of this total in protected in parks.[31] Americans receive an estimated four million tons of junk mail annually and approximately 44 percent of us never open any of it. Every person in the country who receives junk mail has consumed the equivalent of one and a half trees a year. In larger proportions, if only 100,000 people stopped their junk mail, almost 150,000 trees could be saved annually.

This generation of Indian leaders and American officials will need to resolve differences and cooperatively formulate energy policies that do not threaten the tribes. But past exploitative federal policies remind tribal leaders and their people to be skeptical of new federal ideas. In addition, within the last 25 years, we have become dependent on other nations who stand to exploit the United States for dollars.

The end of the twentieth century forced all concerned that natural resources on tribal lands are in enormous demand. The increasing growth of American urban areas and development of rural areas puts an ever increasing demand on tribal natural resources that Native Americans are becoming more acutely aware of. The competition will become even greater for the remaining natural resources. Tribal leaders will wage the most significant battle since the nineteenth century for the existence of their people and to protect their homelands. Oil and coal reserves will be the most likely to be exhausted first, followed by natural gas. Alternative fuels including geothermal, wind, and hydro-electricity will be used, and finally we will be fighting over the air to breathe and water to live. Simultaneously, the economic factor is a part of the decision-making problem for energy tribes weighing the benefits of preserving or developing their natural resources. Tribal trust lands produced $165 million by the end of the twentieth century. Indian trust lands amounted to 56 million acres of the U.S. of the nation's 3,615,210 square miles, with 44 million acres in Alaska . Indian Country is about four percent of the total United States, equaling 156,250 square miles. Besides the primary resources mentioned, tribal lands contain gold, silver, copper, molybdenum, zeolite, phosphate, vanadium, sandstone, basalt, shale, sulfur, limestone, lead, zinc, peat, iron, clay, gypsum, volcanic cinders, sand, gravel, and building stone.

NOTES

1. Andrew Gulliford, *Sacred Objects and Sacred Places: Preserving Tribal Traditions* (Boulder: University Press of Colorado, 2000), 13, originally cited by Edward H. Able Jr., executive director of the American Association of Museums, to the Honorable Daniel K. Inouye, Select Committee on Indian Affairs, September 12, 1988.

2. As an example, for the Diné (Navajo), see Klara Kelley and Francis Harris, "Places Important to Navajo People," *American Indian Quarterly* 17, no. 2. (Spring 1993): 151–70.

3. Winifred Gallagher, *The Power of Place: How Our Surroundings Shape Our Thoughts, Emotions, and Actions* (New York: HarperPerennial, 1993), 23, 96.

4. As an example, for the Diné (Navajo), see Kelley and Harris, "Places Important to Navajo People," 151–70.

5. Gallagher, *The Power of Place*, 23, 96.

6. Indian Mineral Development Act, P.L. 97-382, December 22, 1982, Statutes at Large 96: 1938–40; William J. Broad, "Osage Oil Cover-Up," *Science* 208, no. 4439 (April 4, 1980): 32–33; and *Final Report and Legislative Recommendation*, "A Report of the Special Committee on Investigations of the Select Committee on Indian Affairs United States Senate," Senate Report 101–216, 101st Cong., 1st sess., Senate, November 6, 1989.

7. Kevin Galvin, "Natives Fight Exxon Plan for Valdez," *South Bend Tribune* (South Bend, Indiana), January 16, 1997.

8. News article, *Los Angeles Times*, January 12, 1981.

9. Russell Davis, James E. Wilen, and Rosemarie Jergovic, "Oil and Gas Recovery Policy on Federal and Indian Lands," *Natural Resources Journal* 23, no. 2 (April 1983): 407–09; see also Donald T. Sant, Abraham E. Haspel, and Robert E. Boldt, "Oil and Gas Royalty Recovery Policy on Federal and Indian Lands: A Response," *Natural Resources Journal* 23, no. 2 (April 1983): 417–34.

10. John Butler and Richard LaCourse, "45 Indian Tribes in a Dozen States Form Heartland of Indian Oil Production," *The CERT Report* 4, no. 11 (September 13, 1982): 3–4.

11. J. Butler and R. La Course, "45 Indian Tribes," *The CERT Report* 4, no. 11 (September 13, 1982): 3–4, and Lester Brown and Alan During, *State of World 1990* (New York: W.W. Norton, 1990), 6.

12. Philip Reno, *Mother Earth, Father Sky, and Economic Development: Navajo Resources and Their Use* (Albuquerque: University of New Mexico Press, 1981), 133.

13. *Winters v. United States*, 207 U.S. Reports, 565, 573, 575–577, January 6, 1908.

14. *Arizona v. California*, 373 U.S. 546, (1963).

15. "McCarran Amendment" (1953), 43 U.S.C. §666.

16. Richard Trudell and Joseph Myers, "How Indian Water Rights Are Resolved May Determine Future of Western United States," *The CERT Report* 4, no. 9 (July 23, 1982): 1.

17. "U.S. Supreme Court to Re-examine water rights," *Lakota Times*, March 21, 1989, 11.

18. Zuni River Watershed Act, P.L. 102-338, August 11, 1992, *U.S. Statutes at Large*, Vol. 106, Pt. 1: 866–868.

19. Jicarilla Apache Tribe Water Rights Settlement Act, P.L. 102-441, October 23, 1992, *U.S. Statutes at Large*, Vol. 106: 2237–2242.

20. "San Carlos Apache Tribe Water Rights Settlement Act," P.L. 102-575, October 30, 1992, *U.S. Statutes at Large*, Vol. 106, Pt. 6: 4740–4752.

21. Chippewa Cree Tribe of the Rocky Boy's Reservation Indian Reserved Water Rights Settlement and Water Supply Enhancement Act, P.L. 106-163, December 9, 1999, *U.S. Statutes at Large*, Vol. 106: 1778–1791.

22. Indian Dams Safety Act, P.L. 103-302, August 23, 1994. *U.S. Statutes at Large*, Vol. 108, Pt. 2: 1560–1563.

23. Sharon Illoway, "Lakota Gas Co. Only Indian-Owned Gas Firm in S.D.," *The CERT Report* 4, no. 2 (June 11, 1982): 10.

24. Richard La Course, "Amoco Sohio Seek 'Show Cause Hearing' on Wind River Cancellations," *The CERT Report* 4, no. 8 (July 9, 1982): 2.

25. Daniel Bomberry, "Browning-Ferris Industries Giving Indian Tribes Case of 'Toxic Shock,'" *The CERT Report* 4, no. 10 (August 10, 1982): 8.

26. Amelia W. Irvin, "Energy Development and the Effects of Mining on the Lakota Nation," *Journal of Ethnic Studies* 10, no. 1 (Spring 1982): 90–99.

27. "Report Says New Mexico Energy Development Creates Problems for Tribes," *The CERT Report* 4, no. 2 (February 8, 1982): 18.

28. "Havasupais Fighting Mine Plan," *Lakota Times*, January 10, 1989.

29. Indian Environmental General Assistance Program Act, P.L. 102-497, October 24, 1992, *U.S. Statutes at Large,* Vol. 106, Pt. 4: 3258–3262.

30. "Indian Lands Open Dump Cleanup Act," P.L. 103-399, October 22, 1994, *U.S. Statutes at Large,* Vol. 108, Pt. 5: 4164–4168.

31. Bill Barol and Lynda Wright, "Eco-Activist Summer," *Newsweek,* June 2, 1990, 60.

11

Indian Humor Then and Now

Sometimes it is good to begin things with a good joke. There is nothing like a good Indian joke that causes a spontaneous belly laugh that people cannot hold back. Spontaneously, they cannot help but to laugh. The timing is right and how the joke was told was superb. Among Indians and all groups of people, laughter is good for the spirit of a person and nourishes their well-being. We celebrate life when we have a good belly laugh. An example of this would be:

There are nice relatives and there are mean ones. I once had an uncle when I was a child that all of us cousins respected out of fear. He was mean to all of us kids and he did not have a pleasant personality. In fact, no one really liked him very much. He was that mean, kind of a nasty mean. He was that kind of mean. He was the type that you sometimes wished something bad would happen to him. Well, one day he was out hunting in the woods by himself. Eastern Oklahoma has thick woods of pecan trees, oak and brush, and snakes. Rattlesnakes! Yes, rattlesnakes! As my mean uncle walked in the woods that unforgettable day, a snake lay on a log. A rattle snake, just enormous and five feet long, bit him. For two days, the pain and agony was great! So much suffering occurred, hour after hour, and then finally the rattlesnake died!

STEREOTYPES

Indian people are quite the opposite from the stereotype of the stoic Indian with a stone face. You know the type, the cigar store Indian standing still like a statue. Yet, people who do not know Indians think that they are quiet, at least much quieter than the population of the mainstream in America. Nothing could be farther from the truth. The fact is that most people do not understand the reality of daily life among American Indians. They simply do not know Indians. The following are stories with insights into Indian reality on the fun side. But first we must get past the barriers of stereotypes and the fact of simply not knowing about American Indians.

Stereotypes about Indians are mostly negative. There are at least 38 negative stereotypes and only about 8 positive ones. "Red devil," "savage," "drunken Indian," "dirty savage," "wagon burner," and other negative phrases far outnumber positive stereotypes like "warrior," "steward of nature," "natural man," "environmentalist" or "ecologist." The sources of the typecast views, opinions, and sayings date back to the so-called Indian wars during the late 1600s through the 1800s. These stereotypes have been perpetuated by each generation of non-Indians, especially white Americans. They represent the first barrier to understanding Indian people and their sense of humor. Interestingly, stereotypes tell us more about the people who spout these typecast views. More specifically, they are about "images" of people. In not knowing the people, negative stereotypes have been created and perpetuated to vilify and suppress America's indigenous peoples.

INSIDE INDIAN HUMOR

Lakota activist and scholar Vine Deloria Jr. once said, "One of the best ways to understand a people is to know what makes them laugh."[1] Spontaneous laughter from the depth of a person reveals an insight into how that person sees things and other people. Unable to contain ourselves, hearty laughter exposes our values and bares our true feelings. What we laugh about demonstrates our honest views on any subject. This reveals so much when we cannot contain ourselves from suddenly laughing.

In a similar light, smiling also shows something of our view on humor, but it is not as telling about ourselves. A smile can be used as tactic of diplomacy and can hide one's true feelings. Unlike a hearty laugh, a smile can also be a disguise. A part of this disguise is the unreal laugh that might be used as an ice-breaker or a response in agreement to a statement from another person. Certainly these shallow laughs disguise or hide the feelings of one laughing in such a way.

Understanding Indians means learning about their various cultures and how they are different from tribe to tribe. Tribal traditions and values separate the identities of peoples who live in the same region. Their views, however, are similar due to similar environments in the same region. As a result, their values and what makes them laugh is similar as well. For example, Indians of the Great Lakes region tell jokes with cultural insights that Navajo sheepherders might not understand with the opposite also being true. An Ojibwa from Wisconsin might say they caught a walleye that was two feet long, which might impress a Navajo, while in truth that would be a small fish. On the other hand, a Navajo might brag about his Cherokee brother-in-law having 20 sheep and this would be a small number for most Navajos.

Because of the longevity of the oral tradition among American Indians, telling stories involving myths, legends, oratories, and plain gossip are the vehicles that bonded friends, relatives, and communities. Stories are the unifiers of Indian life. They connect the various parts of Indian life like glue. The power of the story lies in the persuasiveness of the storyteller who tells his or her story in a convincing manner. Embellishing the story, especially if it is a humorous one, is a way of making family and relatives laugh and drawing them closer together. Among Indians, everyone loves a good story.

THE HUMOROUS STORY

The source of Indian humor is "stories." Stories about life involving friends and relatives are the greatest evidence of Indian humor. Native Americans are great storytellers and it is in stories that Indians relive the past. Stories are about experiences involving Indian people, and humorous stories are about foolish things and experiences, such as the tale of the haunted bridge deep in Creek country in eastern Oklahoma. During moonless nights, a ghost rider would jump on the back of a horse, scaring the rider to death. And, it was a frequent happening that the ghost rider would attack! One individual, Asa Harjo, announced his bravery and said that he would kill the rider with his shotgun. Waiting for the appropriate night, he had a few drinks in town to muster his courage then hid his shotgun with a long coat as he rode his horse in the dark night towards the notorious bridge. The horse whinnied, feeling the extra strange weight of the ghost rider. Asa got excited, turned his gun behind him and fired both barrels of his shotgun. The horse reared, threw off Asa, and ran the next mile at a hundred miles an hour to the barn. Asa Harjo finally caught up, running scared all of the way. His wife rushing with a lantern met him in the barn to console the frightened horse that was shivering with fear in its stall. Asa proudly said that he shot the ghost rider as his wife walked around the horse and noticed something, she said, "You also shot off your horse's tail!"

EXTERNAL HUMOR

It is amazing that Indians remain a misunderstood culture. This is because there is much presumption about Indian people. People presume to know about American Indians when they really do not know what it is really like to be Indian. Misinformation and stereotypes, bad ones, are to blame. The first barrier to understanding Indians is stereotypes. Part of getting to know Indians is learning how other people treat them. To experience racism and prejudice is part of being Indian, and Indian people have learned to joke about this.

The forever "cultural gap" between Indians and non-Indians keeps native peoples from being properly understood. This cultural ignorance has maintained the distance between Indians and non-Indians. You have to want to care to begin to learn about real Indian life. Unfortunately most relations between Indians and whites have been marked by hostility on both sides. This hostility is most prominent between Indian and white communities that live close together, thus one can imagine the sayings, views, and jokes about the other side.

The second barrier is cultural ignorance. The rest of the world has criticized the United States for its mistreatment of its First Americans. Yet, Americans do not apologize for their ignorance of American Indians or the disrespect shown to them. Most Americans choose only to know things that pertain to their own life. Thus, learning about other people is not relevant in their views.

These two barriers, stereotypes and cultural ignorance, have maintained the cultural gap between Indians and whites. Yet, Indians can laugh at themselves for not knowing about unfamiliar ways of the white man. Indians who are too proud often find themselves the target of teasing. Indians have found that you have to be able to take a joke.

"Hoka Hey, you gotta have humor," said the Lakota veteran. "Did you hear the story about the relocated Indian who never used an elevator? This Indian just got to the big city, and had to go to the relocation office in a tall building. He never saw an elevator before, and was told to take the elevator to the relocation office on the fifth floor. As he looked at this elevator—at the small room with a button to the side on the wall, a man pushed passed him and rushed into the small room and the doors closed real quick. The Indian watched the dial move above the doors, and then it returned. The doors opened again, and a woman stepped out. The Indian said, 'Man, I'm not going in there, whatever this elevator is called.'" They all laughed, realizing that they all had done something like that when they came to the city. The Lakota veteran got up, smiling at his friends and then he high-fived them as they all laughed.[2]

HUMOR IN THE MEDIA

Indians have long been made fun of in many forms of media, from the television series *F Troop* to the "Poohawks," a dated comic strip in the Sunday newspaper. These efforts poked fun at the old "Cowboy and Indian" cliché, but it is hard for Indians to laugh when they hold the short end of the stick and are the butts of most jokes. For an Indian to tell jokes to other Indians is natural and funny, but for an Indian to tell funny jokes to people of other races and cultures and still be humorous is impressive. In most cases of Indians meeting non-Indians, it seems easier for the Indian person to break the ice. Even in the twentieth century, it seems many non-Indians do not know how to approach an Indian person, much less a group of American Indians.

So much has been said about the Lone Ranger and Tonto. Tonto is the Indian sidekick who the Lone Ranger always verbally kicked in the side when he needed to elevate his superiority while Tonto struggled with English to express himself. This popular radio show and television series of the 1960s finally went off the air, but the two characters became legends. They are also legends in Indian joking. When the Lone Ranger found himself surrounded by Indians threatening to kill him, he said to Tonto: "Tonto, we're surrounded by Indians." Tonto responded with an ironic grin, "what do you mean 'WE, white man!'"

In another Lone Ranger and Tonto joke, the hero cowboy finally asks, "Just what does kimo sabe mean?" "Hm, kimo-sabe, Lone Ranger," says Tonto, "kimo-sabe means, if you ask that dumb question again, I'm going to kick your butt!"

INDIAN COMEDIANS

Indian comedians are the front men of modern Indian humor. Notable native comedians like Charley Hill (Chippewa) and Vincent Craig (Navajo) have become famous. Originally from one of the Chippewa reservations in Wisconsin, Charley Hill has performed throughout Indian Country and in major cities like Los Angeles. He has shared the spotlight with other performers like Johnny Carson, Richard Pryor, and Steve Allen. The ultimate compliment has been paid to his comedic talent with a documentary about him, *On and Off the Res.*

Vincent Craig is another native show business talent who is a humorist, singer, and motivational speaker. He is the creator of the cartoon strip, "Muttonman" and has developed soundtracks for *Jerry's Song* and *The Awakening.* He has worked with the Navajo Nation Rodeo Cowboys Association and Boy Scouts of America, among many activities that concern the future of native youth.

Known nationally, the late Will Rogers, a mixed-blood Cherokee, was a humorist, storyteller, commentator, and jokester. Once asked about his heritage by a proud New Englander whose ancestors came over on the *Mayflower,* Rogers replied, "Well, I am not sure if I had any ancestors coming over on the Mayflower, but I know that I have some who met the boat."

Born in 1879 near Oolagah, Oklahoma, the famed Rogers died in a plane crash in 1935. He was raised on a ranch in northeast Indian Territory before Oklahoma became a state in 1907. Wild as a teenager, Rogers was willing to try anything that interested him. Perhaps, for his reason, he dropped out of high school in the tenth grade, but he went to school when most did not have a formal education, which became more of a privilege in the twentieth century. Rogers learned trick roping form a freed slave while he was growing up, and he became a cowboy showing his roping talent at rodeos. Entertaining appealed to the part Cherokee Indian, and his gregarious personality led to him becoming a star with the Ziegfeld Follies. Becoming nationally known, Rogers was a humorist and syndicated newspaper columnist during the 1920s. As his reputation grew, people also enjoyed his humor as a radio commentator as he helped the radio to become a focal point for families who listened and learned about what was happening in their area and in the country. Rogers's engaging personality earned him invitations to the White House and friendship with celebrities of his time. Of many talents, he traveled around the world three times, wrote six books, and starred in 71 motion pictures before his untimely death. Funny, quick-witted, intelligent, and captivating, Rogers found humor during the difficult years of the Great Depression. Described in various roles as a Cherokee, cowboy, comedian, national figure, and legend, Rogers is famously known for having said, "I never met a man I didn't like."

PLACES OF HUMOR

Indian humor occurs at various places where Indian people gather on a regular basis. Similar to a barber shop or beauty salon, Indian bars, front porches of a home, or the actual site of a funny story are conducive to producing Indians laughter. Each story involves a place with characters interacting with a humorous outcome.

Indian bars are a typical location where much socialization occurs. Some of these sites have become legendary, although some have been closed for many years. The Red Race in Oklahoma City was one such famous bar. Other bars are in the San Francisco Bay Area; the Twin Cities; Gallup, New Mexico; and other urban areas, such as the Shrimp Boat bar in Los Angeles. The list goes on and on.

The important point here is that Indians enjoy the company of other Indians. It is possible to become intoxicated with the camaraderie of friendship. They are friends joking, teasing and enjoying each other's company, especially in a group. This is Indian humor. Laughing in a group where one funny story leads to another one.

When one imagines where Indian humor might exist, it is on the proverbial "Reservation." Indians enjoy making jokes about other Indians and of themselves. Such follies about Indians have a set scene that seems to naturally involve Indian Country, on the nearly 300 Indian reservations throughout the United States.

COYOTE THE TRICKSTER

Trickster tales have been told inside many lodges during winter and on front porches of Indian homes. These accounts are old stories passed down that the present generation does not always find funny, but young people may laugh or smile out of respect about their ancestors using Coyote, the Great Hare, and other animal characters that exemplified humor of the past.

Coyote is the focus of many stories and he is the butt of many jokes. This character is like Wile E. Coyote in the television cartoons. Yet, Coyote has been around for many generations among Indian people. He is human-like and the person that things can be blamed on.

Among the Pubelo tribes, the "clown" is another focal point of humor. He is a being much like Coyote and he represents the irony and truth of society. In this way, the Pueblo learn to laugh at themselves and to not take themselves too seriously. The clown keeps social and cultural norms defined so that the members of the community are reminded of the true way that they were meant to live as a peaceful and respectful people.

Among the plains Indians, the "Heyoka" person who does the opposite of the cultural norms, is a humorous figure. Heyoka is the abnormal and, with the normal, there is a balance in society.

NEED FOR LAUGHTER

We make fun of ourselves to get by in life. We need to make fun of ourselves because of a dire situation that leaves us no other way to respond. Feeling helpless, we make fun of ourselves, but we are not hopeless. Giving in to humble humor is recognition that enough is enough and that something has to be done about getting out of the bad situation.

Poverty is so prevalent among Indian communities that it has become integral to Indian humor. Humor is a means of escape from the white man's reality that has imposed its values on Indian people and measures Indians against white standards. It is an answer to poverty; not the best one, but at least it is a response.

The proverbial "Indian car" is a regular in Indian humor. Indian car jokes are best told when this ethnic automobile is on a reservation. Typically, one Indian might tell tease another that he saw his Indian car sitting at a pawn shop with its one good headlight held together with duct tape, its hubcaps missing, and its fender attached to its old rusted body with baling wire. Do you get the picture? The description goes on and on. Or, it might be a pickup such as a Dakota pickup and the joke becomes more complex with a Crow Indian driving the pickup; he might say that he drove that Dakota to death or that the Dakota finally let him down and would not start.

In the same proverbial sense, the Indian car never dies. Somehow with Indian ingenuity, lots of duct tape and baling wire, the Indian car keeps going like the Energizer Bunny. In 1972 at the AIM takeover of the Bureau of Indian Affairs (BIA), a group of reporters interviewed Floyd Young Horse, a Minneconjou from Eagle Butte, South Dakota, "because of his classic, full-blood face, his red-wrapped braids, and his fine sense of humor. He told reporters he had come in [to Washington] in an 'Indian car' with so many things wrong with it that it shouldn't be up and running at all, but somehow 'its spirit was keeping it going.'"[3]

NICKNAMES AND NAME BRAND HUMOR

Several automobile makers have named models of their cars after American Indians. General Motors Pontiac, Jeep Grand Cherokee, Mazda Navajo, Dodge Dakota, and others carry on the tradition of the Indian car because Indian people use them in jokes. Even the impressive large recreational vehicle, called the Winnebago, is named after an Indian tribe. But why is there no Mercedes Geronimo, or Jaguar Eskimo? At the same time, military hardware has been named after Indians, such as the Apache attack helicopter and the Black Hawk helicopter indicate a "don't mess with me" attitude.

Indian named things in American society describe native peoples in a humorous way. For example, an Indian man who wears an Arrow brand shirt, chews his Red Man tobacco, drives his Dakota pickup, throws down an Andrew Jackson on the counter for a ticket to an exhibition baseball game to watch the Cleveland Indians play the Atlanta Braves in Sioux City, Iowa. Naturally, his wife is named Sue and she is Sioux. As a matter of fact, the Cleveland Indians beat the old Boston Braves, four games to two in the World Series in 1948.

Sometimes the Indian car has a bumper sticker saying, "Custer had it coming!" Bumper stickers are another area of Indian humor. "Red Power!" is an old one that made more sense during the 1960s and 1970s. "Red Power" implied a political statement that Indians were not going to stand by anymore and be told what to do. They would exercise control over their own lives, but the humorous irony is that not a lot has changed since the last 30 or 40 years since the popularity of this bumper sticker. "Fry Bread Power!" is a forever laugh as a reminder that fry bread is a part of most Indian life, especially on the rez.

Fry bread for its easy recipe to make has become a mainstay in American Indian families and you will see it frequently on dinner tables when light bread is not available, usually when someone forgets to get bread at the store. Fry bread become contentious when someone may say she can make fry bread better than anyone. And, a retort might be that "my brother can make fry bread better than you." Since fry bread is almost an Indian universal, it is a way of teasing women about their ability to make it. Mock insults might include that your fry bread looks like a hub cap on an Indian car or that your fry bread can fill the pot hole on the such and such road.

INDIAN TIME

When other people make fun of us, it is not Indian humor. It is ridicule. For example the most worn out joke about Indians is "Indian time." The put-down is that Indians are always late. They are never on time because they never have a watch, and even when they have one, they are still late. Clock time is not important to them because they use to tell time by looking at the position of the sun, and if it was cloudy, then it was okay to be late. Or, Indians use to tell time by the position of the stars or moon at night. One Comanche Indian, when you asked him what time it was, would lean towards a window to check the sun, and then look at his watch in a teasing way before telling you that Mickey's big hand was holding the sun's nose, so that it was about 12:15, just after noon. This is an Indian Rolex watch.

In response to Indian time, Indians claim that whites invented flex time that allows them to be fashionably late. They are not on time either, but it has become a joke among whites that Indians are always late.

White paranoia might possibly explain why such jokes on Indians like Indian time. This is another means of suppressing Indians. It is interesting that whites become a bit uneasy when they see two Indians, mostly Indian men standing somewhere talking. And, they really "look" like Indians! A white person really gets nervous when there are three or four gathered on a street corner. While on the Indian side of this scenario, you can almost hear an imaginary Indian flute beginning to play and then it is replaced by imaginary Indian drumming that gets louder with the increasing nervousness of the white person. You can imagine the heart of the white person beating louder than the imaginary Indian drum. The white feels like Custer when the Indians were going to attack. But, history tells us that Custer attacked first! Who knows, may be Custer got scared, knowing that he was way outnumbered and thought he should attack first. This is like the two greenhorn soldiers in the Cavalry who were thinking about the government's posting saying that $2 would be paid for every pair of Apache ears brought in. As they were riding, not paying attention, and talking about this, they suddenly found themselves surrounded by Apaches! One soldier says to the other, "Hey Jake, look! We're going to be rich!"

INDIAN TEASING

Only Indians can make fun of other Indians, and even this might go too far. In light humor, Indians teasing other Indians strengthens the bond of Indian to Indian. Indian to Indian is seeing someone else who looks physically like you. Someone who is brown skinned with black hair. In this Indian togetherness, it is knowing the other person has endured experiences very similar to you, grew up like you, and identifies with being Indian without having to try to do so.

Indian-to-Indian teasing is a way of testing a relationship such as among cousins and best friends. These gentle put-downs are humorous and mean no real harm. Mostly, they are stories about the other person making a blunder, so that the joke is specifically retelling an experience that happened that had a funny outcome.

In a similar light, there are Indian men and Indian women jokes. The notorious one is the various kinds of Indian women such as the Navajo woman who will walk several paces behind her man. The mixed-blood Cherokee woman will walk beside her husband, feeling equal to him. And the Sioux woman will walk right over her man!

ONE-LINERS

Borrowed white jokes are mostly one-liners levied at particular tribes. For example, the ancient tribal rivalries invite one-line jokes of a Hopi about the Navajos, like "how many Navajos does it take to screw in a light bulb?" A Navajo might ask, "What is three feet tall and a mile long? A Pueblo Grand Entry." These put-downs include an Ojibwa teasing about the Lakota, and vice versa. Lakota having Crow jokes. And, Creeks versus Cherokees. This list of "them" jokes goes on and are obviously most funny when told among a group of Indians sharing the same joke about another tribe.

In addition, one-line quips, quick shots, or pot-shots are mainstream jokes borrowed by Indians. This modern Indian practice is post-1960s with mostly mixed-bloods using this kind of humor.

TRIBE VERSUS TRIBE

These tribal jokes against other tribes might be short stories to put down the other tribe in a humorous way. One Lakota friend tells a story about a group of Crow Indians. He describes that one day the leader of a group of Crow saw a one-eyed dog walking across their path behind them. He said to his Crow friends, "look at that dog behind us with one eye." At that point all of the Crow Indian in the group covered one of their eyes and looked at the dog!

US AND THEM

Indian-on-white joking is taking sides of "us and them." The age-old rift continues between Indians and whites, and jokes have become a part of this cultural and racial difference. Hostilities between Indians and whites have been a long part of their combined history, and humor has become a reminder of these ill relations. The trite joke about whites is that anyone wanting to be Indian says to an Indian that he or she had a grandmother of royalty like a princess and that they think that they are part Cherokee; hence the old Cherokee Princess joke. Get it? So, why does the white man in this case want to be part Indian? The Indian response is for the white man not to cut his little finger on his hand because he might lose all of his Indian blood. Beyond the joking, the wish of "wanna-bes" to experience Indian life is a means of escaping white reality or seeking something that the white world does not offer, such as comfort in finding identity with the natural world. In the face of a psychological need such as this, Indians have something that whites want.

Making fun of anthropologists is a popular target of Indian joking. Because of the continual presence of anthropologists studying Indian people in their communities, the notorious anthropologist has become the butt of countless Indian jokes. An old joke is about the extended Indian family that includes the mother, father, children, a grandparent, and an anthropologist. In modern Indian times, Christmas shopping involves getting presents for everyone in the family, including the anthropologist who hangs out nearby. Because anthropologists have continually exploited Indian people for their own personal gain of writing articles, books, and advancing their careers, there are few native anthropologists.

Vine Deloria Jr. writes that "Into each life, it is said, some rain must fall. Some people have bad horoscopes; others take tips on the stock market. . . . But Indians have been cursed above all other people in history. Indians have anthropologists."[4] But what does an anthropologist look like? Deloria says that

anthropologists can readily be identified on the reservations. Go into any crowd of people. Pick out a tall gaunt white man wearing Bermuda shorts, a World War II Army Air Force flying jacket, an Australian bush hat, tennis shoes, packing a large knapsack incorrectly strapped on his back. He will invariably have a thin sexy wife with stringy hair, an IQ of 191, and a vocabulary in which even the prepositions have eleven syllables. . . . This creature is an anthropologist.[5]

Columbus, Custer, and the BIA are favorite white man targets for Indians poking fun.[6] All three are about being inept. They are incompetent and act stupidly such as the so-called "discovery" of America by Christopher Columbus when Indians were already here. Indians say that they are lucky that Columbus was not looking for Turkey or the Virgin Islands, or else we would be called Turkeys or Virgins! So, what did Custer tell the Indian agent of the BIA before he left to fight the Sioux and Cheyenne at the Little Bighorn? "Don't do anything until I get back!" And the BIA has not done anything since then. Charley Hill's one-liners about Christopher Columbus are an ironic response to the hundreds of years of white mistreatment against Indians. Hill's one-line quips about Columbus—"Goin' Stay Long?" and "Well, there goes the neighborhood!"—remind us that this was only the beginning of the taking of Indian lands by whites. When asked, "what did Indians call America before Columbus arrived, Charley Hill replied, "Ours!"

White oppression of Indians has been a regular target in general for Indian joking, especially in regard to missionaries. Indians remind the larger mainstream about the truth while stating this in a pun or joking statement that often has an ironic edge to it, for example, the white man arrived with a book and Indians had the land, now Indians have the book and the white man has the land. Such an ironic reminder pokes at colonialism and how Christians attempted to save the souls of the "heathen" Indians.

Trying to understand the white man has perplexed many Native Americans and after 500 years of contact, Indians have learned much about their historical suppressor. As a result, Indians have white man jokes like the ones mentioned about Columbus, Custer, and the BIA. But, mainly these types of jokes confirm the Indian effort to try to understand the white man who is often Coyote, the trickster. In fact, many Indians are married to whites, so does this mean that they are married to Coyote?

Among the Western Apache, the white man is an "abstraction" of complicated ideas and values that has caused great confusion for them.[7] The white man is a cultural construct that is everything that is not Indian. Like the contrary in the Heyoka among the Plains tribes, the white man is the opposite and is Coyote who changes his mind and his only objective is what he desires. One time a white rancher and an Indian stood side by side on the rancher's huge spread of hundreds of thousands of acres. The white rancher said proudly, "I have a pickup and I can drive on my ranch for an entire day in one direction and finally reach the end of my land." The Indian looking in the same westerly direction as the sun was going down said pointedly, "You know, I used to have a pickup like that too!"

Indians laugh at this joke and find it funny and ironic. While whites might not think it is funny, Indians have learned to laugh at themselves. The humor is about the pickup since many Indians like owning trucks and the irony is the loss of so much Indian land to the white man.

CONCLUSION

Finally, this is the way Indians are. Being Indian is realizing that you are different from other people, different in a cultural context. In this way, being Indian is learning to laugh at yourself and your own situation. Sometimes, it is making a joke about yourself before the other person does. Indians laugh as much as they cry and feel sad. They laugh because they need to, and sometimes because they do not know what else to do. Sometimes it is the only thing to do when you have almost run out of tears. There is very little difference between the emotional threads of crying and laughing. It is like a fine thin line that is the difference. Tears are involved in both emotions. This human emotion of laughing has sustained Indian people throughout time. It is a way of survival.

Indian humor is also being an optimist in the white man's world. It is being a minority in the mainstream and trying to break the ice to let non-Indians know that you are approachable and that you are just like them. Without humor, the confines of Indian stereotypes and cultural ignorance will continue. To Indians, it is how much they want others to know them. How much do they want to expose of ourselves? Their true feelings? Indians often protect themselves to hide their true feelings, perhaps because this is one of the few remaining things that has not been exploited by other people. Indian-to-Indian or Indians among Indians is an ethnic setting in which only Indians can make fun, tease, or joke in an Indian way about other Indians. It is about identity. It is also about being a minority or person of color in the American mainstream where other people do not look like you. Indian humor when shared is sharing emotions with others. And Indians certainly do not want others laughing at them because that has been done too long, for centuries. Indian humor is the ability to be flexible while sometimes feeling powerless against the government and cultural mainstream in control of your life. Indian humor is being among Indians who are laughing and there is nothing else like it in the world.

NOTES

1. Vine Deloria Jr., *Custer Died for Your Sins: An Indian Manifesto* (Norman: University of Oklahoma Press, 1988), 146; originally published in 1968.

2. Donald L. Fixico, *The Urban Indian Experience in America* (Albuquerque: University of New Mexico Press, 2000), 188–89.

3. Dennis Banks with Richard Erdoes, *Ojibwa Warrior: Dennis Banks and the Rise of the American Indian Movement* (Norman: University of Oklahoma Press, 2004), 136.

4. Deloria, *Custer Died for Your Sins*, 78.

5. Ibid., 79.

6. See chapter on "Humor" in ibid., 146–67.

7. Keith H. Basso, *Portraits of 'The Whiteman': Linguistic Play and Cultural Symbols among the Western Apache* (Cambridge: Cambridge University Press, 1979), 4, reprinted 1980.

12

Bingos, Casinos, and Indian Gaming

Indian gaming has introduced a new era of American Indian history and tribal relations with other peoples. This modern entrepreneurship is a dynamic force that is changing the economics of Indian Country and other communities nearby. In this new world of tribal capitalism, American Indian leaders and their nations are independently altering the course of their history and that of the United States. As a spin-off from Indian self-determination of the 1970s, Indian gaming has resulted from the initiative and resourceful thinking of tribal leaders to emulate the casino owners in Las Vegas, Reno, and Atlantic City. They learned how gambling operated in the mainstream, although games and gambling was much a part of their tribal pasts.

INDIAN GAMES

Among the many Indian nations, the communities play various games of sport and chance. Some of these games date back to prehistoric years. The Cherokee played a game of marbles that archeological evidence dates to A.D. 800. This evidence left clues of a field about 100 feet long contained five holes approximately 10 to 12 yards apart in an L-shape. Players tossed billiard-size balls at the holes with the first team to complete the course being the winning side. Each side had two to four players, and tournaments were held with many teams.[1]

Other Indian games of chance included the Crow plum pit game. Historically and contemporarily Native Americans have been and are

Indians from Columbia Tribe, Colville Reservation, playing a game of chance. Courtesy of Library of Congress.

Navajo Indian and cowboy playing cards. Courtesy of Library of Congress.

great sportsmen. Native peoples enjoy playing games for the pleasure of socialization and solidifying friendships and communities. Indians of the West are great horsemen and horse racing has been one of the ways that plains peoples loved to bet.

Among native peoples, the Nez Perce are well known for breeding Appaloosa horses and many of the 28 Plains tribes are known for their expert equestrianism. Although the Comanche command considerable recognition for their equestrian ability, it remains an unsafe bet to say who are the fastest horsemen among the Indians of the West. Furthermore, Indians and horses changed the West in its course of development.

Games of skill have been prized by Indian people. Victory in most cases came second to the playing experience, which was substantiated by enjoyable anxiety. In surveying the traditional games of chance among American Indians, the dice game was played by an estimated 130 tribes. Roughly 80 tribes played the hand game, and an estimated 60 played the stick game, and about 30 played the moccasin game.[2]

ORIGIN OF BINGO

Bingo developed in Venice, Italy, about 1530 as a common game with numerous versions. Different communities called it "Loo," "housey-housey," or "lotto." As a game combined of letters and numbers on a square playing sheet, Europeans played the game in central Europe in the late nineteenth and early twentieth centuries. An American traveling in Germany whose name has become lost brought some cards and a bag of beans, carrying them back to the small town of Jacksonville, Georgia, just south of Atlanta. He referred to the game as "beano" from using coffee beans placed on the designated squares. The caller picked small wooden disks from a cigar box and called out the numbers. The players placed a bean on the correct number, if they had it. The objective of the game called for completing a line of numbers in either a diagonal, horizontal, or vertical direction. At the same time, you had to be the first successful person calling out "beano!" The prizes during these times were not grand, actually they were quite modest. Typically, the winner won a small Kewpie doll as a prize. The players paid a nickel and the beano caller supervised a game of 12 players. The Kewpie doll was worth about a nickel, enabling the beano caller to earn a 55 cent profit, a good sum during the Great Depression of the 1930s.[3]

Edwin Lowe, a 19-year-old toy salesman from New York, observed beano being played at a county fair. The son of a Polish Orthodox rabbi who came to America, Edwin Lowe was ready to make his way in the new country called the United States. Lowe was bored by the fair at Jacksonville and began to walk towards his Nash automobile to drive north on U.S. 1 when a long line of people caught his attention. Why was there a long line of people waiting to go into a tent with laughter and excitement coming from it? Lowe went inside the town and watched all of the excitement until he got his chance to play. He spent several nickels, despite not winning one game, but the game captured his imagination. He bought a handful of cards from the game supervisor and took them back to New York. He created his own game cards, bought some dried beans, and invited some guests over to play. He called out numbers from a cigar box. One of the players, a young woman, caught onto the game with enthusiasm. She got five beans in a row as the first player, but in her excitement she forgot what to do and the name of the game. Guessing what to shout, she yelled out "bingo!" Lowe recalled later in an interview that at that moment, he decided he would call this game "bingo." He traveled to the patent office to register the Bingo trademark, but was unsuccessful. At some point, Lowe showed his game to a parish priest of a Catholic Church in Wilkes-Barre, Pennsylvania, who saw the promising potential of the game to fill up his church's social hall with people. The Catholic Church became the first big customer of Lowe's idea as it bought bingo cards from his 226 presses in 1934 with 1,000 employees printing cards around the clock. By 1934, roughly 10,000 bingo games were being played each week throughout the United States.

EARLY INDIAN BINGO

The first noted Indian bingo began in Florida with the Seminole Indians. The successful business venture for the Seminoles started with a cigarette shop opened along U.S. 441 in 1975. Soon cars from Fort Lauderdale and Boca Raton brought customers to purchase tax-free cigarettes for $5.50 a carton. The State of Florida lost $2.10 on each carton; the total loss amounted to $2,456,769 from April 1977 to February 1978. The public criticized that the Seminoles were earning money from the addiction of people to smoking, but untaxed cigarettes were also obtained in Florida from military installations and veterans' hospitals who offered untaxed packs, and people could buy them mail order from North Carolina.[4]

With the cigarette business becoming a success, the Florida Seminole Tribe began contemplating bingo as another enterprise. Tribal representatives approached the Bureau of Indian Affairs (BIA) for funding for a bingo hall and government officials refused them. Then, banks refused the Seminoles based on the fact that they could not foreclose on tribal cigarette shops that were in trust status as federal property. Seminole representatives then contacted Eugene "Butch" Weisman and George Simon in 1977. Weisman and Simon, two white businessmen, had been successful in raising $2.5 million for the Seminole Tribe earlier to build a new drive-in facility for the tribe's cigarette business.[5]

In the extreme opposite part of the country, members of the Puyallup tribe in Washington approved of a proposal for casino-type gambling on their reservation. In an unofficial vote of 134 against 89, voters passed the referendum. The Puyallups had more than 400 tribal members who were eligible to vote. By early March, 1979, the tribe submitted their "gaming code" to the Department of Interior for review and approval. Assistant U.S. Attorney Chris McKenna commented that should the Department of the Interior approve of the Puyallup proposal, a precedent would be set for nationwide gambling operations on trust lands throughout Indian Country. Although tribal members had set up individually owned casinos against federal authority, resulting in raids, fines, and convictions, this time the tribe sought federal support and approval. Silas Cross Jr., Chairman of the tribe's gambling commission, believed that gambling could begin later in the summer of 1979.[6]

During these months, the Puyallup Tribe moved their plans for a bingo into action. As soon as news about the Puyallups' gambling proposal became public, the mayor of Tacoma and other officials expressed their opposition. Mayor Mike Parker said that he opposed any casino in Tacoma "because the city would have no control over it."[7]

In the following weeks, Interior Secretary Cecil D. Andrus responded to Senator Henry Scoop Jackson's effort and that of his supporters to halt Puyallup gaming. A powerful U.S. Senator representing Washington in Indian affairs, Jackson had campaigned to run for the U.S. presidency in 1972. The secretary stated that the Assistant Secretary of Indian Affairs had met with the Puyallup Tribal Council on March 27, and that the tribe had "rescinded the gambling code it had earlier prepared, and that the Tribe will not be entering into any type of casino gambling." The Puyallup cited that they did not want to violate federal law, even in regard to card games permitted under Washington State law. Furthermore, secretary Andrus stated that the gaming move was not consistent with the tribal laws and constitution of the Puyallup and with federal law. The secretary cited that the Assimilative Crimes Act applied to Indian reservations, prohibiting gambling within state boundaries which "would be prohibited under similar terms and conditions on an Indian reservation within that state."[8]

FIRST INDIAN BINGO

At the opposite end of the country, the Seminole Tribe pushed forward with their plan to open a bingo operation. The Seminole Tribe negotiated an agreement with Eugene "Butch" Weisman and George Simon to locate financial backers for opening a bingo hall on the Hollywood Reservation, located north of Miami. The agreement called for a split of 45 percent to the financial backers and 55 percent to the Seminole Tribe. Plans called for a bingo hall to accommodate 1,500 players, complete with valet parking, security guards, closed-circuit television, a large announcement board, and climate control. All of this was to be established at Stirling Road and U.S. 441 on the 480-acre Hollywood Reservation, with the doors to open for business in December 1979. The price of admission was $15, but a person could also purchase chances to win from $10,000 to $110,000. Soon, bingo players came by the busloads from as far north as Jacksonville and as far west as St. Petersburg.[9]

Within the first six months, the Florida Seminoles were operating a profitable bingo operation. An estimated 1,200 peopled crowded into the bingo hall, and the Seminoles learned to pamper the players with valet parking, waitresses serving drinks, and armed escorts to players' cars after collecting their winnings. The super jackpot ran as high as $19,000 per night. The Seminoles chartered buses to pick up players as far away as Tampa, who spent an average of $35 per night. In early July, Chief James E. Billie speculated that the tribe would earn $1.5 million, after paying 45 percent of the earnings to Weisman, who held a partnership with the Seminole Tribe.

Since the 1980s American Indian nations and their governments have aroused considerable controversy and support when they entered the gambling industry. When the Seminoles of Florida opened the first bingo hall in 1979, an important precedent occurred to begin a renewed era of American Indian capitalism. Other Indian nations soon followed in opening bingo operations, and many people believed this was acceptable. Others said that it was wrong. Then, Indian gaming operations took off at an explosive rate in the 1990s. In the early 1990s, gaming tribes earned $1.5 to $2.5 billion annually, and by 1999 the intake has risen to over $7 billion a year. By the year 2000, 212 tribes of 558 federally recognized tribes were in business of gaming in 24 states.

CRITICS

Gambling. Should people make their living by it? Is it okay, and legitimate? Is it legal? How is it legal for Indians? Is there a morality involved? What is the government's role? Should Indian tribes benefit from people, including their own, who are addicted to gambling? These are some of the questions raised involving Native Americans and gambling. Everyone seems to have a view on the subject. Many do not understand all that is involved. Due to its controversial nature, this subject of bingos and casinos in Indian Country has provoked the American public and Indian opinions across the United States and into Canada.

In regard to Indian gaming and the future, Colorado's former Republican U.S. Senator Ben Nighthorse Campbell, a Northern Cheyenne, expressed serious concern about Indian values. He remarked about a white backlash of society criticizing that Indians do not have to work because of casino money available to them. "When I see kids, come to a small rural school with $100 bills in their pockets . . . believe me, it creates some problems in the community," Campbell said. "We need to make sure out kids don't lose their way with the greenbacks," said the senator. He worried that some Indian children did not care about furthering their education or decided against going to college because of casino payments distributed to them by their tribe.[10]

In general, gambling is legal in 48 states (except for Hawaii and Utah). In 1994 nearly 100 million Americans gambled $400 billion. Now Las Vegas, Reno, and Atlantic City have to contend with state-authorized casinos and lotteries, where a person can win as much as $100 million. Indian bingos and casinos took in a sizeable portion of the sum spent for 1994, and they continue to do so every year in their more than 125 bingos and casinos, with more scheduled to open. By the end of the twentieth century, Indian gaming had become a part of a new Indian culture. This direction of Native American capitalism caused much discussion and criticism voiced against Indian gaming and Indian people.

Undoubtedly Indian gambling is complex and problematic. Indian gambling involves many people and interests. Governmental interests are involved at the federal, state, tribal, and local levels. Religious groups that operate bingos, other gambling organizations, and even state lotteries, have a stake in the matter. Native American economies are directly affected, but the sudden impact of the success of Indian gaming has also affected local and state economies, and has conflicted with local ordinances and state laws. As the holder of trust responsibilities to Native American tribal governments, the federal government is legally involved to protect the Indian interest. And, within the Indian communities, people are divided over the gambling operations on whether it is morally right or wrong, how they are ran, who is actually benefiting, and a host of other concerns. But, since the passage of the Indian Gaming Regulatory Act in 1988, a National Indian Gaming Commission (located in Washington, D.C.) has been set up and tribes are required to negotiate state compacts with state governments to introduce new gaming operations. These operations are opened according to three categories of gaming.

Class I gaming included traditional forms of Indian gambling usually a part of tribal celebrations and social games for minimal prizes. Class II involved bingo and card games for prizes. Class III included casino gambling, especially baccarat, blackjack, and slot machines. The National Indian Gaming Commission was set up to supervise Class II and III gaming.[11]

THE SEMINOLE CASE

The first test case of Indian bingo involved the Seminoles of Florida, in *Seminole Tribe of Florida v. Butterworth*, 658 F.2d 310 (1981), 246.[12] In this case the State of Florida challenged the right of the Florida Seminoles to operate a bingo operation. The Seminoles had started a bingo operation, which became highly profitable. Florida claimed that it must conform to bingo operations according to Florida Statute that "authorized bingo games operated by certain religious, charitable, and civic groups so long as the entire proceeds from the game were used by the organizations for charity."[13] The court ruled in favor of the Seminoles that the State of Florida had no authority to regulate the Indian bingo operation.

CABAZON CASE

On March 3, 1983, in Riverside County in Southern California, the Cabazon Tribe of 25 enrolled members opened Cabazon Bingo Palace for the first time as they entered in the gambling business. For three years, the Cabazon Band operated a bingo room according to a management agreement with an outside firm until 1986. The Morongo Band of about 730 enrolled members had a similar agreement, Morongo Band of Mission Indians Tribal Bingo Enterprise Management Agreement, in running its bingo operation. An Executive Order of the president created the Cabazon Reservation on May 15, 1876, and a similar reservation was created for the Morongo Band of Mission Indians in the same manner.

In California, the local and county governments regulated card games because they were legal. On May 6, 1983, the Riverside County Sheriff closed down the Cabazon gambling establishment and Judge Waters issued a preliminary injunction against the county. The Cabazon tribe received bad publicity when a takeover was attempted by Wayne Reeder, Peter Zokosky, John Patrick McGuire, and Jimmy Hughes and the conflict was reported on Geraldo Rivera 20/20 show. On February 25, 1987, the U.S. Supreme Court ruled that high-stakes bingo and other gaming on Indian reservations could not be regulated by state and local governments, if state law allows such forms of gaming by anyone.[14]

Furthermore, the State of California argued that it was one of the original five states under P.L. 280. This law gave the right of criminal and civil jurisdiction over Indian reservations within its boundaries. States tried to intervene into the locked relationship of federal–Indian relations.

In 1987 unregulated "high stakes" bingo faced a serious test in the court case, *Cabazon Band of Mission Indians et al. v. California*, 480 U.S. 202 (1987), 205, 215, 247.[15] In this case, two Indian groups or communities, the Cabazon and Morongo Bands of Mission Indians, opened successful bingo operations in Riverside County, California. The State of California contested the bingo operations when the Cabazon Band opened a card club, offering draw poker and other card games to the public, which was predominately non-Indians. The State of California sought to apply two state ordinances, Cal. Penal Code Ann. §326.5 (West Suppl. 1987), although the statute did not prohibit the playing of bingo.

On February 25, 1987, the Supreme Court of the United States handed down a major decision in favor of Indian gaming tribes. Justice Byron White stated the ruling of the Court with Chief Justice Rehnquist and Justices William Brennan, Margaret Marshall, Harry Blackmun, and Lewis Powell in agreement. Opposed opinions included Justices John Stevens, Sandra Day O'Connor, and Antonin Scalia.

FOXWOODS

The Mashantucket Pequot's Foxwoods Resort and Casino in Connecticut stands today as the grandest of Indian gaming casinos. It has grown rapidly since its inception. One day after the Fourth of July in 1986, the Pequot opened their doors for bingo. Congressman Sam Gejdenson cut the red ribbon to officially open the bingo parlor with closed-circuit television, electronic scoreboards, and fried-chicken dinners for players. Thousands of New Englanders passed through the doors to play bingo. The crowds did not stop coming to Ledyard to gamble. By the end of 1987, the Pequot bingo parlor grossed $20 million a year with 25 percent accounting for pure profit. The tribal population stood at about 100 members, which resulted in an estimated $60,000 for every man, woman, and child on the reservation. Foxwoods had become the world's most profitable casino by the end of the twentieth century.

The man behind the growing Pequot gaming empire was Richard "Skip" Hayward. Born the day after Thanksgiving in 1947, Skip was one of nine children of Theresa Plouffe Hayward. Theresa Plouffe had married Richard Hayward, a navy man. While Richard Hayward served in the navy, the family lived at Quonset Point, Rhode Island. Theresa brought her young, large family to visit their grandmother at the reservation. Skip recalled the difficult conditions, of cold floors, thin walls, and no hot water or electricity. His grandmother's house had been built in 1856. Skip's father intended for his son to attend the U.S. Naval Academy, but at the final hour, Skip was convinced that the navy would send him to Vietnam. Upon graduation from high school in North Kingston, Rhode Island, Skip went to work for $229 a week as a pipe fitter and welder at Electric Boat, a submarine manufacturer, in Groton. During these years, Skip spent more time with his grandmother, who died on the reservation on June 6, 1973. Skip received his Indian blood from his mother's side, placing his blood quantum at about one-sixteenth.[16]

Skip Hayward had visited the Seminoles in Florida to observe how they had built their casinos. With their advice in mind, he set out to obtain federal recognition for the Mashantucket Pequot tribe and to build a casino. He did both with much work and careful business strategy. Following the expansion of Foxwoods, Hayward set out to build a tribal museum for the Pequot. At a near cost of $200, this venture succeeded as well. Tribal politics among the Pequot led to his stepping down from the leadership of his tribe and he turned his attention to run his personal business.

THE INDIAN GAMING REGULATORY ACT

Two events helped to bring about a final act of Congress to settle the growing differences between states and tribes. The Democrats regained control of the Senate in 1986, which helped to enable Senator Daniel Inouye (D-HI) to replaced Senator Mark Andrews (R-ND) as chairman of the Select Committee on Indian Affairs. During October 1986, Senator Andrews introduced an amendment to H.R. 1920. Andrews claimed that his amendment gave states more control over Class III gaming. In response, Inouye strongly advocated the protection of Indian sovereignty.[17]

The second event involved the declining health of Representative Morris Udall (D-AZ), who told his staff that he did not believe that he could effectively be a part of the committee. As a result, he chose to go along with the new legislation.[18]

On February 19, 1987, Senator Inouye introduced S. 555, six days before the Supreme Court decided the landmark *Cabazon* case. On the floor of the Senate, Inouye stated,

The issue has never really been one of crime control, morality, or economic fairness. . . . At issue is economics. At present Indian tribes may have a competitive economic advantage. . . . Ironically, the strongest opponents of tribal authority over gaming on Indian lands are from States whose liberal gaming politics would allow them to compete on an equal basis with the tribes. . . . We must not impost greater moral restraints on Indians than we do on the rest of our citizenry.[19]

On September 15, 1988, the Senate passed S. 555 in a voice vote. Eleven days later, the House of Representatives voted on the bill. Representative Udall called S. 555 a "delicately balanced compromise" and said that while he understood the frustration of Indians, he "felt that this bill is probably the most acceptable legislation that could be obtained given the circumstances." On September 27, the House passed the bill by a vote of 323 to 84 and President Reagan signed S. 555 into law on October 17, 1988, resulting in Public Law 100-497, the Indian Gaming Regulatory Act (IGRA).[20]

The IGRA defined three kinds of gambling: Class I gaming included traditional forms of Indian gambling usually a part of tribal celebrations and social games for minimal prizes. Class II involved bingo and card games for prizes. Class III included casino gambling, especially baccarat, blackjack, and slot machines. The National Indian Gaming Commission was set up to supervise Class II and III gaming.[21]

In addition, the IGRA is an act "to establish federal standards and regulations for the conduct of gaming activities within Indian country;" [and] "as a means of promoting tribal economic development, self-sufficiency, and strong tribal governments," "to shield it [Indian gaming] from organized crime and other corrupting influences, . . . to assure that gaming is conducted fairly and honestly by both the operator and players," and to establish a National Indian Gaming Commission.[22]

Following the passage of the IGRA of 1988, 70 casinos began operations in 16 different states. By 1998, 260 casinos existed in 31 states.[23]

TRUST STATUS

Legally the Indian nations have interpreted the trust responsibility of the U.S. government to Native Americans to serve their gambling operations. The legal rights of Indian people derive from the 371 ratified treaties and agreements signed between them and the federal government. In order to began operations, an Indian tribe needs a land base that also requires trust status. In regard to the law at the federal, state, tribal, and local levels, Indian tribal governments are having to respond to limitations and interpretation of "sovereignty" and legal responsibilities of the federal government.

Locally, for the most part communities are upset with Native American groups. The response has been largely due to the gambling clientele that would frequent Indian bingos and casinos. Furthermore, Indian gambling has proven to compete too successfully with local church-operated bingos. Yet, Indian gaming has brought more jobs and improved local economies.

Morally, religious organizations and Christian individuals have opposed Indian gambling. It is a sin and promoting it is wrong in their eyes. Native Americans who are Christians agree. These people and organizations believe that American Indians should pursue some other avenues to better their communities. They also claim that promoting Indian gaming operations also encourages gambling addicts, who frequent Indian bingos and casinos.

THREATS OF ORGANIZED CRIME

A swirl of controversy and criticism of Indian gaming has assaulted gaming tribes throughout Indian Country. Whites argue that organized crime had infiltrated Indian gambling, that Indians are feeding off of gambling addicts, and that the tribes themselves are in trouble due to mismanagement and infighting. In response the tribes charge that state governments and the federal government are out to limit Indian sovereignty and legally over-regulate the Indian gaming industry.

On March 18, 1992, a report from the Department of Justice to the Senate Select Committee on Indian Affairs concluded that organized crime had not infiltrated gaming operations ran by tribes. Based on several years of investigation by the FBI, no substantial evidence of organized crime existed in Indian gaming.[24]

ADDICTION

One of the serious problems of gambling has been addiction. Both whites and Indians are addicted to gambling, thus these people visit Native American bingos and casinos. Ed Looney, the executive director of the New Jersey Council on Compulsive Gambling, stated that "about 70 to 75 percent of people who go into a casino do so socially—they have fun, lose some, and it's OK." Unfortunately, an estimated 20 percent have some gambling addiction. "That group will steal, embezzle or borrow to gamble," said Looney. He said compulsive gamblers go through three stages: "a big winning phase when the action is intoxicating, followed by a losing phase when they borrow money and can't stop until finally desperation sets in with even larger betting to recoup losses." In the last phase, Looney said that 90 percent of the compulsive gamblers will commit crimes "to feed their habit."[25] In a meeting on regulating gambling casinos held in Detroit on November 25, 1996, Michigan State Racing Commissioner Nelson Westrin, also named interim executive director of the Michigan Gaming Board, said "There are hidden social costs. It's hard to tell children that hard work pays off when we're all involved in gambling."[26]

Rena Comeslast, seventy-eight years old, who has raised dozens of foster children in Poplar, Montana, said that "There'll be a lot of food stamps for sale this week," as she referred to the first of the month when welfare and child aid checks are issued on the reservation.[27]

John Pipe, a member of the Fort Peck Tribal Council, remarked that "Parents are already selling food stamps to go to bingo. And who suffers? The children."

Economically, bingos and casinos have been a financial windfall for Native American nations, which have tried other industrial ventures in the past. They now bring in over $2 billion on the whole per year. But, is Indian gaming a boon? How long will it last? During the 1990s, Indian gaming was a success, and even challenged Atlantic City, Reno, and to some extent Las Vegas. The famed business tycoon Donald Trump even filed a suit against one Indian gaming operation. What is the future of Indian gaming heading into the twenty-first century, now that Indian gaming is more than 25 years old?

Indian gaming has become a part of American life. Usually Indian Country and what happens there is not newsworthy to the rest of the nation, but such large Indian-owned gambling operations as Foxwoods, owned by the Mashantucket Pequot Tribe of Connecticut, cannot be ignored. When television shows refer to Foxwoods, then Indian reality has intersected with public reality as fictitiously portrayed on television, which is reality for many viewers. In essence, Indian gambling has made an impact on the American public and caused it to take notice of Indian Country, and it has also affected local economies.

JOBS

Another plaguing question for the tribes is what the benefits of gaming are for tribes. One response is decrease of unemployment. Whereas some reports show that unemployment on reservations averages 40 to 60 percent, and as high as 80 percent during winter, bingo has decreased unemployment on some reservations as a trend. Among the Seminoles in Florida, the unemployment rate decreased by as much as 50 percent in the 1980s as the tribe enjoyed much prosperity from the leadership of James Billie.[28]

STATE COMPACTS

The passage of the IGRA did not immediately regulate gaming throughout Indian Country. What followed was the most strict limitation of Indian affairs since the "competency" years of Indian allotment at the turn of the twentieth century. Before the creation of the Indian Gaming Commission, as prescribed in the legislation, many reservations continued to ignore government threats to close their operations and they offered bettors computerized games that looked like and played like slot machines. Such computerized games in Florida, Arizona, California, and other states put Indian gaming tribes in opposition to state and federal officials. In particular, California officials seized hundreds of machines from California tribes. In November 1991, California seized 100 machines from the Table Mountain Reservation. "The state of California has been opposed to all forms of Indian gaming from the outset," said Howard Dickstein, attorney for California's Table Mountain reservation. He continued saying, "The state continues to treat Indian people and Indian tribes like children. It's an outmoded and racist approach."[29]

The tremendous growth of the Indian gaming industry under the protection of trust with the federal government forced state governments to try something new. Feeling threatened by the increasing economic power of gaming tribes, states sought to intrude into the legal status of American Indian nations. As of 1996, 97 tribes had compacts with 22 states for casinos with Class III gaming.[30]

TRIBAL IMPACT

The Indian gambling industry has changed Indian Country remarkably. The direct impact has been tribal economies have been uplifted by the tribes themselves. The obvious result is the evidence of financial windfalls, with some distribution to all tribal members in some successful Indian tribes. Gambling profits have enabled tribes to fund needed programs to help all of their people such as in health care, educational scholarships for college, agricultural assistance programs, care for the elderly and youth, and other related programs. In the process, the tribes have become less dependent on the federal government for funding. Importantly, this era of Indian gaming has advanced Indian sovereignty and tribal self-determination.

Overall, Indian Country has changed as a result of gaming, and more change is forthcoming. Additional construction of Indian bingos and casinos is in progress, and the values of Indians and white are on the line as Native Americans and the American mainstream society have become increasingly optimistic for luck to help change their lives for the better. Such optimism has made people in casinos increasingly addicted to take a chance to win in casinos. At this date, the history of Indian gaming is by no means over.

INDIVIDUAL IMPACT OF GAMING

It is ironic that gaming tribes can earn tremendous wealth while members of all gaming tribes are not benefiting from such windfalls. The problem is that tribes have been compelled to reinvest their earnings into expanding their gaming operations and funding programs that help their tribes as a whole.

The real issue to outsiders is per capita payments paid to tribal members from tribal gaming earnings. When only one-fourth of the gaming tribes succeed to turn profits out of more than 330 Indian gaming operations, there is a small percentage of the successful tribes who are able to make per capita payments to their tribal members. This raises the next question for many tribes, and that is, "who is a tribal member?" People on the outside are asking, how can I prove my membership in tribes, especially one successful in gaming?

The quick answers are that the tribes themselves determine who their tribal members are and who can become a tribal member. Secondly, strong evidence of relatives who were members is pertinent to any case involving desired tribal membership. It is the burden of the outsider to prove his or her heritage to possibly become a tribal member.

Poor conditions that are far below the level of modern standards still exist on most reservations and now urban Indian ghettoes are found in virtually every large city. In spite of such problems as high unemployment, substandard health, alcoholism, insufficient education, and discrimination from the mainstream, American Indians have made substantial progress. Tribal governments on reservations now resemble business corporations whose leadership is sophisticated. American Indians have always learned to adapt to circumstances for survival as an enduring people. Whether they are content is a relevant question to them, but according to outside values of the mainstream it will always appear that native peoples are not doing as well as they could. A part of this presumption is the overall Indian effort to thwart more than 500 years of such stereotypes as the plight of the poor Indian.

CONCLUSION

As the Indian gaming industry moves into the twenty-first century, this native venture is now more than 25 years old. The so-called "new buffalo" has already lived a healthy life with ill wishes from some critical non-Indians who would like a part of the action. It is the hope of many native peoples that gaming does not lead to the downfall of their nations and communities. Thus the pressure increases on tribal leadership and business managers to continue to guide their people into the white man's business world as Indian capitalists. The long-term success of the Indian gaming industry relies on the age-old value of human greed to want to be rich with little effort. Yet, the gaming industry is about Indian people developing a respectable entrepreneurship that provides for families and communities in a non-Indian business world. It is the combination of operating within two value systems and being able to make smart business decisions and following through to make successful deals.

NOTES

1. Each player rolled one marble underhanded to land in the proper hole, or to knock another player's marble out of the way. A player had two chances to knock each of the opposing team's marbles away from a hole, and after a player was hit twice, he was considered "dead." A Cherokee National Holiday Marble Tournament is held each year during Labor Day weekend in the Cherokee Nation and marble fields are in Adair, Cherokee, Delaware, and Mayes County in Oklahoma; "Marbles is an old and complex game," *News from Indian Country: The Nations Native Journal* (Hayward, WI) 10, no. 23 (mid-December 1996): Sec. B, 11B.

2. Eric Henderson, "Indian Gaming: Social Consequences." *Arizona State Law Journal* 29 (1997): 205–250; originally quoted in Stewart Culin, *Games of the North American Indians,* in *Twenty-Fourth Annual Report of the Bureau of American Ethnology to the Smithsonian Institution, 1902–1903* (New York: Dover, 1975), 49–327, originally published in 1907.

3. Kim Isaac Eisler, *Revenge of the Pequots: How a Small Native American Tribe Created the World's Most Profitable Casino* (New York: Simon and Schuster, 2001), 91.

4. James W. Covington, *The Seminoles of Florida* (Gainesville: University Press of Florida, 1993), 253.

5. Ibid., 254.

6. "Puyallups OK Casino Plan—U.S. Approval Is Pending," *Seattle Press-Intelligencer,* March 11, 1979, Henry Jackson Papers, Acc. No. 3560-5, Box 83, Folder 8, University of Washington Allen Library, Archives Division, Seattle, Washington.

7. "Tacoma Mayor Opposes Casinos," *Seattle Times,* March 14, 1979, Henry Jackson Papers, Acc. No. 3560-5, Box 83, Folder 8.

8. Cecil Andrus to Henry Jackson, March 30, 1979, Henry Jackson Papers, Acc. No. 3560-5, Box 83, Folder 9.

9. Covington, *Seminoles of Florida,* 254–55.

10. Sandra Chereb, "Campbell Warns about Greenbacks," *News from Indian Country: The Nations Native Journal* (Hayward, WI) 10, no. 23 (mid-December 1996): 6A.

11. "Indian Gaming Regulatory Act," P. L. 100-497, October 17, 1988, U.S. Statutes at Large, 102: 2467–88.

12. *Seminole Tribe of Florida v. Butterworth*, 658 F.2d 310 (1981), 246.

13. Robert Clinton, Nell Jessup Newton, and Monroe Price, *American Indian Law: Cases and Materials*, 3rd ed. (Charlottesville, VA: The Michie Company, 1991), 621.

14. Ambrose I. Lane Sr., *Return of the Buffalo: The Story behind America's Indian Gaming Explosion* (Westport, CT: Bergin and Garvey, 1995), 126–27.

15. *Cabazon Band of Mission Indians et al. v. California*, 480 U.S. 202 (1987), 205, 215, 247.

16. Eisler, *Revenge of the Pequots*, 55–56.

17. W. Dale Mason, *Indian Gaming: Tribal Sovereignty and American Politics* (Norman: University of Oklahoma Press, 2000), 61.

18. Ibid.

19. Ibid., 62.

20. Ibid., 63–64; "National Indian Gaming Commission Report to Congress," December 31, 1991, White House Office of Records Management, Subject File "Indians," Box 3, Folder 296253-301061, George Bush Presidential Library, College Station, Texas.

21. "Indian Gaming Regulatory Act," P.L. 100-497, October 17, 1988, *U.S. Statutes at Large*, Vol. 102: 2467–2488.

22. Ibid.

23. Tom Meager, "Opponents Bet They Can Defeat Casino," *Lawrence Journal World*, August 14, 2000, 2B.

24. Wilmer, "Indian Gaming," 96; originally quoted in Statement by Paul L. Maloney, Senior Counsel for Policy Criminal Division, before the Select Committee on Indian Affairs, U.S. Senate, March 18, 1992.

25. "Compulsive gambling Council to Make Pitch," *South Bend Tribune*, November 25, 1996, B7.

26. "Experts: Be Strict Regulating Casinos," *South Bend Tribune*, November 26, 1996, B5.

27. Carolin Vesely, "Poplar's Prairie of Dreams," *Montana's Indians Gambling on Gaming*, "A Special Report by the School of Journalism," Billings: University of Montana, ca 1993, 30–31.

28. Covington, *Seminoles of Florida*, 255.

29. "Reservations Bucking States, Taking Gamble with Gambling," *Vicksburg (Mississippi) Sunday Post*, December 29, 1991, D3.

30. "Cherokee Nation Adopts Act; Ready for Class III Gaming," *Cherokee Advocate* (Tahlequah, OK) 20, no. 1, January, 1996.

13

HEALTH, MEDICINE, AND CURES

American Indians have undergone a tremendous transition from treating their own people with native cures to relying on Western medical practices. This transition is still going on and it is a major decision in each individual case of illness for an Indian person to seek out Western medical help while foregoing native cures. Throughout the twentieth century, Native Americans have learned to become dependent upon the federal government and outsiders for health services. This decision has not always been easy due to limited health facilities available. In the context of history, at the turn of the century it was not easy for native people to turn to the mainstream for health care when it was not too long ago that Indian people were at war with the United States.

NATIVE CURING

American Indians have a lot of trust and faith in their medicine makers. They continue to practice, curing members of their tribal communities and other Indians who come to them for help. As previously mentioned, Black Elk of the Lakota was a powerful medicine maker who was born in the 1800s and lived into the twentieth century. Philip Deer, a Muscogee Creek, was a spiritual leader for the American Indian Movement (AIM) in the 1970s. Sanapia (1895–1968), a Comanche eagle doctor during the 1960s, helped to heal the sick among her people and Severt Young Bear of the Lakota and Left Handed of the Navajo are among the many medicine makers of the twentieth century with literature written about them.

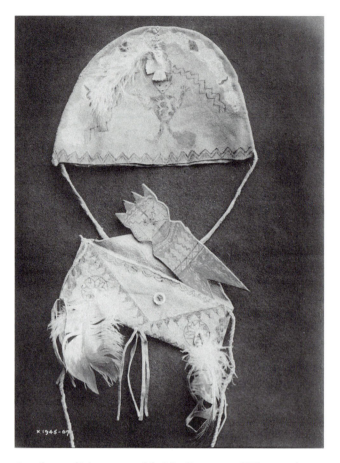

Apache medicine cap and fetish. Courtesy of Library of
Congress.

EUROPEAN DISEASES

Diseases introduced by Europeans to Native Americans were devastating in causing enormous loses in population. Smallpox was the well-
known killer that wiped out indigenous communities in the East to
the Great Plains. Some tribes were able to survive this illness, but after
losing substantial numbers of their communities. Tuberculosis, the flu,
and the common cold also proved devastating because native peoples
had never encountered them before and had no immunity to them.

It also became practice to trade blankets infested with smallpox to
Indian tribes. Shocked at the numbers of their people falling to the
strange disease, native leaders were not sure what to do. Their curers
and medicine makers attempted to take care of their sick and failed.
A common belief was that the medicine people had failed in some part

of their own life for not being able to cure their sick, or that the Creator was punishing the people for some wrongdoing.

EARLY FEDERAL ASSISTANCE

Federal support of Indian health care began in the early eighteenth century. As early as 1832, the U.S. Congress appropriated $12,000, a large sum for those days, for medical attention for Native Americans. This legislation provided limited medical services to the Ottawa and Chippewa Indians who had signed treaties that placed them on reservations in Michigan. There was no time limit on this treaty provision for medical support as the federal government adopted a policy to continue this support to the two groups. Two years later, nearly half of the Indian agencies had a physician. Interestingly, Indian health was transferred from the U.S. Department of War to the Department of the Interior in 1849. The first federal hospital for Native Americans was constructed in the 1880s in Oklahoma. By 1900, the Indian Medical Service had 83 doctors attending Indian patients. Dental service for American Indians began in 1913 when five traveling dentists were assigned to visit reservations and schools with Indian students.[1]

EARLY YEARS

As the nation transformed from an agrarian society to an urban one, the American Indian was attempting to survive. Typical Indian life was poor allotees or traditionalists eking out a living on destitute reservations. In 1901, 29 agencies and nonreservation boarding schools reported epidemics of smallpox, measles, influenza, and whooping cough. All were contagious diseases. In 1913 the mortality rate reached it highest when it peaked at 32.42 percent per 1,000. Trachoma, a disease which causes granules to grow on the inner surface of the upper eyelid, was detrimental to Indian youths. Its first stage was small grayish-white follicles developing usually on the upper lid, and then granules appeared which emitted a watery substance which clouded the eyes, giving a grayish eye coloring. Next, the tissue irritated the eye.

During the following years, tuberculosis and trachoma prevailed among students at Indian schools. In the Southwest, Dr. J.F. Perkins verified that the 50 percent of the pupils at the Pima boarding school had trachoma. At Pima day school, had 75 per cent were affected; at Mescalero Apache boarding school, 50 percent; at San Carlos boarding school, 40 percent; and Papago (Tohono 'Odom) day schools, from 60 percent to 100 percent. Sherman Institute had 20 percent, Phoenix boarding school up to 25 percent, and of the entire population at Taos pueblo, 20 percent had the disease. Zuni boarding school was spared and had no evidence of trachoma. Other diseases included measles, scarlet fever, and smallpox.

Navajo shaman gives medicine to participant used in sweat bath. Courtesy of Library of Congress.

From 1910 to 1920, influenza killed 2 percent of the total Indian population at about four times the rate of whites. For these years, no statistics for tuberculosis exist, but a public health nurse noted during her visits to Indian schools that tuberculosis was contagious via the school's living quarters and lack of prevention precautions and that treatment was careless treatment. Afterwards the children were sent home when it seemed certain that they would not improve. Overall the death rate in Indian country was 35 for each one 1,000, as compared to 15 of 1,000 Americans.

The status of the majority of Oklahoma Indians depended on seasonal employment. They picked cotton at 75 cents per day. Malnutrition, starvation, and diseases including pellagra and tuberculosis affected the people. Three-fourths of children were undernourished. The diets of those fortunate enough to have food consisted of dry salt meat, beans, and bread. The Cheyenne even resorted to using diseased horses for food. The Depression had devastated Oklahoma, causing a large number of people to journey to California as described in John Steinbeck's *The Grapes of Wrath*. Poor Okies often stole chickens belonging to Indians as they passed by.

Serious problems remained in Indian Country. For example, Indian health concerned Commissioner of Indian Affairs Charles Rhoads as a major concern. In a report to the president, he stated that 140 physicians worked in Indian health, which included 15 specialists in eye, nose, and throat disorders. More than 400 field nurses covered most rural communities. A total of 96 hospitals existed with a total bed capacity of 3,600 patients. Another six hospitals were authorized by Congress. Responding to these services, more than 37,000 Indians received treatment during 1929.[2]

In spite of such efforts, in 1931 conditions for Indians turned worse. During the summer, a drought and swarms of grasshoppers devastated Nebraska, North and South Dakota, and eastern Montana. Starting in November, the Red Cross contributed $192,260 over several months. The U.S. Army, called upon by the Bureau of Indian Affairs (BIA), sent 55 carloads of surplus supplies, consisting of overcoats, jackets, gloves, wool trousers, underwear, shirts, socks, shoes, and blankets. Working during the winter months, the army distributed approximately 6,190,000 pounds of flour and 5,500,000 pounds of crushed wheat for stock feeding. The Western states did not escape nature's punishment. In the southwest, an unprecedented series of storms engulfed New Mexico and Arizona during November and continued until January. Hazardous roads forced an airplane drop of 30,000 pounds of food to the Navajos, whose reservation was covered by a large blanket of snow.[3] The living conditions of American Indians had turned worse.

The first half of the century witnessed a host of illnesses inflicted upon American Indians. In the early decades, influenza, measles, whooping cough, and diphtheria plagued the Indian population. Tuberculosis proved to be the greatest killer of Native Americans in the United States. Accidents continued to cause death or crippling conditions. Otitis media, an infection of the inner ear, impaired the hearing ability of American Indians, especially during the 1950s and 1960s.

Following World War II, considerable changes occurred in the federal government involving Native Americans. The patriotic service of 25,000 Indian men in the military convinced federal officials that American Indians were ready for assimilation into the rest of the country. A movement began to cut back on federal programming for native peoples. Indian health care was transferred from the BIA to Public Health Service in 1955. Improvements needed to be made.

After the transfer of Indian health care to the Public Health Service, 27 new hospitals and 84 outpatient facilities were built as a continuing trend to increase the number of health installations to serve Indian communities. This trend continued until the 1970s when tribes began to contract with the federal government to build their own hospitals and clinics.

BIRTH RATE

Poor living conditions produced health problems for Native Americans, especially for children. In 1960, the American Indian population was youth oriented with the average age at 17.3 years for all Indians and 16.3 years for Alaska Natives. For the entire United States, the average age of the population was 29.5 years. For American Indians, the birth rate was 39.2 per 1,000 and for Alaska Natives the rate was 31.5 per 1,000, almost twice the rate of the rest of the country which was 17.5 per 1,000.[4]

Although the infant mortality rates for Indians and Alaska Natives have been declining rapidly, the rates are still much higher than for the rest of the country. In 1967 the infant mortality rate for American Indians was 30.1 per 1,000 live births and 55.6 per 1,000 for Alaska Natives. For the general mainstream population during the 1970s, the rate was 22.4 per 1,000 births.[5]

In regard to dental health, in the 1960s only 54 percent of Indian children (rural and urban) under the age of 20 received dental care.[6] As an example, from 1963 to 1967, the pediatric service of the Public Health Service Indian Hospital in Tuba City, Arizona, received 4,355 admissions of children under five years of age. Of this number admitted, 616 had diagnoses related to malnutrition, 44 had kwashiorkor or marasmus (serious forms of malnutrition), and the other 572 had weights or heights below the average of their ages.[7]

The 1970 census reported a total of 355,738 Indians with an estimated 45 percent living in urban areas. While health conditions among Indians had improved significantly over the last two decades, according to government statistics, American Indian health remained far behind that of mainstream Americans. For example, the Indian life expectancy at birth increased from 60 years to 64 years between 1950 and 1970, while life expectancy for whites rose from 69 years to 71 years. The main reason for this significant improvement was the sharp decrease in the infant death rate among Indians, which was nearly halved—from 62.5 to 30.9 per 1,000 live births—between 1955 and 1970, according to figures from the U.S. Public Health Service. However, infant mortality among Indians still was 40 percent higher than for all Americans, according to the health service, but in 1955 it was 140 percent higher.[8]

The average age of death for American Indians remained still only 44 years, far less than for non-Indians. For American Indians, Eskimos, and Aleuts, the level of health continued to lag 20 to 25 years behind the health advances of the general population in America. American Indians were eight times as likely to suffer from tuberculosis as the rest of the population, and deaths due to influenza and pneumonia were nearly 2.5 times for American Indians. There were 3.5 times as many homicides and twice as many suicides among American Indians as there were among the general population. If one was an American Indian in 1970, he was 10 times more likely to suffer from rheumatic fever, strep throat, and hepatitis. The incidence of otitis media, a middle ear disease which causes permanent hearing loss, was far more prevalent among American Indians than among any other people in our society. Twenty-eight percent of all

Indian homes still lacked running water and an adequate means of waste disposal. The average American Indian family of five or six members lived in a one- or two-room house, and only about 24 percent of the dental care needs of American Indians were being met.[9]

CAUSES OF DEATH

The ten leading causes of death among American Indians and Alaska Natives in the United States for 2002 are as follows:

1. Heart disease
2. Cancer
3. Unintentional injuries
4. Diabetes
5. Stroke
6. Chronic liver disease and cirrhosis
7. Chronic lower respiratory disease
8. Suicide
9. Influenza and Pneumonia
10. Homicide[10]

HEART DISEASE

On May 9, 2005, the First Conference on Cardiovascular Disease and Diabetes took place in Denver, Colorado. Dr. James Galloway, Director of the Native American Cardiology Program and senior cardiologist for the Indian Health Service, stated, "Cardiovascular disease has become the leading cause of death of American Indians and Alaska Natives." He continued, saying, "Diabetes is the most important risk factor. In addition, the roles of high cholesterol, high blood pressure and tobacco abuse must be addressed both in those with diabetes and others."

The leading cause of death among American Indians and Alaska Natives is heart disease. Related to this cause is stroke, the fifth leading cause of death. Diabetes is listed as the fourth leading cause of death for American Indians and Alaska Natives. Judy Goforth Parker, RN, Ph.D., and alternate chair of the Tribal Leaders Diabetes Committee said, "As tribal leaders, we must take a proactive stand and provide interventions that will help to combat the devastating effects of cardiovascular disease. No longer can we look at diabetes as being the single most significant health enemy of our people."

ALCOHOLISM

Alcohol and alcohol-related incidents are among the leading killers of the American Indian population. Indian people have incurred this problem since the beginning of trade relations with Europeans during the 1600s through the 1800s when they received trade items, including alcohol, in exchange for their pelts. In the twentieth century, alcoholism persisted as a serious problem for tribal communities and for individual Indians. Almost all 562 federally recognized tribes have dealt with alcoholism, and it is an individual struggle that each community, family, and individual faces. The following describes the efforts of the Muscogee Creek Tribe in Oklahoma in dealing with alcoholism.

Too frequently the sociocultural transition from Creek nativism to a hybridization with white mainstream resulted in unhappiness. Alcoholism increased acutely among the Muscogee Creek populace, especially during the 1940s. A concerned Woman's District Conference of the Indian Mission of the Methodist Episcopal Church urged Oklahoma Senator Josh Lee to introduce a bill to prohibit the sale of intoxicant beverages to the Muscogee Creeks. Assistant Commissioner of Indian Affairs William Zimmerman Jr. responded that nothing could be done because an act in 1934 repealed the special Indian liquor law in Eastern Oklahoma. The Creeks themselves were alarmed at the rise of alcoholism within the Tribe. On July 27, 1944, the Council adopted a tribal resolution consisting of 12 points and presented it to the House Subcommittee of the Committee on Indian Affairs.

SUICIDE

Alcoholism and depression have been associated together in regard to American Indians. American Indians experience both alcoholism and depression on reservations and in urban Indian areas. It was a too-frequent occurrence during the 1960s and 1970s when urban Indians became frustrated then depressed with the difficulty of fitting into the urban mainstream. Depressed alcoholics contemplated suicide as a means to end their frustration and their lives. In such situations, the conversation is much about personal problems and suicide. Unfortunately, these conversations and frustrations continue today.

An alarming 800 American Indians and Alaska Natives end their own lives every year. In many cases, accidents such as auto wrecks are involved, as is alcohol. From 1997 to 1999, the suicide death rate for American Indians and Alaska Natives was almost twice the rate for other Americans.

Suicide has become the eighth leading cause of death for all American Indians and Alaska Natives. For Native American males, it is the fifth leading cause of death. For American Indians and Alaska Natives between the ages of 15 and 24, suicide is the second leading cause of death.

OBESITY

One of the main health concerns of native peoples is obesity. This is an increasing problem among Indian people and it is causing stress on the heart of every person carrying too much weight. With less exercise more fat builds up in the body and becomes a potential source of danger, leading to heart problems and diabetes. In many cases, it is a personal decision for each individual to implement a daily exercise routine. A daily walk for 30 minutes at the minimum is sufficient to exercise the respiratory system. Playing sports and other exercise on a routine basis has been reported to extend one's life, add energy, and help produce a positive outlook on life. Increasing rates of obesity have been found in many American Indian and Alaska Native communities. Both diet and physical activity have changed for many members of American Indian and Alaska Native groups over the past several decades. Native diets are higher in fat and calories than in typical American meals, and physical activity has decreased noticeably.

The Office of Minority Health discovered that approximately 30.3 percent of children (ages 6 to 11) are overweight and 15.3 percent are obese for all children. For adolescents (ages 12 to 19), 30.4 percent are overweight and 15.5 percent are obese. Excessive weight in childhood and adolescence has been found to predict overweight in adults. Overweight children, aged 10 to 14, with at least one overweight or obese parent were reported to have a 79 percent likelihood of overweight persisting into adulthood.

In comparing males and females, overweight occurs more often in boys (32.7 percent) than girls (27.8 percent). Among adolescents, overweight conditions are about the same for females (30.2 percent) and males (30.5 percent). The prevalence of obesity quadrupled over 25 years among boys and girls. Among American Indians and Alaska Natives ages 45 to 74, over 30 percent of women were overweight and over 40 percent of women were obese. Being overweight or obese increases the risk of heart disease, Type 2 diabetes, high blood pressure, stroke, breathing problems, arthritis, gallbladder disease, sleep apnea (breathing problems while sleeping), osteoarthritis, and some cancers.

DIABETES

By the 1980s, one out of four Native Americans had diabetes. Compared with white Americans of the same age, American Indians and Alaska Natives are 2.2 times more likely to have diabetes. A report by the Indian Health Service disclosed a 106 percent increase in diabetes among adolescent American Indians and Alaska Natives over a 11-year time period during the 1980s and 1990s.

Increased sugar in people's diets has changed the body chemistry of American Indians. Insulin is needed to break down sugar to be supplied to the blood to produce energy for the body. The change in eating habits with too much sugar calls for the body to produce more insulin and this is the problem. Too much temptation from mainstream foods that are sweet, plus alcohol, has increased sugar consumption for many Indian people. Diabetes was the sixth leading cause of death in 2000 for all Americans. In fact, more than 17 million Americans have diabetes. More than 200,000 people die each year of related complications. Diabetes is a collection of diseases with high levels of blood glucose resulting from insulin secretion or insulin action. Type 1 diabetes was formerly called insulin-dependent diabetes mellitus (IDDM) or juvenile-onset diabetes. Autoimmune, genetic, and environmental factors are a part of the development of Type 1 diabetes.

Type 2 diabetes was formerly called non-insulin diabetes mellitus (NIDDM) or adult-onset diabetes. Type 2 accounts for almost 90 to 95 percent of all diabetes cases. Factors leading to Type 2 include older age, obesity, family history of diabetes, evidence of gestational diabetes, glucose tolerance, physical inactivity, and race or ethnicity. Overall, Hispanic/Latinos are 1.9 times more likely than the mainstream to have Type 2 diabetes. African Americans are twice as likely, and American Indians/Alaska Natives are 2.6 times more likely. Diabetes contributes to several leading causes of death among Native Americans and Alaska Natives, including heart disease, stroke, pneumonia, and influenza. Certain tribes have much higher rates. For example, 50 percent of Pima Indians in Arizona who are between the ages of 30 and 64 have Type 2 diabetes.

INDIAN HEALTH SERVICE

Health services for members of federally recognized tribes developed from the unique government-to-government relationship between the federal government and Indian tribes. This relationship was established in 1787 and based on Article I, Section 8 of the U.S. Constitution. This legal obligation received support for funding from the Snyder Act of 1921, authorizing funds "for the relief of distress and conservation of health . . . [and] . . . for the employment of . . . physicians . . . for Indian Tribes throughout the United States." In 1975 Congress passed the Indian Self-Determination and Education Assistance Act, P.L. 93-638, to provide Tribes the option of either assuming from the IHS the administration and operation of health services and programs in their communities, or remaining within the IHS-administered direct health system. Afterwards, Congress passed the Indian Health Care Improvement Act (P.L. 94-437), which is a health-specific law deriving from P.L. 93-638.[11]

P.L. 437 extended the quantity and quality of health services necessary to elevate the health status of American Indians and Alaska Natives to the highest possible level and to encourage the participation of tribes in the planning and managing of such services. The IHS clinical staff consisted of about 2,700 nurses, 900 physicians, 400 engineers, 580 pharmacists, 300 dentists, and 150 sanitarians. The IHS also employs various allied health professionals, such as nutritionists, health administrators, and medical records administrators. The IHS has a vacancy rate of about 12 percent for health professional positions, ranging from a vacancy rate of 6 percent for sanitarians to 24 percent for dentists. Through the Indian Self-Determination and Education Assistance Act contracts, American Indian tribes and Alaska Native corporations administer 15 hospitals, 179 health centers, 9 residential treatment centers, 117 health stations, and 180 Alaska village clinics. The IHS currently provides health services to approximately 1.5 million American Indians and Alaska Natives who belong to 562 federally recognized tribes in 35 states.

In 1988 the Indian Health Service reported a comparison of seven causes of death per 100,000 population within the United States among all races. The outcome was that the causes of death for American Indians were significantly higher, as illustrated:

1. alcoholism—433 percent greater
2. tuberculosis—400 percent greater
3. diabetes mellitus—155 percent greater
4. accidents—131 percent greater
5. homicide—57 percent greater
6. pneumonia and influenza—32 percent greater
7. suicide—27 percent greater

Accidents were the leading cause of death among Indian youth and are about three times the national average. For the children age one to four, accidents are four times the national average. For those age five to fourteen, the rate is nearly twice the national average.

Overall, heart disease was the leading causing of death, followed by accidents. Diabetes is a major cause of death and is almost three times that of the general population in the country.

In early 1992, 352 cases of Acquired Immune Deficiency Syndrome (AIDS) existed among American Indians and Alaska Natives. An estimated 55 percent of the cases were among homosexual or bisexual males and 19 percent were among intravenous drug users.

To improve the health of American Indians, Congress passed the Indian Health Care Improvement Act, P.L. 102-571, on October 29, 1992. This was an act which amended the previous Indian health care act. The amendment authorized appropriations for Indian health programs and declared health objectives: "The Congress hereby declares that it is the policy of this Nation, in fulfillment of its special responsibilities and legal obligation to the American Indian people, to assure the highest possible health status for Indians and urban Indians and to provide all resources necessary to effect that policy."[12]

As the year 2000 began, the Indian Health Service helped roughly 1.5 million patients. This was an increase from 1.2 million in 1990 IHS employed about 15,800 workers and 62 percent were American Indian. The HIS medical staff included an estimated 840 physicians, 100 physician assistants, 2,580 nurses, 350 pharmacists, 380 dentists, 60 optometrists, 45 physical therapists, 7 nutritionists, 80 dieticians, and 285 medical technologists. The IHS had 49 hospitals and 492 outpatient facilities.

TRIBAL EFFORTS

Since the mid 1970s the dire need for Indian health care caused an explosion of Indian health care facilities throughout the nation. During the years when Presidents Nixon and Ford were in office, the federal government appropriated the following dollar amounts to the Indian Health Service: $143 million in 1971, $170 million in 1972, $198 million in 1973, $216 million in 1974, and an estimated $293 million for 1975.[13] In 1976 an estimated $3 million was spent on Indian health care. During this year, the House of Representatives entertained a bill entitled the Indian Health Care Improvement Act. The measure intended to request $355 million for Indian health. Whereas urban Indians were reluctant to apply for health care, Title V of the legislation "would provide for a program of contracts with Indian organizations in urban areas for the purpose of making health services more accessible to Indians."[14]

Two years later, legislation provided $5 million for Indian health. Most of the budget of the Indian Health Service, however, went to the reservations where approximately $420 million annually was distributed in the late 1970s.

Construction for a new capitol complex began on the north side of Okmulgee and within the next few years, the Claude Cox administration flourished into a growing bureaucracy. Chief Cox envisioned a tribal complex that would serve the entire Creek Nation and he believed the Creek Tribe could assume a leadership role among all tribes. The newly completed complex included the tribe's administrative offices, BIA, Housing Authority, Indian Health Service offices with a dental health clinic, and an Environmental Health Office. In June 1973, the tribe hired an executive director to supervise all tribal programs and to be the executive administrator reporting to Chief Cox. Several vocational and educational programs listed for the 1974 fiscal year included Indian Action Team, Indian Children's Education Program, and Comprehensive Employment Training.

In October 1975, the Creeks held a dedication ceremony for the tribal complex. A new dental clinic began operating and additional plans called for extended health care. Previously, low income and high unemployment had hindered good health among the Creeks, but by 1975 four clinics were operating at Wetumka, Holdenville, Okemah, and Sapulpa. At Eufaula a large medical and dental health clinic was negotiated to be leased from the General Services Administration. Two years later, the tribe began an ambulance service to transport ill and injured patients from their homes to public hospitals, nursing homes, and Indian Health Service facilities. In addition the tribe introduced a mobile clinic. Local communities were visited periodically and offered clinical services. The mobile unit was staffed with a physician's assistant, registered nurse, licensed practical nurse, and driver. The crowning touch was the beginning of construction on a 39-bed hospital at Okemah and after its completion; the tribe officially dedicated the hospital on May 13, 1978. In other areas of progress, a new 52-bed medical center was officially opened in Henryetta. The new center replaced the old 44-bed Henryetta Hospital and clinic. The new medical center included an obstetrical unit, an intensive care unit, and a 24-hour emergency room.

Following the cutbacks of the Reagan administration in the 1980s, the federal government proved to be more helpful during the 1990s. For example, Congress passed the Tribal Development Student Assistance Revolving Loan Program Act, P.L. 102–325, on July 23, 1992. This was an act to

establish a revolving loan program to be administered by a tribe or tribal organization for the purposes of increasing the number of college graduates available to work in tribal businesses, tribal government, and tribal services such as schools and hospitals; to conduct research in postsecondary education; and to encourage development, through grants in addition to loans, transitional and follow up services added to encourage persistence in postsecondary education.[15]

ASSOCIATION OF AMERICAN INDIAN PHYSICIANS

The Association of American Indian Physicians (AAIP) is a national organization of Indian physicians that is making efforts to recruit more young Indians into the medical field. By the 1980s only 80 physicians in the United States were identified as American Indian. Furthermore, less than 10 doctors in the Indian Health Service were Indian. On the average, there were 5 Indian doctors for every 100,000 American Indians, while there were 173 physicians for every 100,000 people of the mainstream population.

As the twenty-first century begins, much more work needs to be done to recruit Native Americans to become nurses, doctors, and dentists. In spite of many more doctors, nurses, and other native personnel needed in medicine, Native Americans have made great strides since Dr. Carlos Montezuma (Yavapai) received his medical degree in 1889 andDr. Charles Alexander Eastman (Dakota) received his M.D. in 1890. The Navajo have had their first woman surgeon in Dr. Lori Arviso Alvord.

CONCLUSION

The relationship of native peoples with the outdoors has undoubtedly made them healthy. Life on the reservation remained rigorously demanding at the turn of the century and in the early decades. The strong survived, which has been nature's way for Indian people who have spent a long time dealing with hardships. This is nature's way of testing men and women. As harsh is may seem, native people have learned from nature and watch for signs of forthcoming bad weather. Nature's way is the Indian way. With this point made, Native Americans have experienced an easier life in the latter decades. As times change, Indian people find themselves more often inside air-conditioned buildings and homes during warm summer months and in warm homes during winter's cold. The adaptability of Indian people is being a changed to their previous relationship with nature as Thomas Bancaca warned in the Hopi prophecy for the world in 1992 at the United Nations. Perhaps, the way to well-being in mental, spiritual, and physical health is within ourselves and lies in trying to find the balance between the physical and the metaphysical.

NOTES

1. Alan L. Sorkin, "Health and Economic Development on American Indian Reservations," in *Public Policy Impacts on American Indian Economic Development,* ed. Matthew Snipp, 145 (Albuquerque: Native American Studies Institute for Native American Development, 1988).

2. Commissioner of Indian Affairs Charles Rhoads described Indian health, August 6, 1930, John Collier Papers, microfilm, Reel 47. Originals at Yale University, New Haven, Connecticut.

3. Annual Report of the Commissioner of Indian Affairs, Charles Rhoades, June 30, 1932, microfiche, p. 3. Copy available in Special Collections, Marquette University, Milwaukee, Wisconsin.

4. Helen M. Wallace, "Health of American Indian Children: A Survey of Current Problems and Needs," *Clinical Pediatrics,* 12, no. 2 (February 1973): 450.

5. Ibid.

6. Ibid., 453.

7. Ibid., 86.

8. Lawrence Feinberg, "U.S. Indian Total Up 51% in Decade, '70 Census Shows," *Washington Post,* November 10, 1972, Box 27 (ab27), Folder 1, James Abourezk Papers, Special Collections, University of South Dakota, Vermillion.

9. Proceedings and Debates of the 91st Congress, second Session, *Congressional Record,* Vol. 116, No.110 (July 1, 1970): 1–2.

10. Indian Health Care Improvement Act, P.L. 102-571, October 29, 1992, *U.S. Statutes at Large,* Vol. 106, Pt. 106: 4526–4579.

11. Indian Health Service, U.S. Department of Health and Human Services, www.ihs.gov. Accessed October 10, 2005.

12. Indian Self-Determination and Education Assistance Act, P.L. 93-638, January 4, 1975, *U.S. Statutes at Large,* 88: 2203–17.

13. Paul H. O'Neil to Ted Marrs, memorandum regarding Indian Health Service, March 25, 1975, IN Indian Affairs 8/9/74–11/31/74 Folder, Box 1,

White House Central Files, Gerald R. Ford Presidential Library, Ann Arbor, Michigan.

   14. Marjorie Lynch to John Rhodes, letter, June 30, 1976, Health Care Legislation (S. 522) Folder, Box 2, WHCF, Ford Library.

   15. Tribal Development Student Assistance Revolving Loan Program Act, P.L. 102-325, Part E, July 23, 1992, *U.S. Statutes at Large,* Vol. 106, Pt. 1: 809–812.2

14

BEING INDIAN IN THE TWENTIETH CENTURY

Being Indian in the twentieth century has been difficult for true Native Americans. It is a challenge and it is being challenged. Real native identity is obvious when an Indian person physically looks like an Indian. This is being Indian by blood. Being a person of color in the white American mainstream means to stand out whether you like it or not. As one young Indian person once said, it is like being a spot and everyone notices or chooses to ignore it. In this sense, it is like being less than a person, but rather an object. This odd feeling is dehumanizing and Indians are treated like they have no feelings.

American Indian identity is also confusing and complex, beginning with the question of "who" is an Indian? But who determines this? While this is under discussion, the debate leads to the underlying question of "what" is an Indian? There needs to be a working definition for discussion's sake at least. And, there is more than one definition. There are legal definitions, that even define what a tribe is, and there cultural definitions and self-definition, according to anyone who considers themselves to be Indian. The definition of "Indian" for the U.S. Census used in 2000 was based totally on self-identification for "American Indian" and "Alaska Native." This definition referred to anyone by self-definition who had origins in any of the indigenous peoples of North or South America who maintained a tribal affiliation or community membership.

An "Indian" to outsiders is a person who naturally looks Indian without trying to enhance one's physical features with hair color, jewelry, or some other cosmetic means. There is no doubt about the person who personifies being a member of a tribe and it may even be discernable which tribe it is because certain tribes have particular physical traits. Furthermore, the real Indian-looking person has generally grown up with their tribal traditions and ways. Hence, the outside appearance of this native person is convincing enough for everyone that he or she is a genuine Indian. Yet, it must be pointed out that even natives who are Indian-looking have been Christianized, urbanized, and de-Indianized. They might be called an "apple" in Indian Country for being red on the outside and white on the inside, meaning that mainstream values have been adopted in toto.

The "internal Indian" is a person who feels Indian on the "inside" and who knows his or her culture. This person was born Indian, but is a mixed-blood and may only look like they have a trace of Indian appearance. This is different from "going native," meaning that the person adopts Indian ways and appearance for a particular reason. This person already knows his or her people and about the tribal ways of the past. This innateness is also about being connected to one's people. Self-examination or outsiders looking in is internalizing what it means to be Indian. The outside world and outsiders remind you that you are Indian and you feel the stress and pressure, although their idea and your idea of being Indian are quite different. The color barrier separates the two sides of Indian and white, while the native person finds himself or herself trying not to yield to the pressure from the mainstream.

Being Indian means actually being an Indian by blood and culture. And there are people who want to be Indian for psychological or spiritual reasons. The latter might even be followers of the New Age movement and others who want to be Indian for a short time, or perhaps even their lifetime. But why do they want to be Indian? Perhaps, in all of our lives at some time, we want to be someone else. Naturally mainstream individuals would want to be Indian, but being Indian all of the time would be too much for them. There is too much stress, pressure, and stereotypes, plus the struggle against prejudice and racism. Being Indian is hard, swimming against the mainstream, and being the only Indian in a room with other people, at work, or in a crowd is very difficult. Being Indian outside of your community means being alone a lot of the time.

THE IRONY

The irony here is that sometimes non-Indians want to be Indian, as just mentioned. There can be any number of reasons for this desire. Psychologically, it is interesting that people would want to be Indian and it is usually for personal reasons. Possibly they want to know what it is like to be the underdog, the victim, or the martyr, or the person who is not likely to come out on top such as in playing cowboys and Indians. This situation is a matter of perspective, because Indian people do not feel this way and this is an external projection on Native Americans. However, some native people tend to believe that Indians are second-best at most everything, sometimes third best, but never the first.

Metaphorically, it is the cowboy wanting to be the Indian. Furthermore, it is amazing how many people identify with Indians. They want to enjoy a part of the "shared experience" of what it is like to be Indian. Perhaps, they have even grown up playing with Indian children. They have been around Indians all of their lives and they do not want this to change. These people find the characteristics of Indian people to be good and appealing. Or, perhaps they want American Indians to be treated fairly. To them, Indians are fun to be with and there is a sense of belonging that attracts them and they want to be included in the group. In some cases, they have no one else and feel the discomfort of being in the mainstream.

WANNA-BES

For many non-Indians, an Indian psychosis compels them to want to be Indian. The real reason may not be understood, but the choice has been made by the individual trying to be a Native American. For some individuals, it is almost a lifelong choice that they want to be Native American. These people find themselves being more comfortable being Indian than being a member of the mainstream society or whatever group that they are a member of.

One main reason for wanting to be Indian is the fear of or actual rejection from the American mainstream. They are or feel outside of the mainstream set of values and norms. Daniel Boone was one of the best historic examples of this situation. A legend of a frontiersman in Kentucky, Boone found it more to his liking to be on the other side of the frontier where Indians lived, particularly the Shawnees. Furthermore, Boone felt rejection by the white man's civilization. He was a misfit and did not act like a gentleman. He was criticized by others and there was no doubt he was marginal, on the edge of civilization.

Another explanation for others wanting to be Indian is an attraction to the naturalness of being Indian. In a way, people say they feel psychologically that they meant to be born Indian. In their heart they are Indian. Because they are non-Indian, they function seemingly well with the mainstream, but they really prefer to be among Indian people. If given a choice of being born again, they want to be Indian.

HOBBYISTS

Hobbyists are certain individuals who admire and respect American Indians, their cultures, and their histories. Sometimes, hobbyists know more about Indians than Indians themselves because of their unquenchable thirst for knowledge and details. They wish to know everything about the Indians; they study and act like Indians.

For example, the hobbyists in Germany set up their own tribal camps. Their interest in Indians is due to the work of Karl May (1842–1912), an early German writer who wrote many novels about Indians and the American, while he served time in prison and afterwards. In his late years of life, May finally made the journey to America that he should have made long before. His influential books about the adventures of Winnetou, an Apache, and his fair-haired companion, Old Shatterhand, and others in his volumes ignited the German people, generation after generation, as they expressed their curiosity about native peoples by learning more about them. In 1962 German studios produced *The Treasure of Silver Lake,* and this led to 11 films being produced from the works of Karl May, in which American actor Lex Barker played Old Shatterhand and French actor Pierre Brice played Winnetou. They wanted the truth and today students and scholars in German universities study American Indians, teach courses about them, and write about them.

Hobbyists are also present in England, but to a lesser degree. Their interest in "Red Indians" as they call American Indians is more about the knowledge of Indian ways. The British American Studies Association holds annual conferences and sessions are held on Native Americans on a regular basis. To a lesser degree, there is a growing interest in American Indians in Australia and Japan. The latter especially has been sending students and scholars to the United States to study American Indians, their cultures, and histories.

There are also hobbyists in the United States, but they are less evident since they have the advantage of being able to visit Indian communities on reservations. Ironically, hobbyists are more interested in traditional Indians and express almost no interest in urban Indians, although two-thirds of the entire native population lives in urban areas of the United States. It is the romantic appeal of living with nature that draws German hobbyists and others to imitate American Indians during their golden era of cultural expression. Holding camp allows hobbyists to act out their fantasies as Indians, mostly as Plains Indians. In search for something that is lacking in their lives, hobbyists find satisfaction in being Indian for the weekend as warriors of past glory.

American Indians tolerate hobbyists, even accept the situation, since they act in the most sincere way to seek knowledge about native people. Hobbyists are respectful of Indian ways and traditions, and in an interesting irony they honor Indian people by wanting to be like them.

WEEKEND WARRIORS

Every weekend, countless boys and men become weekend warriors whether playing games like football, playing or other competitive games, or being in the National Guard. The weekend warrior escapes his weekly job, duties, and responsibilities. It is being away from one's civilization of certain expected norms and being free to express oneself in a male sort of way. This is a means of getting in touch with nature as a primordial man. Strength and endurance are called upon in living with nature. Being a part of Nature is the process of becoming a warrior, at least in the mind of the weekend warrior.

To be recognized as a warrior is a status to be desired. Some boys' teams are named "Warriors" and they try to fill their roles as warriors by claiming victory on the field. In football, baseball, and other sports of keen competition, a team of warriors no doubt has to possess athletic skills as real warriors stood the test of manhood, protecting, hunting, enduring, and holding a spiritual strength. Historically, the traditional status of warriors among tribes accounts for this desired status. War or military societies perpetuated this upbringing as boys prepared to become warriors to risk their lives for the sake of protecting their families and homelands.

NEW AGERS

During the late 1970s and early 1980s, a New Age group of individuals, consisting of mostly non-Indians, began to practice American Indian ways of culture. They are mostly interested in sweats and religious practices of Native Americans and have gone as far as excluding Indians in their quasi-ceremonies. In some instances, they have consulted with medicine leaders who offer their assistance to introduce New Age believers to Indian ways. Such self-professed individuals have been called "plastic medicine men" by Indian critics.

The problem is that New Agers have borrowed cultural ways and ceremonies without respecting the origins of them. Sweats and ceremonies are held by New Agers professing to be the experts of these activities. These rituals are misinterpreted and given new meanings, resulting in cultural exploitation of religious beliefs.

PATERNALISM

Due to their suppressed state at the end of the nineteenth century, American Indians were forced to become dependent upon the federal government for almost everything. As prisoners of war on reservations during the late 1800s, the U.S. military stripped every possible resource that might assist Native Americans from going to war. In return for agreeing to live on the reservations, tribes signed 371 treaties and agreements with the United States. Annuities that arrived late, or never, for example, compelled Indians to become frustrated with the Bureau of Indian Affairs (BIA). Native peoples became increasingly convinced that treaty after treaty was being broken by the United States.

In addition, federal policies and programs were forced on Indians, making native people feel like Uncle Sam told them what they could do and what they could not do. No doubt, the letters "BIA" have been said to really mean, "Boss Indians Around." Federal paternalism proved to be frustrating and it usurped Indians of their rights and inherent sovereign freedom. The BIA became the target of Indian criticism and this feeling has not changed even though American Indians have been appointed to the highest position as assistant secretary of the Department of Interior since 1978 during the Jimmy Carter administration.

A twisted irony is that part of the paternalism is for the good of Indian people in reference to the federal trust relationship to protect individual and tribal business investments. There is a long history of depriving Indians of their lands and properties, and this trust prohibits certain Indians with trust lands from selling or leasing lands without authorization from the Secretary of the Interior. This situation has also been equally frustrating to Indians who say justifiably that they cannot take care of their own business affairs or find someone else who will help them. Arguably many educated mixed-bloods find trust restrictions holding them back waiting for BIA approval to develop their properties and lands, but many elders with trust lands are actually protected by the same binding restrictions. How the government handles the trust relationship and has lost accountability for millions of dollars in accounts for native peoples is another controversial subject.

PAN-INDIANISM

The federal government's iron control over Indian people and their affairs compelled a native leadership to form various organizations throughout the 1900s in response. Such organizations became local, regional, and national, but were political in nature. Their voices proved most effective at the national level; they got the government's attention and forced bureaucrats to listen to Indian demands. Non-Indians supported the rights of Indians and their tribes as early 1882 when the Indian Rights Association (IRA) was formed. The IRA acted as a clearinghouse in the early 1900s for appeals of all sorts with a general mission to protest on behalf of Indian rights (Indians, as a group, were not even citizens of the United States until 1924).

Founded in 1923 in New York City, the Association on American Indian Affairs (AAIA) communicated Indian issues to Indian Country during the 1970s. It involved prominent Indians and non-Indians acting to bring about reform for Indian tribes and their people overall. Its original purpose was to provide legal and technical assistance to Indian tribes throughout the United States.[1]

In Denver, Colorado, in 1944, the National Congress of American Indians emerged and endures to the present. It is the longest continuing national Indian organization and continues to address nationwide issues via tribal representation at its annual meetings. Twenty years later, the

American Indian Historical Society began in San Francisco. Under the supervision of Rupert Costo and Jeanette Henry, the society assessed and attempted to correct the historical portrayal of American Indians through its own journal publication called the *Indian Historian,* sponsoring conferences and voicing the need to tell the truth about American Indian history. A few years later in 1970, the American Indian Law Center was launched in Washington, D.C. It was established to render legal services through research and offered training to tribes, individuals, and various agencies interested in federal Indian law. In 1971, tribal leaders from 55 tribes met in Billings, Montana, to form the National Tribal Chairmen's Association. This national Indian organization met in response to the government's need to address Indian issues with an Indian response.

Only a couple years earlier, the National American Indian Court Judges Association was formed in Washington, D.C. The association began as a means to improve the tribal court systems by gathering knowledge about law in order to protect the rights of tribal people. In the area of law, the American Indian Law Center started in 1970 at Albuquerque. The center provides services, primarily through research and training of a broad legal nature in preparing law students in federal Indian law. In the same year, the Native American Rights Fund began in Boulder, Colorado. This organization has continued to legally represent Indian individuals as well as tribes with its battery of lawyers and paralegals.

By the mid and late 1970s, regional Indian organizations began to emerge. Such organizations as the United Southeastern Tribes (USET) find themselves to be more effective as collection of tribes, consisting of the remaining members of the Five Civilized Tribes in the region, Cherokee, Chickasaw, Choctaw, Creek, and Seminole. Other Indian regional groups included the Northern Pueblos Tributary Water Rights Association; Confederation of Indian Tribes of the Colorado Tribe; Five Central Arizona Indian Tribes; United Indian Tribes of Western Oklahoma; and Intertribal Council of California. In Oklahoma, there is the Intertribal Council of the Five Civilized Tribes, and the eight tribes of the northeastern part of the state founded the Inter-Tribal Council, Inc., in 1967. The council consists of the Peoria, Modoc, Ottawa, Eastern Shawnee, Miami, Seneca-Cayuga, Quapaw, and Wyandotte. The mission of the ITC is "to enlighten the public towards a better understanding of the Native American race, to preserve Native American cultural values, to enhance and promote general educational and economic opportunities among members of the ITC." Its programs assist low-income American Indians within the jurisdiction of the eight tribes in order to attain a self-sufficient standard of living to become a productive member of the Indian community. In the western part of Oklahoma is the Wichita and Affiliated Tribes, consisting of the Wichita, Waco, Takakoni, and Keechi.

ROMANTICS

Admirers and romantics are a part of Native American lives. In some instances, they have championed Indian causes. They respect the ways of native peoples. Indians' closeness to nature, spiritualism, and mysticism are some reasons for attracting romantics, who appreciate the traditional ways of Indians more than the contemporary ways. Native people have studied the ways of nature for many centuries and have great knowledge of herbs and the life ways of animals. They are a part of the natural world and admirers and romantics find this compelling to learn more about.

Others might be in admiration of Indians because of certain individuals like Crazy Horse, Tecumseh, and other native leaders who gave their lives in defense of their peoples and homelands. These martyr heroes sacrificed the ultimate for causes that they believed in. These types of heroes are irresistible to some people who champion the underdog. In a way, it is human to respect such individuals who have given their human life for others.

PREJUDICE

To be prejudiced is to be human. Biased attitudes have unfortunately been an obstacle for American Indians and have arise largely because most people know very little about Native Americans and they operate on what they have heard or seen about them. Being prejudiced on the part of the mainstream is not allowing an understanding or expressed point of view from Indian people. It is also unfortunate that prejudice is steeped in cultures and this becomes a part of ethnicity, especially when the other side is very much unlike yourself.

Even more, some Indians are prejudiced against other Indians. Tribe versus tribe is one situation of comparison, mixed-bloods are often critical of full-bloods and vice versa, certain families are critical of other families and all of this makes Indian politics very interesting.

RACISM

Racism begins with the perception of the human eye and how we see other people based on our knowledge about them. It is also unfortunate that racism knows color differences and puts an emphasis on the importance of color. To see other people different in color from ourselves is the start of racism and American Indians have encountered more than their share since they are a minority and are looked at by the mainstream on a daily basis.

As much as white Americans are racist against American Indians, the opposite can also be true. In fact, some tribes are racist against other tribes. This is an inter-ethnic racism that undermines tribal relations. Due to the many past injustices and personal experiences, some American Indians are anti-mainstream and anti-white.

PRIDE

American Indians who are close to their traditions are proud to be Indian. It is a sense of being able to assert yourself to let others know that you are Indian, in spite of what they may think. Such pride calls for self-confidence. It is not always easy and it is actually difficult for much of the time, especially since many Americans know little about Indians and are left to believe the stereotypes that they may have heard or seen about Native Americans. Thus, they may not think highly of Indians and may believe that Indian people are not capable of accomplishing very much.

Being Indian is trying to overthrow the second-class status that is a constant presumption, that being Indian is not being as good as the mainstream. This is a psychological obstacle that has two concerns. The first is that the native individual must be able to overcome the possible feeling of being inferior. This is a struggle in itself and a defeatist attitude harms any progress in personal development, Some native people never overcome this presumption. They have great self-doubt and they do not give themselves much of a chance to succeed in the mainstream or even in their own Indian community.

The second concern is that the mainstream must be ready to accept the Indian person socially, in business, intellectually, and psychologically. It is unfortunate that even an Indian person with zealous confidence might be socially rejected by a mainstream person or group due to their unreadiness to accept someone outside of their culture and ethnicity. The proposed "melting pot" concept of the American experience that was introduced in the early eighteenth century has been the reality of the twentieth century. Since the protest years of the 1960s, the mainstream has been more tolerant of American Indians and have accepted them more on equal terms whereas once they fought wars against each other as late as 1890, a little over a hundred years ago. Meanwhile, Indians have learned to be patient.

OUTSIDE OF INDIANNESS

Indian people have learned to be patient and to endure a lot over the years. Being a minority is not being in control of the mainstream and having limited power to even regulate your own life. Yet, it is being in control over you and learning to contain yourself until the best opportunity comes to improve one's life or situation.

Being Indian on the outside is conducting yourself in a respectful way that is both acceptable to others and to yourself. Most of the time, outsiders already have their minds made up about Indians due to stereotypes both good and bad, but unfortunately most of them are negative. Native Americans are marginal to the mainstream because their culture is a combination of Indian and white. Thus, this means there is a constant comparison between the two sides that dates back to the first encounter between Columbus and the Arawak Indians of the Caribbean. Naturally there is a presumption of which one is superior and the mainstream presumes that it is always better. This logic accounts for the assumption that Indians are inferior to members of the American mainstream.

One might think that this extraordinary encounter has been over for more than 500 years and that much social progress has been made in the great diversed United States. However, this same encounter occurs daily when an Indian person meets a white person who has never really been around American Indians or knows very little about them. This would mean that non-Indians need much more exposure to indigenous peoples and their traditional cultures, but this has not been an established need at the level of other subjects that are taught in classrooms and programs aired on television. For the present, the mainstream media and textbook companies believe that they offer enough about American Indians. Thus, if the mainstream wants to know more about Indians, then an individual effort must be made to decided to learn more about Native Americans.

INSIDE OF INDIANESS

Being Indian on the inside is a constant self-analysis for the simple fact of being a minority in a mainstream linear western world. It is not an Indian way of doing things. But being Indian means realizing this fundamental difference permeates all things in Indian–white relations, even for those mixed bloods who are part white. It means feeling Indian and being Indian in a tribal community or urban Indian area in a close sense that exudes a kind of communal feeling. It is a sense of belonging to a group that renders identity and helps to define who Indians are and who their people are. Being Indian on the inside is knowing that you are connected to the community, tribe, and the shared past of your people.

CONCLUSION

The lives of American Indians are more complex than most people would believe. Theirs is a dual identity of living as Indians and functioning in the mainstream society. It is living a balanced life as much as possible in two realities that host different sets of values and possess a different ethos. As Indians work with other peoples of the mainstream, they go home to their Indianness, even if they are not married to an Indian person. This is typical of minority ethnic groups in the American mainstream. The difference is an array of ironies that all of this continent was once Indian land, buying real estate and paying property tax on land that your tribes use to own. To watch land areas being exploited, bulldozed, or open-pit mined is having immense tolerance as an Indian. Being Indian is hard. Being Indian is reminding other people that you are still here.

NOTE

1. Theodore W. Taylor, *American Indian Policy* (Mt. Airy, MD: Lomond Publications, 1983), 132.

Glossary

Allotee An Indian tribal member whose tribal lands were surveyed, allotted, and distributed to individuals as a part of Dawes Act of 1887 to individualize and civilized Indians for assimilation and citizenship in the American mainstream.

Assimilation The integration or absorption of a person or group into another group.

Autonomy The ability of a person or group to exercise full freedom of cultural or political expression or to act in a similar manner.

Citizenship The official membership in a tribe or membership as a citizen of the United States with all of its understood rights, privileges, and responsibilities according to the U.S. Constitution.

Clan Individuals related by lineage and identified according to an animal or plant totem.

Colonization The processing of an indigenous person or group to become like another group, according to its beliefs, values, and ideas.

Community A group of people based on common concerns, values, and culture.

Competency The status determined by a federal court that a person is able to run their own business affairs; *incompetency* is the same process, but with the court stating the person is not able to run their business affairs.

Council   A governing group selected according to cultural procedure to represent all members of the group, band, or tribe.

Dichotomy   A situation where two individuals, communities, or groups are distinctively different, according to sets of values, beliefs, government and leadership.

Ethos   A defined view of seeing the world based on a mindset determined by one's cultural beliefs.

Federal paternalism   The firm handling of business affairs of a group by another group or organization due to certain legal restrictions placed on the first group.

Indian Country   Geographic regions referred to collectively that includes reservations, traditional tribal areas, and sometimes urban Indian areas.

Indianness   A state of condition pertaining to being American Indian.

Leasing   An individual or group allows another to pay to use or reside on certain properties.

Metaphysical   A reality of native people pertaining to spirits, visions, and deities.

Native   The state of condition or identity of being indigenous in North America.

Natural Democracy   All things acknowledged in an Indian universe based on respect.

Natural world   All things of plants, animals, physical, human, and spiritual, in an inclusive context.

Oral tradition   A continual process of told stories, myths, legends, and accounts of experiences passed from one generation to the next.

Pan-Indian   A national occurrence, event, organization, or state of being existing throughout Indian Country.

Per capita   Payment of a certain amount of money to members of an Indian tribe from the tribe or the federal government.

Relocatee   An Indian person who signed up for relocation and moved to an urban area to improve his or her life with federal assistant in finding a job and housing.

Relocation   An official urbanization program of American Indians from reservations to cities starting in 1952 and lasting until 1973 with the federal government finding jobs and housing for individuals who signed up voluntarily for this program.

Rez   A common word for Indian reservation.

Royalty   Monies received as a percentage of lands leased, mined, or used to generate income, but usually referring to funds paid to individuals or tribes per agreement for using natural resources.

Self-determination   The right and recognition of a tribe to exercise its full independence to govern itself and its members and to develop its own programs, policies, and laws.

Sovereignty   The legal state of recognizing the full freedom of another entity such as one sovereign nation acknowledging the full rights of another sovereign nations and vice versa.

Sweat   A purification procedure for the human body usually performed as a ceremony, but can also be nonceremonial in nature.

Termination   Started by House Concurrent Resolution 108 as a federal policy approved in 1953 by Congress to end the trust status once and for all between the U.S. government and a tribe usually, but also a community, band, or individual who has land or properties in trust with the United States.

Traditional   In reference to the old customs and ways of a tribe, including its beliefs and values and how it performed ceremonies.

Treaty   Usually refers to an agreement between tribes and the U.S. government. There are a total of 371 treaties and agreements, and there are also treaties between states and tribes and tribes with other nations, whereupon both sides agree to the same provisions, and whereas the U.S. Congress has ratified its treaties with tribes.

Trust   The binding agreement produced by a treaty that both sides, such as the U.S. government and a tribe, will honor the provisions legally and respect them.

Wardship   The legal relationship such as that of the U.S. government serving via the Bureau of Indian Affairs as the trustee over Indians or tribes regarding their lands and properties.

FURTHER READING

Basso, Keith H. *Portraits of 'The Whiteman': Linguistic Play and Cultural Symbols among the Western Apache* Cambridge: Cambridge University Press, 1979, reprinted 1980.

Berkhofer, Robert, Jr. *The White Man's Indian: Images of the American Indian from Columbus to the Present.* New York. Alfred A. Knopf. 1978.

Brophy, William, and Sophie Aberle. comps. *The Indian, America's Unfinished Business: Report of the Commission on the Rights, Liberties, and Responsibilities of the American Indian.* Norman. University of Oklahoma Press. 1966.

Brown, Joseph Epes. *The Spiritual Legacy of the American Indian.* New York: Crossroad, 1988.

Caroll, James T. *Seeds of Faith: Catholic Indian Boarding Schools.* New York: Garland, 2000.

Cash, Joseph, and Herbert T. Hoover. *To Be an Indian: An Oral History.* St. Paul: Minnesota Historical Society Press, 1995.

Champagne, Duane, ed. *The Native North American Almanac: A Reference Work on Native North Americans in the United States and Canada.* Detroit: Gale Research, 1991.

Chaudhuri, Joyotpaul. *Urban Indians of Arizona: Phoenix, Tucson, and Flagstaff.* Tucson: University of Arizona Press, n.d.

Crow Dog, Mary, and Richard Erdoes. *Lakota Woman.* New York: Grove Weidenfeld, 1990.

Danziger, Edmund, Jr. *Survival and Regeneration, Detroit's American Indian Community.* Detroit: Wayne State University Press, 1991.

Davis, Mary B., ed. *Native America in the Twentieth Century.* New York: Garland, 1994.

Deloria, Philip J. *Indians in Unexpected Places.* Lawrence: University Press of Kansas, 2004.

———. *Playing Indian.* New Haven: Yale University Press, 1998.

Deloria, Vine, Jr. *For This Land: Writings on Religion in America.* New York and London: Routledge, 1999.

Deloria, Vine, Jr., and David E. Wilkins, eds. *Tribes, Treaties, and Consitutional Tribulations.* Austin: University of Texas Press, 1999.

Drinnon, Richard. *Dillon S. Myer and American Racism.* Berkeley: University of California Press, 1987.

Ellis, Clyde. *A Dancing People: Powwow Culture on the Southern Plains.* Lawrence: University Press of Kansas, 2003.

Fixico, Donald L. *The American Indian Mind in a Linear World: Traditional Knowledge and American Indian Studies.* New York: Routledge, 2003.

———. *The Invasion of Indian Country in the Twentieth Century: American Capitalism and Tribal Natural Resources.* Niwot, Colo.: University Press of Colorado, 1998.

———. *Termination and Relocation: Federal Indian Policy, 1945–1960.* Albuquerque: University of New Mexico Press, 1986.

———. *The Urban Indian Experience in America.* Albuquerque: University of New Mexico Press, 2000.

Foster, Morris W. *Being Comanche: A Social History of an American Indian Community.* Tucson: University of Arizona Press, 1991.

Fuchs, Estelle, and Robert J. Havinghurst. *To Live on This Earth: American Indian Education.* Garden City, N.Y.: Doubleday, 1972.

Garroutte, Eva Marie. *Real Indians: Identity and the Survival of Native America.* Berkeley: University of California Press, 2003.

Gordon, Milton M. *Assimilation in American Life.* New York: Oxford University Press, 1964.

Grobsmith, Elizabeth S. *Indians in Prison: Incarcerated Native Americans in Nebraska.* Lincoln: University of Nebraska Press, 1994.

Hauptman, Laurence M. *The Iroquois Struggle for Survival: World War II to Red Power.* Syracuse, N.Y.: Syracuse University Press, 1986.

Hertzberg, Hazel W. *The Search for an American Indian Identity: Modern Pan Indian Movements.* Syracuse, N.Y.: Syracuse University Press, 1971.

Hosmer, Brian. *American Indians in the Market place: Persistence and Innovation among the Menominees and Metlakatlans, 1870–1920.* Lawrence: University Press of Kansas, 1999.

Hosmer, Brian, and Colleen O'Neil, eds. *Native Pathways: American Indian Culture and Economic Development in the Twentieth Century.* Boulder: University of Colorado Press, 2004.

Huhndorf, Shari M. *Going Native: Indians in the American Cultural Imagination.* Ithaca, N.Y.: Cornell University Press, 2001.

Iverson, Peter. *"We Are Still Here": Ameriacn Indians in the Twentieth Century.* Wheeling, IL: Harland Davidson, 1998.

———. *When Indians Became Cowboys: Native Peoples and Cattle Ranching in the American West.* Norman: University of Oklahoma Press, 1994.

Jackson, Deborah Davis. *Our Elders Lived It: American Indian Identity in the City.* DeKalb: Northern Illinois University Press, 2002.

Katz, Stanley N., and Stanley I. Kutler, eds. *New Perspectives on the American Past: 1877 to the Present.* Boston: Little, Brown and Company, 1969.

King, C. Richard, and Charles Fruehling Springwood, eds. *Team Spirits: The Native American Mascots Controversy.* Lincoln: University of Nebraska Press, 2001.

Lassiter, Luke Eric, Clyde Ellis, and Ralph Kotay. *The Jesus Road: Kiowas, Christianity, and Indian Hymns.* Lincoln: University of Nebraska Press, 2002.

Levine, Stuart, and Nancy O. Lurie. *The American Indian Today.* Baltimore: Penguin Books, 1965.

Lewis, Bonnie Sue. *Creating Christian Indians: Native Clergy in the Presbyterian Church.* Norman: University of Oklahoma Press, 2003.

Light, Steven Andrew, and Kathrun A. L. Rand. *Indian Gaming and Tribal Sovereignty: The Casino Compromise.* Lawrence: University Press of Kansas, 2005.

Maracle, Brian. ed. *Crazywater: Native Voices on Addiction and Recovery.* Toronto. Penguin Books, 1993.

McNickle, D'Arcy. *They Came Here First: The Epic of the American Indian.* New York: Harper and Row, 1949.

Nagler, Mark. ed. *Perspectives on the North American Indian:* Toronto: McClelland and Stewart Limited, 1972.

Neils, Elaine M. *Reservation to City: Indian Migration and Federal Relocation.* Chicago: University of Chicago, Department of Geography, 1971.

Nurge, Ethel. ed. *The Modern Sioux Social Systems and Reservation Culture.* Lincoln: University of Nebraska Press, 1970.

O'Brien, Sharon. *American Indian Tribal Governments.* Norman: University of Oklahoma Press, 1989.

O'Neil, Colleen. *The Working Navajo Way: Labor and Culture in the Twentieth Century.* Lawrence: University Press of Kansas, 2005.

Parman, Donald L. *Indians and the American West in the Twentieth Century.* Bloomington: Indiana University Press, 1994.

Prucha, Francis Paul. *The Great Father: The American Indian and the United States Government.* Lincoln: University of Nebraska Press, 1986; abridged edition.

Sorkin, Alan L. *American Indians and Federal Aid.* Washington, D.C.: The Brookings Institution, 1971.

———. *The Urban American Indian.* Lexington, Mass: Lexington Books, 1978.

Spicer, Edward H., ed. *Navajo: Perspectives in American Culture Change.* Chicago: University of Chicago Press, 1961.

St. Clair, Robert, and William Leap, eds. *Language Renewal among American Indian Tribes.* Rosslyn, Va.: National Clearing House for Bilingual Education, 1982.

Stanbury, W. T. *Success and Failure: Indians in Urban Society.* Vancouver: University of British Columbia Press, 1975.

Stein, Wayne J. *Tribal Controlled Colleges: Making Good Medicine.* New York: Peter Lang, 1992.

Steiner, Stan. *The New Indians.* New York: Dell, 1968.

Stewart, Omar C. *Peyote Religion.* Norman: University of Oklahoma Press, 1987.

Straus, Terry, and Grant P. Arndt, eds. *Native Chicago.* Chicago: McNaughton and Gunn, 1998.

Szasz, Margaret Connell. *Education and the American Indian: The Road to Self-Determination since 1928.* Albuquerque: University of New Mexico Press, 1974.

Tyler, S. Lyman. *A History of Indian Policy.* Washington, D.C: U.S. Department of Interior–Bureau of Indian Affairs, 1973.

Weaver, Thomas, ed. *Indians of Arizona: A Contemporary Perspective.* Tucson: University of Arizona Press, 1974.

Weible-Orlando, Joan. *Indian Country, L.A.: Maintaining Ethnic Community in Complex Society.* Urbana: University of Illinois Press, 1991.

White, Jon Manchip. *Everyday Life of the North American Indians.* New York: Dorset Press, 1979.

Wilkinson, Charles. *Blood Struggle: The Rise of Modern Indian Nations.* New York: W.W. Norton, 2005.

Wilson, Edmund. *Apologies to the Iroquois.* With a study of the "Mohawks in High Steel" by Joseph Mitchell, New York: Farrar, Straus and Cudahy, 1960.

Young, Richard K. *The Ute Indians of Colorado in the Twentieth Century.* Norman: University of Oklahoma Press, 1977.

INDEX

About the Author

DONALD FIXICO is Distinguished Foundation Professor of History at Arizona State University. He is the author of numerous articles and several books of which some are, *Termination and Relocation: Federal Indian Policy, 1945–1960* (1986); *The Invasion of Indian Country in the Twentieth Century American Capitalism and Tribal Natural Resources* (1998); *The Urban Indian Experience in America* (2000); and *The American Indian Mind in a Linear World: Traditional Knowledge and American Indian Studies* (2003).